THE UNCONSCIOUS AND ITS NARRATIVES

T0374697

Zvi Giora

THE UNCONSCIOUS AND ITS NARRATIVES

T–Twins Publishing House
Budapest
1991

Published by T–Twins Publishing House in cooperation with the Institute of Psychology of the Hungarian Academy of Sciences and the Department of Psychology, Tel Aviv University

HU ISBN 9789637977060

MIX
Paper | Supporting
responsible forestry
FSC
www.fsc.org   FSC® C013604

FOREWORD

Professor Zvi Giora's book *The Unconscious and its Narratives* is published on the occasion of two important scientific events taking place in Budapest in the summer of 1991: the Second European Congress of Psychology, in July, and the world meeting of psychologists of Hungarian origin in August. Its publication was made possible by the joint efforts of the Tel Aviv University, the Institute of Psychology of the Hungarian Academy of Sciences and the T-Twins Publishing House.

The main topic of Professor Giora's book, the Freudian theory is one of the most important heritage of modern European psychology. In particular, he deals with the cornerstone of psychoanalysis, the theory of the unconscious. The "unconscious and its narratives" – dreams, literary creativity and pathogenic factors leading to neurosis – are examined here from a critical perspective in light of the new developments in cognitive psychology. Giora carefully analyzes the merits and limits, as well as the major achievements and contradictions of Freudian theory in understanding these "narratives".

Professor Giora's work is an important and original contribution to discussions on the scientific status of psychoanalysis as well as to the philosophy of science. Thus, the book is recommended to all readers who are interested in the revival, re-evaluation and further development of the European psychological tradition.

May 10, 1991

Dr Ferenc Erős
Institute of Psychology
of the Hungarian Academy of Sciences

ACKNOWLEDGEMENTS

Grateful acknowledgements are given to the following publishers who have kindly permitted to quote from their copyrighted material as follows:

Academic Press from B. T. Ho, D. W. Richards, D. L. Chute (eds.) *Drug discrimination and state dependent learning*, 1983.

Lawrence Erlbaum Associates from J. D. Lichtenberg and S. Kaplan (eds.) *Reflections on self-psychology*, 1983.

Alfred A. Knopf Inc. from B. Bettelheim, *The uses of enchantment: The meaning and importance of fairy tales*, 1976.

The Editor of *The Psychoanalytic Study of Child* from M. Katan, A causerie on Henry James' The turn of the screw, 1962, and M. Edelson, Language and dreams, 1973.

The Editor of *Psychological Reports* from M. R. Westcott and J. H. Ranzoni, Correlates of intuitive thinking, 1973.

Princeton University Press from *The basic writings of Jung*, 1958.

Routledge Publishing from C. G. Jung, *Modern man in search of a soul*, 1939.

The Sigmund Freud Copyrights Ltd., The Institute of Psycho-Analysis and The Hogarth Press from the Standard Edition (1960–1974) of the *Complete Psychological Works of Sigmund Freud*.

Verso Editions from S. Timpanaro, *The Freudian slip*, 1974.

I also wish to thank the Rector of Tel-Aviv University, Professor Itamar Rabinovitz and the Chairman of Psychology Department, Faculty of Social Sciences, Professor Chanan Frenk for their generous support of my research.

TABLE OF CONTENTS

PREFACE

In a lecture delivered at the Third International Congress of Psychology in Munich, Lipps (1897) stated that the problem of the unconscious is less a psychological problem than *the* problem of psychology. Earlier, in "The basic facts of mental life", Lipps (1883) declared that "unconscious mental processes are the basis of conscious ones ... conscious processes rise out of the unconscious when conditions are favourable, and then sink back again into the unconscious" (p. 149). Such statements, echoing as they did the ideas originally proposed by one of the most influential psychologists of the 19th century in Germany and the father of the concept of the threshold of consciousness, "which a representation has to trespass in order to proceed from the state of complete suppression to that of actualized presentation" (Herbart, 1824, p. 175), were no innovations for Freud. For Freud, as a high-school student, studied from Lindner's (1859) "Textbook of Empirical Psychology by Genetic Method" (Jones, 1953), which was characterized as a compendium of the Herbartian psychology.

While agreeing with these ideas of Herbart-Fechner-Lipps, to mention only the most important of his predecessors, Freud (1900) also made it clear that "his" unconscious, as he put it, "is not the same as the unconscious of philosophers or even the unconscious of Lipps" (p. 614). Lipps, though, carries things beyond the position of his colleagues, "But it is not in order to establish *this* thesis that we have summoned up the phenomenon of dreams and the formation of hysterical symptoms" (p. 614, emphasis in original). Dreams and symptoms prove "that there are two kinds of unconscious, which have not yet been distinguished by psychologists ... One of them, which we term the Ucs. is also *inadmissible to consciousness,* while we term the other the Pcs. because its excitations – after observing certain rules, it is true, and perhaps only after passing a fresh censorship ... – are able to reach consciousness" (pp. 614-615, emphasis in original).

The Freudian Unconscious, then, the *Ucs.* in contradistinction to the unconscious of philosophers, is inadmissible to consciousness. The mental contents of this unconscious do not submit to this banishment from consciousness but rather, press unceasingly for their reappearance and actualization. This pressure, indeed, may succeed, but only under the condition that the repressed mental content, as indicated in the above quotation, yields to the demands of a hidden censorship, that is, becomes disguised and distorted. It is only by means of a compromise between what seeks for expression and what denies the right for expression that the seals of the repression may be broken. To put it simply, repressed mental contents cannot and never again will be conscious in their original form. In their original form they are inadmissible to consciousness - this assertion was the only reason and justification for conceiving a second, Freudian, unconscious.

The contents of the repressed *Ucs.*, then, are unknowable. If there is a possibility to disclose the repressed thoughts and feelings in their original form and meaning, then one should agree that there is no Freudian unconscious. If, however, Freud was correct in elaborating his *Ucs.*, then he and we cannot know anything of the psychic "thing in itself", neither of its nature, of the laws prevailing there, nor of the true meaning of its contents. But Freud knew that the laws governing mental events in the *Ucs.* differ from those of the consciousness, and that the repressed thoughts and feelings relate mainly to the Oedipal conflict. For example, in his paper on constructions in analysis, Freud (1937) suggested that in hallucinations "something that has been experienced in infancy and then forgotten returns ... probably distorted and displaced owing to the operation of forces that are opposed to its return" (p. 267). Our problem now is clear. Some early memory is redeemed from the chains of repression, and it may be re-experienced again consciously under the condition, however, that it will be unrecognizable. How can then one be sure that one understood the meaning of the original experience? But an understanding of the original meaning of the repressed experience is the essence of the psychoanalytic theory of psychopathology and psychotherapy.

One way out of this dilemma may be to agree that, indeed, due to the nature of the repressed unconscious and its interaction with consciousness, one is prevented – figuratively speaking – from putting one's hand on the original meaning of the repressed experiences and, as also indicated in the title of Freud's paper, one has to construct them. Freud's writings abound in statements to this effect. In the case-history of Dora, Freud (1905/a) conceded that one usually cannot conclusively prove the unconscious origin and the meaning of a neurotic symptom and one has to be content with the fact that one's interpretation fits in "quite extraordinarily well" with the situation (p. 77). In the case-history of the Wolfman, Freud (1918) wrote that "so far as my experience hitherto goes, these scenes from infancy are not reproduced during the treatment as recollections, they are products of ... construction" (p. 194). In his "Constructions in Analysis" Freud (1937/b) observed that quite often patients are unable to recollect repressed experiences. "Instead of that, if the analysis is carried out correctly, we produce in him an assured conviction of the truth of the construction which achieves the same therapeutic result as a recaptured memory" (p. 266).

The opposite way is to insist that difficulties in proving notwithstanding, it is possible to get to know the original meaning of a repressed experience. Freud held both these views. We have just seen his conciliatory approach. But in the same "Construction in Analysis" where he indicated that for want of recollections because of their beneficial therapeutic influence, constructions are recommended, he also wrote that "our construction is only effective because it recovers a fragment of lost experience" (Freud, 1937, p. 268). And in the same case-history of Dora where he was satisfied that his interpretations-constructions fit in with the circumstances, (Freud (1905/a) also wrote that he followed the example "of those discoveries whose good fortune is to bring to the light of day

... mutilated relics of antiquity. I have restored what is missing, taking the best models known to me from other analyses; but, like a conscientious archaeologist, I have not omitted to mention in each case where the authentic parts end and my construction begins" (p. 12).

It is apparent that Freud was correct either in admitting that the pathogenic "scenes" from infancy are not, because they cannot be, reproduced by the patient but are constructed by the therapist or, to the contrary, he was justified in contending that psychoanalysts, like archaeologists, recover fragments of repressed experiences in their original form – but not in both cases. Besides, only by disregarding the very reason for conceiving "his" unconscious, could Freud have claimed to have discovered the original and true meaning of some repressed wishes. Either the possibility for making such discoveries or the concept of the *Ucs.* – this was the dilemma before Freud, but he deemed it possible to have it both ways.

People usually were not aware of this self-contradiction because, by a slight adjustment of the concept of repression, the acuteness of Freud's predicament seemed mitigated. Quite often, repression is understood to denote some gaps in memory. Had he only been interested in finding a term for describing the process of motivated forgetting and preferred for this purpose "repression" over the then very popular "dissociation", Freud (1937/b) would not have written that, as quoted above, "something ... forgotten returns ... probably distorted and displaced owing to the operation of forces that are opposed to its return" (p. 267).

Clearly, any attempt to identify repression with the non-availability of some memories due to the well-known "opposing forces", overlooks the element which really distinguishes repression from dissociation: the distortions and displacements imposed on the repressed mental content, which is on its way to becoming conscious again. Freud's readers, at any rate, are aware of his warning that the "mechanism of repression becomes accessible to us only by our deducing that mechanism from the *outcome* of repression" (Freud, 1915/b, p. 154, emphasis in original).

Indeed, in an interesting paper, in which he tried to prove that the abandonment by Freud of the "seduction" theory was inevitable, and not, as Masson (1984) suggested, personally motivated, Schimek (1987) stated in a manner of approval: "The overcoming of resistances and the lifting of repression through the psychoanalytic process does not lead to the emergence of early experiences and conflicts in their original form but, at best, as less distorted derivations. Most of this had become standard analytic theory ..." (p. 955). But then, what status should we assign to statements concerning the contents and manners of the Freudian, repressed, unconscious? Are they consensually validated facts or subjective constructions for private usage?

For a great part of this century this question, while not dormant, seems not to have preoccupied Freud and psychoanalysts in general. Lately, however, more and more authors admit that as this question comprises the very foundation of the psychoanalytic theory of behavior, an answer to it is not only important but urgent. Eagle (1984) put it in rather strong terms by saying that "there is simply no way that psychoanalysis can shrug off problems of accountability ... and there is no way, I believe, that psychoanalysis can legitimately and comfortably content itself simply with the status of a hermeneutic endeavor" (pp. 326-7). In a similar manner, Blight (1981) opposes evading the issue created by the very definition of repression and dynamic psychology by a "retreat", as he put it, to hermeneutics. "To anyone whose views derive from a more or less empiricist tradition, this may well be the central paradox and hence stumbling block, of the hermeneutical program: logic and truth itself become, if not quite arbitrary, at least plastic, perhaps infinitely so" (p. 167).

Yet, I have found the most penetrating diagnosis of the predicament Freud created by conceiving "his" unconscious in the Foreword Wallerstein (1981) wrote to Spence's (1982) Narrative Truth and Historical Truth: "... Spence is signally one of the very few among us who reminds us that our 'data' are not self-evident, their nature not at all to be taken for granted, and who in fact calls into question ... our total enterprise ..." (p. 10). While Eagle and Blight would not agree to disregard or belittle these problems, nevertheless they sound optimistic. They demand an honest effort precisely because they believe that there is, and there must be a solution acceptable both to Freudians and philosophers of science. Wallerstein, however, was less confident. Spence, he wrote, "maybe (guardedly) optimistic more than is inherently warranted by the nature of the case he himself has built concerning the possibility (let alone the feasibility) of truly unpacking the psychoanalytic text ... on this most central issue, Spence does not convincingly answer his own troubling question, nor can we just on reading his book" (p. 13).

This, indeed, is the conclusion suggested here: the "troubling question(s)" created by the definition of the *Ucs.* do not seem solvable. In the three essays of this study I discuss the most important narratives, supposedly originating in the *Ucs.*: dreams, literary creativity, and the pathogenic factor leading to neuroses and necessitating psychotherapy, and try to show that these and related questions are better dealt with without the construct of *Ucs.* than with it.

While each essay is an independent unit, and can be read separately, I would like to suggest the essay on dreams be read first. In order to prevent repetition, what was explicated in the first essay is only dealt with in brief in the second. Only by reading in this order will the reader have a comprehensive picture of the view suggested here.

A NEW LOOK AT AN OLD TOPIC: DREAMS AND WHAT THEY TEACH US

What a dream is

Every child knows, and surely no grown-up would have doubts about the meaning of sleep. Only the experts cannot make up their minds. Corner (1984) called it "a thorny question". "A thorny question ... how the word 'sleep' be defined?" (p. 50). Also Meddis (1979) agrees that "for the present we must simply accept that sleep, as a behavioral ... and electrophysiological affair, is still only a moderately coherent concept. The question 'What is sleep' remains fairly open" (pp. 103/4). Corner's and Meddis' succinct statements are, by no means, peculiar to them. The chairman of a symposium (Chase, 1972) on the sleeping brain reflected on this question in the following way: Time, and probably disinclination, prevented us from pursuing the question of a definition of sleep. My impression was that there is a definite uneasiness about any rigid definition. During the symposium we heard terms such as "behavioral sleep", "sleep-like state" and "dormancy" used to describe the behavior of non-mammalian vertebrates. These euphemisms reflect uncertainty as to the sufficient and necessary signs of sleep, and they are honest admissions that we simply do not know, at this point, what the essence of sleep is.

As an afterthought to this discussion, Molinari observed that it would be nice to have a future symposium on what a dream really is and how to define it. Such a symposium was not held, and people continue to rely on their intuitive understanding of the nature of dreams. It may happen though that the intuitions of the people participating in an experiment and that of the researcher are not exactly alike. For example, Foulkes (1962) first asked his subjects in the sleep laboratory whether they had dreamt and, on being told that they had not, asked them to report whatever was going through their minds because "Not all cognitive and perceptual phenomena occurring during sleep are labelled by subjects as 'dreams'."

Although never explicitly decided, it was apparently agreed that in order to qualify as a dream, the mental product should have certain distinguishing features. While the Foulkes' question as to whether or not, before awakening, anything was going through the subject's mind, indicated a disagreement with the subjects' intuitive understanding of dreams, he eventually did seem to have accepted their intuition, for he allocated their reports into "two distinct classes", as he put it, namely "dreams" and "thoughts".

Reports of visual, auditory, or kinesthetic imagery Foulkes called "dreams"; reports in which such imagery was lacking but in which the subject either assumed an identity other than his own or felt that he was in a physical setting other than the laboratory, were also accepted as "dreams". Reports lacking sensory imagery and changed identity or setting he classified as "thoughts".

Freud (1900) seems to have been aware of the possibility of such a distinction between "dreams" and "thoughts" since he related to it - and rejected it. It was his opinion that "not every dream exhibits this transformation from idea into sensory image. There are dreams which consist only of thoughts but which cannot on that account be denied the essential nature of dreams" (Freud, 1900, p. 595). In fact, Freud thought that every dream is a mixture of "dreams" and "thought" for, "in every dream of any considerable length there are elements which have not ... been given a sensory form, but which are simply thought or known, in the kind of way in which we are accustomed to think or know things in waking life" (p. 595) – It is rather clear that an intuitive understanding of what a dream is, ends in misunderstanding. We need a clearly formulated definition. As it happens, we have one and, it will be worth considering why it is too often disregarded. "According to Aristotle's accurate but bold definition, a dream is a thinking that persists ... in the state of sleep" (Freud, 1900, p. 550).

Unlike Aristotle and Freud, who defined any product of thinking generated in the state of sleep, and not just one class of these, as dreams, Foulkes' subjects seem to have believed in what Dorus, Dorus and Rechtschaffen (1971) felicitously termed "the strange, fantastic, otherworldliness of dreams" (p. 364). It was then rather consistent with this view of dreams that they disregarded what did not fit their expectation and, if asked about their dreams did not report them. Foulkes, however, was engaged in an important mission: he was on his way to correct this mistaken notion of dreams. His compliance with his subjects' intuition warrants some questioning: why, indeed, did he follow their suit?

The view prevailing among workers of laboratory sleep and dream research at that time was that dreams are vivid, sensory, and strange. "Presuming to know what a dream was, the investigators took it as their task to find when in sleep it could be found. The REM dream (actually the 'apex' of most vivid dream) came to define all dreaming. In effect, the more vivid and striking REM dream was accepted as the definition for the standard dream, and so it was the 'apex' REM dream that was searched out in all stages. This might have predetermined where it would be found – in REM sleep almost exclusively" (Herman, Ellman, and Roffwarg, 1978, p. 71). It was Foulkes who in his study challenged this view, first, by substituting "what was going through your mind" for "did you dream", thereby, eliciting reports of mental activity during both REM and non-REM periods, and second, by concluding that "Dreaming ... might conceivably occur continuously in the sleeping human and REMs might be useful only in differentiating different kinds of dreams, rather than [being] signs of dreaming versus non-dreaming" (p. 15). These "different kinds of dreams" were a few pages later relabelled into reports classifiable as "dreams" and "thoughts".

"Foulkes", Herman et al. (1978) observe, "in effect sidestepped the issue of when, and to what extent, dreaming occurs. From the definitional (really conceptual) point of view, it is clear that at first he felt unwilling to classify a dream as any particular sort of mental activity" (p. 71). In fact, as we have seen, he did classify dreams according to Aristotle and Freud and, at the same time he "sidestepped" the issue. Apparently, he wavered between actually abandoning, challenging, and working with this stereotyped notion of the "otherworldliness," which dominated the minds of naive people as well as of influential researchers. The facts, though, as displayed by Foulkes himself should have prevented such a collaboration. For, if one is interested to know how the mind works while one is asleep, then one has to consider all that the mind is producing in this state. Foulkes ingeniously devised the proper method for such a consideration and convincingly stated the meaning of his finding, namely, that there are two kinds of dreams. Here, however, he stopped. Instead of calling them by names which would bear out his distinction between kinds of dreams, like strange and simple dreams, he preferred to speak of "dreams" and "thoughts", as if agreeing with the very conception he was challenging, namely that a dream should conform with or at least approximate the "apex REM dream".

It is difficult to know what would have happened if Foulkes had suggested names for different kinds of dreams rather than the labels "dreams" and "thoughts". Snyder (1969), Dorus, Dorus, and Rechtschaffen (1971), Rechtschaffen (1978), and myself (Giora, 1981, 1989) have presented data which should have demolished the definition of dreams by means of the "apex REM dreams", yet I am afraid that a survey of opinions, including those of psychotherapists, might reveal a surprising and frustrating stability of views. Thus, for example, in his interesting book on the dreaming brain, Hobson (1988), in complete disregard, as it seems, of the evidence proffered by the authors quoted above, defined dreams as befitting the "apex REM" tradition: "The cardinal features of all dreaming – detailed sensory imagery, the illusion of reality, illogical thinking, intensification of emotion, and unreliable memory – constitute its form ..." (p. 230); then he conjectured that "Although the precise cerebral basis of the *distinctive cognitive disorders of dreaming* is not yet fully understood, it is tempting to see these failures as perhaps related to the cessation of activity in the modulatory neurons" (p. 209), emphasis added). Let us, then, explore again the findings of Dorus and associates, and Snyder, and their possible impact on the definition of dreams.

Dorus et al. (1971) tackled this issue in an impressively systematic way. In order to establish whether or not dreams, in general, are strange and different from our waking thinking, they evaluated the novelty of each element of manifest dream content and of the overall theme of the dream relative to the experiences of the individual dreams. Six novelty categories were devised: the dream element (or overall dream) is an exact replication of something previously experienced – is a replication of something previously experienced, but with minor changes from the original – with major changes from the original – has not been previously experienced, but the dreamer could readily imagine its being experienced (e.g., "A couple whom I don't know", etc.) – has not been previously experienced, and it is not very likely that such an element could occur in the dreamer's experience (e.g., "There were thousands of snakes on the ground") – has not been previously experienced, and it is extremely unlikely that it could occur in the dreamer's experience (e.g., "The Indian made a big dash through the village gyrating wildly so that the arrows might hit him but the force of his motion in another direction would make it ineffectual").

Their subjects slept in a sleep-laboratory, were awakened from their REM periods and asked: "What was going through your mind just before I awakened you?" Immediately after the dream report, the subjects were questioned about how novel each of the specific settings, objects, characters, interactions, and activities of the dream was in their own personal experience. The results, as the authors were able to conclude, emphasize the rarity of the bizarre in dreams. "Evidently, the occurrence of elements which are very novel both in the sense of not having been previously experienced and in the sense of being strange and highly improbable is very rare in dreams" (p. 366).

It is yet to be pointed out that these results were obtained by collecting dreams from REM periods of sleep only. It is reasonable to assume that dreams collected from non-REM periods of sleep would have added further strength to the conclusion reached by Dorus et al. After all, it was not by mistake that Foulkes labelled non-REM dreams as "thoughts". The authors did not explain why they restricted themselves to reports from REM periods. But we may surmise that the exclusiveness granted to REM periods in most laboratory dream research is the last remnant of the early marriage between the stereotype of the "otherworldliness" of a dream and the information that only REM periods of sleep are a fitting substrate for such an occurrence. Now we know that dreams generated during REM periods, and certainly during non-REM periods of sleep, are not what they are supposed to be and, while the preference of REMs over NREMs in dream research still awaits a justification, we may at least admit that by concentrating their efforts on REMs researchers made the puzzle of discrepancy between the facts and views held on the nature of dreams even more salient.

This discrepancy was already pointed out by Snyder (1969). In his research on the "phenomenology" of dreams, he also wakened his subjects from the REM sleep and asked them to report their dreams. He found – very much to his own surprise – that most dreams were acceptable as realistic depictions of experienced and possible occurrences. Snyder, and Dorus et al., then established a fact of far-reaching consequence: most of our dreams are not what they are expected to be. "The general impression left by [Snyder's] study", as Schwartz, Weinstein, and Arkin (1978) related it, "is that dreams 'are not so dreamy after all'" (p. 150). How can one account, they ask, for the differences between these findings and the general impression of dreams as strange and uncanny? Likewise, Dorus et al. (1971), having concluded that "the appearance of the unusual in dreams seems grossly exaggerated in popular conceptions" (p. 368), wonder what could explain this exaggeration? Indeed, it is a puzzle and puzzles require an explanation. By our very make-up, we are intrigued by what seems to defy reason for we are sure that everything is comprehensible and that eventually all mysteries will lose – to use again this term – their other-worldliness.

Quite naturally, I too, was puzzled by the persistence of the stereotyped notion of dreams – and of a few other stereotypes, too – yet my attention was soon diverted from this puzzle to another one. Foulkes spoke of "dreams" and "thoughts": Snyder, and Dorus et al., found that most, but not all, dreams are neither strange nor otherworldly. In effect, then, these researchers poi. ᵔd to the existence of two kinds of dreams – logical and bizarre. A theory of dreams has to account for, has to make sense of this diversity. Why do we generate two kinds of dreams and what conclusions may we draw from this phenomenon? This is the basic question a theory of dreams has to deal with.

At the beginning of my own dream research, I too was under the spell of what seemed to be a fortunate meeting of psychoanalysis and REM literature. Freud's theory of dreams nurtured expectations which REM-researchers seemed to have succeeded in realizing. The construct of a peculiarly working unconscious, indicated by the strangeness of dreams and the conception of "apex" REM dreams, seemed so suitable that an enthusiastic approval of both of these lines of research seemed almost inevitable. With the passing years, having seen over one thousand dreams, my enthusiastic approval turned into a firm rejection of the theory of the "otherworldliness" of dreams, which together with my acceptance of Aristotle's definition of dreams eventually led me to conceive of a new theory of dreams.

A theory is judged by the merit of the solution(s) it offers and, while I think of the theory to be presented here as worthy of consideration, nevertheless, I would like to emphasize and draw attention to the question which instigated the theory: why do we generate two kinds of dreams? Others may succeed in suggesting more convincing answers than the one I shall elaborate here, but nobody should continue to disregard the most basic and, at the same time the most neglected, fact of dream psychology, *the heterogeneity of dreams.*

Styles of dreaming and styles of thinking

Dreams may be reported in the course of psychotherapy, in a sleep laboratory, immediately after the dreamer is roused while the memory of the mental events is, as it were, still fresh or, by means of entries made in a diary immediately upon awakening. Which way is preferable, which method will allow us to have a faithful picture of what went through the mind of the sleeper?

Let us here be reminded that in physics the hope of describing objects objectively had to be abandoned with the birth of the new quantum-mechanics. It was proved that the observation of an atomic system disturbs it and introduces an unpredictable change in some important feature of the state of the observed particle. In order to know, one has to observe, but to observe means to interact and, interacting means introducing changes in the phenomenon studied. Clearly, "objectivity" should be used in a more modest manner than is usually the case: it may mean the attainment of a minimum possible interaction with the phenomenon studied which, of course, is still an interaction.

With these considerations in mind, let us now turn to the question of how to collect dreams. Privately, very few people pay attention to their dreams and usually are unable to recall them. Counteracting spontaneous forgetting by asking one to keep a diary and record, for a period, every dream recalled after awakening, may induce some changes in dreaming too. While it is difficult to know what changes will occur – spontaneous dreaming and forgetting, in order to be spontaneous, cannot be observed and therefore cannot be compared with dreams generated under different conditions – we have reasons, as indicated above, for expecting change.

The next step in intensifying the interactions between an experimenter and his subject is to awaken the subject in a laboratory one or more times during a night's sleep and let him report what he was dreaming. To begin with, as a sign of the emotionally charged relationship, subjects in laboratories often dream of the experimenter. Further, and more pertinent to our topic, laboratory dreams contain a mean of 2.63 characters per dream versus 1.95 for those dreamt at home and reported later. References to food, drink, and eating are more frequent in the laboratory. In laboratory dreams, there is less aggression and it is more often only witnessed by the dreamer than in home dreams. Also, sexual elements are more frequent in home dreams. On the other hand, the number of bizarre elements is much more prevalent in laboratory dreams (Domhoff and Kamiya, 1964). And finally, subjects who at home are not able to recall dreams (a feature often misinterpreted by people not involved in dream research as a sign of not dreaming rather than non-recalling), were able to recall their dreams in the laboratory (Witkin, 1969).

The strongest interaction between the one who relates his dream and the one who listens occurs in the course of psychotherapy. Here, the observer's influence on what will be dreamt and reported reaches its peak. This danger and its implications were spelled out with admirable clarity by Stekel (1913). Examining the dream material with which a patient had supplied him during an "industrious analysis" that went on for fourteen months, Stekel came to the conclusion that patients dream the dialect of the therapist who happens to be treating them. The dreams are "made to order", are produced in the form that will best please the analyst. That is why the dreams of a patient familiar with his therapist's pet theories must never be taken as confirmation of these theories. Sadger's patients, Stekel stated, will dream about urinary eroticism; his own, perhaps, of the symbolism of death and religion; Adler's of "top-dogs" and "under-dogs" and of the "masculine protest", Svoboda's student will dream of beautiful periodicity, and Silberer will be provided with fascinating instances of threshold symbolism and functional symbolism.

Obviously, one would arrive at different conclusions about dreams and dreamers if one related only to dreams recounted in psychotherapies, or to dreams reported anonymously by means of a diary to an unknown investigator. For example, the intriguing finding that laboratory dreams do have bizarre elements might cause one to hesitate in abandoning the stereotype of dreams. However, knowing that dreams at home contain less bizarre elements, one may look for other explanations. For example, Tart (1969) is of the opinion that the expectations of dream researchers, unintentionally conveyed to the subjects, may explain the rise in bizarreness in laboratory dreams. Is it, then, possible to talk of dreams, in general? Clearly not. The same dreamer may have different dreams under different conditions, and we have to decide which product to accept as our frame of reference for an understanding of dreaming and dreams.

The above analysis of the grades of interaction between observer and the observed naturally leads one to the conclusion that the commendable way to study dreams is through dream diaries kept at home for reasons which are not specified and by subjects who are not knowledgeable enough to know of the "pet theories" of the experimenters. This is the way I have been collecting dreams for years. Volunteer subjects, students, are asked to keep a dream-diary for two weeks; that is, first thing every morning to write down, as fully as possible, every dream they are able to remember; each dream on a separate page. I ask them please not to read them later on again. For reasons which immediately will be clarified, I use only diaries which contain at least five dreams. If there are more than five dreams, I analyze the first five only. By using the word "analyze", I do not refer to any method of interpreting, as may happen in psychotherapy but rather to classifying dreams as logical or bizarre.

The criteria used for classifying dreams follow, with only one modification, the categories suggested by Freud (1901). In an essay, written in the wake of his Interpretation of Dreams, Freud suggested that there are: (1) dreams which make sense and are intelligible, "which, that is to say, can be inserted without further difficulty into the context of our mental life.

We have numbers of such dreams"; (2) dreams which in spite of having "a clear sense, nevertheless have a bewildering effect because we cannot see how to fit that sense into our mental life": (3) "dreams which are without either sense or intelligibility, which seem disconnected, confused and meaningless. The preponderant majority of the products of our dreaming exhibit these characteristics" (pp. 642/3).

I united Freud's first two categories and labelled them "logical" dreams since whether an event happened to me or the others, it is still an experienced or a possible event which conforms with logic and reality testing. To his third category, comprising, as it does, impossible elements which are unacceptable by logic or reality testing and, sudden, unexplained, shifts in setting, I gave the name "bizarre".

Since dreams may be either bizarre or logical, one may be interested in knowing whether there are individual differences in the propensity to generate dreams of this or that type. Dorus et al. (1971), reported of their subjects, who slept for two consecutive nights in the laboratory that the distribution of "novelty categories in their dreams was a stable individual characteristic". Since I collected five dreams from every subject, I was able to verify that indeed, the proclivity to dream logical or bizarre dreams is a stable feature of one's personality. If all his/her dreams were bizarre, the subject was identified as having a bizarre style of dreaming; if all his/her dreams were logical, then the subject had a logical style of dreaming, and if some of them were logical and some of them bizarre, then the subject was identified as having a mixed style of dreaming. In one study, the details of which will be presented later on, the distribution of these styles of dreams was as follows (N=30); 60% had a mixed, 27% only logical and, 13% only bizarre styles of dreams.

To qualify as logical, the dream story should be plausible and show an orderly sequence of events. To be classified as bizarre, it is enough for one of these criteria, plausibility of elements or sequence of events, to be violated. Since it is easier for a dream to be classified as bizarre, one may expect, for this reason alone, a "preponderance", as Freud put it, of bizarre dreams. In fact, however, this advantage notwithstanding, bizarre dreams proved to be fewer in number than the logical ones.

In order to test the stability of one's style of dreaming, Miriam Rass (1983) asked 50 volunteers to keep a dream diary for two weeks. 42 subjects were able to report five or more dreams. 66% had a mixed style, 21% only logical, and 12% only bizarre dreams. Six weeks later, these subjects were requested to write down, again for two weeks, every dream they could remember. 16 subjects returned their diaries with five dreams or more; of these, 14 subjects had the same style of dreaming in both diaries. One bizarre dreamer on the second occasion showed a mixed style and one subject with a mixed style became a logical dreamer. We may then state that one's style of dreaming is a stable feature of his personality.

Speaking of personality in the context of dreams, one has to be aware of the ambiguity surrounding such statements. Does this stability relate to the sleeping state of mind only or did I indicate some feature which is identifiable in wakefulness and sleep as well? While we are accustomed to suggestions and assertions that differentiate between sleep and wakefulness as two separate realms of existence, each one of them character- ized by its own aims and modes of mental working, I think that even those who are firmly convinced of the necessity of such a distinction may agree that, alert or asleep, and, in fact, which ever state of mind we would turn to, all people are not alike. Individual differences are the base and essence of any theory of personality. Every person is truly an individuum: similar to his fellow persons in some aspects and unique in some others. Sleep, then, does not abolish the differences between people and the only question yet to be decided is whether it creates new ones while wiping out the differences prevailing in wake- fulness or leaves untouched the personality of wakefulness?

Considering the range of behavioral phenomena, such a question may easily be defined as not solvable since partisans of each view may find indications substantiating their respective views. In order to see whether waking and dreaming mental activity are continuous or not, one has to ask specific questions rather than be content with sweeping generalities. Here a sentence of Freud (1900) quoted above may be of help: "According to Aristotle's accurate but bold definition, a dream is a thinking that persists ... in the state of sleep" (p. 550). A specific question, perhaps, "the" question since it relates to the concept of dreaming itself, may be thus formulated: Is thinking different in sleep and wakefulness or does it remain the same? Even this question may turn out to be too broad. Let us than split it into two steps and ask first: Does one's characteristic style of thinking in wakefulness, prevail in dreaming too or, perhaps, turn into a different one?

The term "style of thinking" may require some explanatory remarks. The principle of individual differences leaves one expecting to find these differences not only in regard to abilities but also regarding the ways used in solving problems and thinking in general. Moreover, even people who are similar or identical in their intellectual capabilities may differ in the strategies implemented in learning about he world or making decisions. For some proceed analytically and some proceed in a global-intuitive manner. Individuals of analytic style proceed in measured steps, looking back, time and again, checking the data once more. Their decisions may be accompanied by limiting and qualifying remarks and take time to be arrived at. They are alert in identifying contradictions between their assumptions and the data subserving them, and without any delay would try to find compatibility between them; having failed in this attempt, analytic persons would not hesitate to reconsider their position. In contrast, individuals of global-intuitive style proceed in leaps on the basis of relatively little information. They are guided by a sensitivity and responsiveness to information which, while not consciously represented, is trusted and relied upon. Decisions are made quickly and, are accompanied by a sense of confidence; contradictions are easily disregarded. They would not deny that A cannot also be B at the same time, but are ready or better, able to suspend, for quite a while, their need for harmony between the conflicting information. Unlike their analytic counterparts, they can "live with" contradictions.

Some researchers, dealing with these same differences, suggested other terms for designating them. Bruner, Goodnow, and Austin (1951) described a "whole hypothesis" strategy and a "part-hypothesis" one. Individuals whose strategy of "concept attainment" is holistic, Bruner et al. observed, if confronted by unfavorable evidence, stuck to their views for a longer time than do individuals with partist strategy. Gardner and Long (1962) contrasted the extensive with the limited "scanner". Individuals who extensively scan their mental or physical field are "preoccupied" with verification, exactness, and acceptability of their decisions. The limited scanner is less hesitant and less punctilious. All these terms are of equal value, and my decision here in favor of analytic – intuitive was influenced by a practical consideration. The latter pair of terms is better known; both researchers and laymen use and understand it. It seemed then warranted to prefer it.

There is yet one issue to be mentioned. Like so many other mental functions, styles of thinking are also understood to be a continuum of related phenomena and not discrete points. Some people are characterized by being punctilious, hesitant and proceeding stepwise, and some people decide quickly, without hesitation and are not easily perturbed by contradictory evidence. In between these two extremes, we may expect to find people, the majority, who are neither vigilant in searching for inconsistencies, nor blithely content with them and who, although moderately, are able to think both analytically and intuitively.

Coming back to the dreams, the question now is whether or not one's style of thinking, analytic, mixed, or intuitive, will remain the same while asleep and dreaming.

Among the many features comprising styles of thinking, the

manner of one's adherence to a hypothesis threatened by contradictory evidence is, perhaps, the easiest to follow up. It was for this reason that I have used repeatedly over the years the guessing game introduced by Shouksmith (1965). In this experiment the subject is presented with white and red disks, one at a time, and must guess whether or not the experimenter will present a red disk next. Four separate conditions were used. Under condition A, the red disk was presented on every alternate trial, beginning with the second one. Ten trials were given; thus the sequence was repeated five times. Under condition B, the red disk was shown on every third trial, beginning with a third. Fifteen trials were given; thus the sequence was repeated five times. Under condition C, the red disk was presented on trials 2, 5 and 16. Thirty-three trials were given so that the sequence was repeated three times. Under condition D, the red disk was presented on trials 4, 6 and 9, with the sequence recurring three times.

As one may see, conditions A and B aroused an expectation for simply structured sequences of the disks. Thus, only alert individuals already feel the need to generate a new hypothesis under condition C. Individuals who can "live" with self-contradiction, demonstrate this ability of theirs by abandoning their first hypothesis only later, under condition D. Summarizing, then, all the successful predictions over the conditions, one may expect that individuals who adjusted their hypothesis of the sequences already during the course of condition C, will succeed more than their global-intuitive counterparts.

This difference in the overall correct guesses was used in an experiment by Miriam Rass (1983). Her subjects also kept a dream-diary for two weeks (and six weeks later for another period of two weeks). Thus, it was possible to match their speediness or slowness in harmonizing between these expectations and the changing reality and their styles of dreaming. As the results of planned comparison tests show, the average of correct guesses of the subjects who dream logical dreams only was 3,000, those of mixed style of dreams 1.6786, and the average of the dreamers of bizarre dreams only 0.800. A one-tailed analysis of variance showed a high-level correlation (p<0.0001) between success in eliminating hypotheses contradicted by new evidence and styles of dreaming.

We see here a continuance between one's style of thinking while awake and asleep. Styles of thinking and styles of dreaming are the reflections of the self-same personality variable in different states of mind. Individuals whose style of dreaming is logical are the most vigilant in observing the rules of logic whether asleep or awake. Individuals whose styles of dreaming is bizarre are the most relaxed if the truthfulness of their hypothesis is challenged; under the condition of sleep this relaxed manner in dealing with violations of logic becomes even more salient, resulting in bizarre dreams only. Between these two extremes dwell the majority, who are neither vigilant nor unconcerned but rather situationally influenced, and ready to be a companion once to this and another time to that party.

I am reminded here of a description of the nature of dreams by the noted psychologist, Dostoevsky. In his *The Idiot*, one may read the following beautiful exposition of the stereotype of dreams: "You remember first of all that your reason did not desert you throughout the dream; you remember even that you acted very cunningly and logically through all that long, long time, while you were surrounded by murderers who deceived you, hid their intentions, behaved amicably to you while they had a weapon in readiness, and were only waiting for some signal; you remember how cleverly you deceived them at last, hiding from them; then you guessed that they'd seen through your deception and were only pretending not to know where you were hidden; but you were sly then and deceived them again; all this you remember clearly. But how was it that you could at the same time reconcile your reason to the obvious absurdities and impossibilities with which your dreams was overflowing? One of your murderers turned into a woman before your eyes, and the woman into a little, sly, loathsome dwarf – and you accepted it all at once as an accomplished fact, almost without the slightest surprise, at the very time when, on another side, your reason is at its highest tension and showed extraordinary power, cunning, sagacity and logic?"

Writing at about the same time, Nietzsche (1878) felt that he was in a position to clarify this puzzle. Dreams, he wrote in his "Human, all-too-human" are arbitrary and confused, constantly confound things on the grounds of the most fleeting resemblances. But with the same arbitrariness and confusion, Nietzsche suggested, the ancients invented their mythologies, and even at the present day travelers are accustomed to remark how prone the "savage" is to forgetfulness, lies and nonsense. But in dreams we all resemble the savage. Therefore, "I hold that as man now still reasons in dream, so men reasoned also when awake through thousands of years ... Dream-thinking is now so easy to use because during immense periods of human development we have been so well drilled in this form of fantastic and cheap explanation."

In a similar vein, Havelock Ellis (1899) thought that "In our dreams we are taken back into an earlier world. It is a world much like that of the savage, the child, the criminal, the madman ... Through our dreams we may realize our relation to stages of evolution we have long left behind" (p. 721). We know that Freud held similar views. However, the facts displayed here do not support this contention. Some of our dreams, indeed, fit these descriptions by Dostoevsky, Nietzsche, Ellis, and Freud, but only some of them. The majority of dreams stand up to the scrutiny of judgment and reasoning expected to prevail in wakefulness. Such a difference between dreams, quite understandably, does not allow an explanation along the lines suggested by these authors, namely, one kind of thinking for everybody while awake and another one, again, for everybody while asleep. *Rather, it seems that people differ in their strategies of thinking, and these differences are carried on from one state of mind to the other one.*

The heterogeneity of dreams faithfully reflect the heterogeneity of strategies available for getting knowledge. The use of one of these strategies or the interchangeable implementation of them is a stable characteristic of one's personality, which does not change with the change of one's state of mind. One's style of dreaming is one's style of thinking.

Styles of thinking and beyond

"In biology", Kagan and Kogan (1970) observed, "the cell and the genes are the basic units, and the principles of biochemistry describe their function ... Psychology's units may turn out to be cognitive structures, and laws about cognitive processes will describe how these units function" (p. 1275). To put it differently, cognition, in general, and the differences in cognition, in particular, describe and explain important areas of one's personality make-up. We have motives, will, abilities, a body, and are surrounded by an environment. A person is what he could have been and what, in the course of his interactions with his world, he became to be. Neither motives, nor abilities, or cognitive styles are encompassing enough to explain the life of a person.

Yet, cognition and its styles influence what one may become, for they determine many of the results of interactions with the environment. Clearly, one may experience the world differently and the world may react differently if, for example, one proceeds cautiously and is always ready to retreat and turn to a new avenue, or to the contrary, decides quickly and is unperturbed by the voices of dissent. There are a few studies available which deal with these effects of cognitive styles. Shapiro (1965) described the correlations, in fact, a causal relationship, between styles of thinking and styles of neuroses. Hysterical neurosis is characterized by a global manner of thinking which is lacking in precise details, and further, by a readiness to decide in a quick, impressionistic, manner. Conversely, the hallmark of obsessive neurosis is a sharply focused attention and a prolonged search for detail. Understandably, decisions tend to be postponed and are accompanied by doubts. It is Shapiro's (1981) understanding that hysterical and obsessive neuroses are styles in behavior determined by one's style of thinking. "Symptomatic behavior", as he put it, by referring, for example, to the constant doubting, worrying, or regretting of obsessional people, is "a reflection of how individuals characteristically think and see things" (p. 13).

Incidentally, this understanding should leave one expecting a different term. To speak of "symptomatic behavior" makes good sense in a psychodynamic but not in a cognitive-style-approach. Shapiro, indeed, saw the main motive of his study in explicating precisely this difference: "It gradually became clear to me that the view of symptomatic behavior as a reflection of how individuals characteristically think and see things is in certain ways not only different from but actually contrary to the traditional dynamic view. The possibility of understanding the specific form of symptomatic behavior – for example, the constant doubting, or regretting of obsessional people – as derived from characteristic ways of thinking and points of view, reveals something fundamental about the nature of such behavior and, so to speak, the responsibility for it" (p. 3). It is apparent that in spite of his usage of the term "symptomatic behavior", it is Shapiro's understanding that one's style of thinking is responsible for one's "choice" of neurosis, and that the behaviors which differentiate between hysteric and obsessive neuroses are, in fact, ways of experiencing determined by one's style of thinking both in health and illness.

Another study to be mentioned here is the work of Westcott and Ranzoni (1963). These authors were able to show a correlation between styles of thinking and some dimensions of personality. Regrettably, this study did not receive the attention it deserved. For this reason, but also because of its pertinence to what will be discussed in this chapter, I shall here recapitulate the results of the Westcott and Ranzoni study.

They presented their subjects with a series of problems and asked them to find the solutions by using as little information as possible. The amount of information demanded as well as the success with which the problems were solved were recorded. Not surprisingly, though worth mentioning again, the amount of information demanded was found to be consistently unconnected to the level of success attained. We see then again that styles of thinking, that is, whether one proceeds in leaps and needs a relatively small quantity of information or proceeds slowly and relies upon a relatively large amount of information, are a different dimension than what is measured by I.Q.

Having chosen the extreme performers of the intuitive and analytic groups only, Westcott and Ranzoni asked these subjects to answer a personality-attitude questionnaire, an adjective check list, and to agree to be interviewed for approximately an hour. Below are the results of the attitude-questionnaire.

TABLE 1
Items which Differentiate Ss Who Demand Much
Information From Those Who Demand Little Information Before Attempting Solution to Problems (p <.05 All Items)

Item No.
More "True" responses from low information demanders

10. I have had periods of days, weeks, or months, when I couldn't take care of things because I couldn't get going.
12. I work under a great deal of tension.
74. At times I have been so entertained by the cleverness of a crook that I have hoped he would get away with it.
81. Sometimes without any reason or even when things are going wrong I feel excitedly happy, "on top of the world."
139. I have periods in which I lose sleep over worry.
153. I like men who antagonize me somewhat.
165. I easily become impatient with people.
183. I sometimes keep on at a thing until others lose patience with me.

More "True" responses from high information demanders

1. I always see to it that my work is carefully planned and organized.
25. I am very careful about my manner of dress.
61. I have had very few quarrels with members of my family.
116. I am happy most of the time.

Reproduced with permission of authors and publisher from: Westcott, M. R., and Ranzoni J. H., "Correlates of intuitive thinking." *Psychological Reports*, 1963 12, 595-613, Monograph Supplement 5–V12.

The interviews yielded some interesting comparisons or rather, differences between the two groups. The question, "Do you like to take chances?" elicited 100% positive answers from the intuitive subjects. Only 36% of the analytic individuals tolerated risk. The risk-taking of the intuitive individuals ranges from physical danger to "ego risks", as the authors put it, of battling for lost causes. Also the answers to the question as to whether they were influenced by others differentiated the groups. The intuitives acknowledged being changed by some influential others, but not the analytic group.

The self-descriptions, obtained by means of an adjective check list, showed that the intuitives think of themselves as alert, demanding, sharpwitted, and quick. The analyticals described themselves as anxious, cautious, kind and modest. Breaking down both of these groups into two subgroups: intuitive-successful problem solver (Group 1); intuitive-unsuccessful problem solver (Group 2); analytical-successful problem solver (Group 3); analytical-unsuccessful problem solver (Group 4), their self-description was as follows: Group 1 members think of themselves as alert, quick, resourceful, confident, foresighted, informal, spontaneous, and independent. Members of Group 2 evaluate themselves as being alert, quick, cynical, and headstrong. Group 3 members say they are cautious, kind, modest, confident, foresighted, resourceful, and spontaneous. Group 4 members lack self-confidence, but are kind, modest, and cautious.

Integrating these results into a comprehensive description, Westcott and Ranzoni suggest that intuitive individuals are unconventional and ready to accept challenges. They can live with doubt and uncertainty, and even enjoy risk and instabilities. They are deeply involved emotionally in what they are doing and emotions are observable in their behavior, in general. They are prone to fluctuations in their emotions. In their interactions with the world they are spontaneous; they are open to influence by others.

Analytic individuals are well-socialized and while they

rarely behave erratically, can entertain the possibility of incautious behavior. Generally, however, they are cautious, conservative and modest. They are confident of their place in the world and not involved in altering it. They acknowledge almost no profound influences on their lives.

These, then, are the general characteristics of individuals whom I would label as having pure styles of thinking. To be put between these two categories are the ones, in fact the majority, with a mixed style of thinking who are not as unconventional and emotional but also not as well-socialized and cautious as those individuals.

Applying now the results of Shapiro and Westcott and Ranzoni to the differences in dreaming styles, it seems reasonable to assume that individuals who habitually dream bizarre dreams belong to the intuitives (Groups 1 and 2) and have their characteristics, whereas those who habitually dream logical dreams are analytical (Groups 3 and 4) and have the corresponding characteristics. If neurotic, dreamers of bizarre style most probably will suffer from hysteria, and dreamers of logical style probably will be obsessive. The neuroses of individuals with a mixed style of dreaming will less easily be classifiable since they will contain features of both hysteric and obsessive neurosis.

Indeed, this is the picture which emerges from the studies of Nurit Lavi (1988) and Ariela Mamon (1988). They collected, by means of diaries kept at home, five dreams from 30 freshmen who consequently performed on the Rorschach and Draw A Person tests. The dreaming styles were categorized with the following results: 27% had only logical, 60% mixed, and 13% only bizarre dreams. Of the 167 Rorschach characteristics considered, fourteen differentiated between the three styles in a statistically significant manner. In five cases the logical and mixed styles of dreaming formed one group and were contrasted with the bizarre style of dreaming; in none of these statistically significant differences were the mixed and bizarre styles together contrasted to the logical style of dreaming. That is to say, although dreamers of a mixed style differ in their style of dreaming and personality characteristics from dreamers of both of the pure styles, they are nevertheless somewhat closer to the logical style and its personality.

Table 2 presents the statistically significant difference between the three styles of dreaming. Table 3 presents the differences between the bizarre and logical styles of dreaming only.

TABLE 2
One-Tailed Analysis of Variance Between
the Three Styles of Dreaming and Test Rorschach

Duncan*	Bizarre 3 Means (SD)	Mixed 2 Means (SD)	Logical 1 Means (SD)	P	F(d/f)	Dependent
3>1,2	0.75 (0.5)	0.16 (0.38)	0 (0)	0.005	6.43 (2/27)	FMC+
1>2	1.25 (1.25)	0.44 (0.7)	2.5 (3.92)	0.09	2.61 (2/27)	FC+
3>1,2	7 (12.02)	0.83 (11.5)	0.5 (0.75)	0.02	4.01 (2/27)	Σc
3>1	0.75 (1.95)	0.27 (0.57)	0 (0)	0.1	2.43 (2/27)	mf
3>2	1.25 (0.5)	0.16 (0.51)	0.62 (1.06)	0.02	4.36 (2/27)	WS
3>1,2	2.5 (1)	0.8 (1.36)	0 (0)	0.005	6.47 (2/27)	DS
3>1	3.25 (2.21)	1.83 (1.58)	1.12 (0.99)	0.09	2.53 (2/27)	M+
3>2	5.5 (2.08)	2.61 (1.94)	2.87 (2.99)	0.08	2.66 (2/27)	ΣM
3>1,2	0.75 (0.5)	0.05 (0.23)	0.25 (0.46)	0.004	6.78 (2/27)	Symmetry
2>1	46.5 (0.7)	60.77 (11.69)	47.5 (8.87)	0.05	3.65 (2/14)	F%>40
3>1 2>1	97.5 (2.12)	93.09 (6.1)	87.14 (4.18)	0.03	4.1 (2/17)	TF%>80
3>2	2.16 (0.57)	0.77 (0.64)	1.25 (1.62)	0.04	3.37 (2/27)	M : ΣC
3>1,2	1.88 (1.45)	0.67 (0.77)	0.6 (0.75)	0.04	3.43 (2/27)	M : FM

* Test Duncan; for establishing between which groups the differences are significant.

TABLE 3
Rorschach

Logical Dreams		Bizarre Dreams		Difference Statistically Significant
0.62	WS	1.25	WS	*
No	DS	2.50	DS	*
47.5	F%	46.5%	F%	-
No	FMC +	0.75	FMC+	*
2.5	FC +	1.25	FC +	-
87.14	TF%	97.5	TF%	*
1.12	M%	3.25	M +	*
No	mf	0.75	mf	*
2.87	ΣM	5.5	ΣM	-
0.5	Σc	7	Σc	*
0.25	Symmetry	0.75	Symmetry	*
0.6	M:FM	1.88	M:FM	*
1.25	M:ΣC	2.16	M:ΣC	-

The first impression one gets from the results detailed in Tables 2 and 3 is that the personalities of the different dreaming styles are indeed different. The group of bizarre dreamers is characterized first by some tensions and inner conflicts. They are independent, imaginative, self-sufficient and prefer their own ways of understanding; also, they are inclined to critically view the world around them and to behave, time and again, in unconventional ways (M; M:C; WS; DS). However, this self-assured individualism and sometimes provocative poise is contradicted by an almost as strong need of dependency (Symmetry) and an almost insatiable urge for affection (c). They are vulnerable to emotional pressures; if under stress, they will try to control their emotions rather strictly, yet the efficiency of this control is unstable (TF%, mf). They are, then, not steady in their behavior; one may even say that from time to time they surprise their environment by their unpredictable reactions. While usually at ease with themselves, they also know the pressure of their self-criticism and the resultant feelings of inadequacy (M:C; WS; DS).

In contrast, members of the group of logical styles of dreaming are stable and predictable. They are not critical but rather feel comfortable in the world they live in (no DS). They need the support of their environment; however, this need will not be felt as a pressure (few indications of Symmetry). Also, generally speaking, inner conflicts and tensions do not trouble them (no mf; low c; no FMC). If under stress, their control of emotions will be flexible and efficient. Unlike the dreamers of bizarre style, members of the logical group are not swept away and dominated by emotions. Less imaginative and less individualistic than the group of bizarre style of dreaming, dreamers of the logical style get along smoothly with other people, and with themselves too. They get along smoothly, but from a distance. While dreamers of the bizarre style are interested in, from time to time, and even desperately need intimacy, dreamers of the logical style are less emotionally involved. If emotion does appear here it is a fear of closure.

Dreamers of a mixed style, as already pointed out, are closer in their behavior to, but not identical with, the group of logical style. The most distinguishing feature of the mixed style is their rigid controls (F% 40; TF% high) of emotions, stricter than the ones applied by the group of logical style.

Comparing the results of the Westcott and Ranzoni study with those of Nurit Lavi and Ariela Mamon, one immediately sees a high degree of agreement between them. Westcott and Ranzoni described the intuitive individual as an emotional, unstable person whose enthusiasm opens him/her up to influences from outside, yet at the same time is self-determined, non-conformist, preferring challenges and changes over tradition, and is ready to live with, in fact enjoys doubts and uncertainties. Lavi and Mamon were able to show that individuals whose habitual style of dreaming is bizarre are emotionally unstable, spontaneous, imaginative, self-sufficient non-conformists, who at the same time strongly need affectionate ties and support.

Analytic individuals, as described by Wescott and Ranzoni

are well-socialized, conservative, and modest. Though it was not emphasized by these authors, I would like here to remind you of the last item of Table 1: high information demanders said they are happy most of the time. Intuitives, on the other hand, have their high tides and low ebbs. People of a logical style of dreaming, Lavi and Mamon have found, are well-controlled, well-socialized individuals who though in need of emotional ties, will be strained by close intimacy. One does not then stretch one's point by summarizing that dreamers of bizarre dreams are intuitives and are characterized by the corresponding personality style, as detailed by Westcott-Ranzoni and by Lavi and Mamon, and similarly, dreamers of logical style have the characteristics of analytical individuals.

In fact, rather than stretching the conclusions beyond what the facts would support, one has to be aware of the risk of collecting more evidence than either logic or aesthetics would deem necessary. Nonetheless, I would like to mention one more finding which bears out the thesis suggested here. In differentiating "up" from "down", we rely on two sources of information: the visual field and the inner experience of gravity on the body. By creating incongruence between the upright, indicated by the surrounding visual field, and the upright, indicated by body sensation, Witkin, "a leader among psychologists who sought to identify stylistic differences among people in perceptual and cognitive functioning" (Goodenough, 1968, p. 11), was able to demonstrate that people consistently use this or that source for resolving this ambiguity.

Field-dependent persons characteristically rely more on information that comes from the world around, while field-independent people are self-referent and autonomous. These strategies of decision making were found to be correlated with important dimensions of one's behavior. Field-dependent persons are interpersonal in orientation and socially sensitive; their perception is dominated by the field as an unarticulated whole, so that its parts are not experienced in discrete. This global mode of perception is indicative of their holistic-intuitive cognitive style. In contrast, field-independent people are often inept and offensive in their personal relationships; their style of perceiving is characterized by an ability to articulate their field and differentiate parts from their organized background; their style of cognition is analytical. If psychotic, field-dependent patients produce hallucinatory symptoms, field-independent patients are prone to delusional symptoms.

"I once heard", Messick (1986) observed, "a noted perceptual psychologist remark that cognitive styles were exciting concepts, but that too many unfulfilled promissory notes had been issued in their name. This may well be true for some cognitive styles ... but it is not true for field dependence-independence" (pp. 116/7). Indeed, the countless number of papers and books that studied or related to this construct may vouch for its value and usefulness. Starker (1973) applied it in his research on the individual differences in daydreaming and reported that the daydreams of field-dependent people, as compared with that of field-independent people, are more bizarre. Subsequently, Starker (1974) reported a statistically significant correlation between dreams and daydreams. Starker's subjects wrote down, upon arousal, every dream they could recall on 16 consecutive mornings. These dream diaries were analyzed by two independent judges for "bizarreness", among other things. The judges had to estimate to what extent the dream departed from reality on a scale from 1 (a "realistic" dream) to 5 (a dream characterized by "wild and impossible happenings"). The results, as indicated, were statistically significant: subjects who had realistic daydreams also had realistic dreams, while subjects who had bizarre, improbable daydreams, had bizarre, improbable dreams.

It seems apparent that one's style of dreaming is but a reflection of one's cognitive style, and that aware and interacting with the environment, or absorbed in reveries, or sleeping and dreaming, one's style of cognition and the correlated styles of behavior prevail across the different states of mind.

Holograms, microgenesis and mental effort

At a closer look, the criteria for classifying dreams may turn out not to be of equal value. Unlike an element of dreams which violates logic or reality testing, the criterion of sudden, unexplained shifts in the sequence of events is perhaps less reliable in distinguishing between logical and bizarre dreams. As an analysis of daydreams shows, it may happen that while the story recalled is one of sudden jumps, nevertheless, logic prevailed and all the missing links were, in fact, at their proper places. In the study by Varendonck (1925) of his own daydreams, there are quite convincing hints to this effect. It will suffice here to detail one of his reveries.

Two events of the day preoccupied his mind at the time he was engaged in daydreaming. He had returned to the front (in the First World War) from a special leave, which he was granted because of a telegram informing him of his son's illness. He had to bring with him a medical certificate to prove the veracity of the telegram. Although he had submitted such a certificate, he was still worried since something in it "was not quite in order". The same day a soldier provoked him to intense anger. The soldier conveyed a request by the head-nurse, "but spoke and behaved so impolitely that I flatly refused to grant it". The soldier was insistent and even threatened him with the vengeance of the head-nurse who, incidentally, was a countess, and he knew that the chief medical officer "was at her mercy". Varendonck immediately wrote a report to his commanding officer, demanding the punishment of the soldier.

Now, in his fantasy, Varendonck sees, [as he assures us: "at a certain moment all the images stood before me with the vividness of real dream pictures" (p. 460)], his commanding officer's office. The commander is conveniently absent, a colleague of Varendonck opens the envelope, reads the certificate and the report of the incident with the soldier and forwards it to the general headquarters. The scene changed, now he is in another office and sees a secretary filing his certificate without his little fraud being detected. Suddenly, he writes a letter to the head-nurse. He sees very distinctly the lines of his letter and himself enclosing his visiting-card in the envelope. Then he is back in his office again which he shares with another officer. Varendonck asks this officer to send his corporal to the hospital with the letter. The officer objects at first, but eventually agrees. Now he is talking to the head-nurse, and tells her his view of the events.

While the change of scenes between the first and second officer is perhaps acceptable as a quick transition following, as it were, the path of documents, the letter-writing and return to his own office do not seem to fit this sequence. If, however, we read the report of these visualized fantasies together with its full verbal text, one may see that there were gaps in the visual presentation but not in the underlying thoughts.

The first visualized scene ended by him having seen an officer forwarding Varendonck's report of the incident with the soldier; in the third scene, suddenly, he writes a letter to the head-nurse. Let us now listen to Varendonck's recollection of his fantasies: "To whom will Major H. transmit my report? Either to the chief medical officer [or the administrative] officer; ... not to Countess V. Still, the latter will have her say in the matter. What if I warned her so as to dispose her in my favor and arouse her feelings against the culprit? I begin to compose the letter which I intend to write her with this purpose, but am interrupted by the idea: what if I enclosed my visiting-card (with my academic title)? What if I asked Captain X to send his corporal with the latter to the hospital? And I might add a copy of my report to it ... But what if I went to see her myself? I shall have to put on my best uniform. I'll send the orderly to ask her for an interview and tell him to give her my visiting-card" (pp. 458/9).

In the visualized scenes there is no indication of "what if I warned her". Instead, suddenly he writes her a letter. Again, in the visualized scenes there is no trace of his hesitation between sending a letter to the head-nurse or visiting her.

Instead, there appear two disconnected acts. "The if is dropped at once", Varendonck observes, "for I perform in fancy the act which is only introduced hypothetically in the text ... The if is forgotten as soon as thought, and swifter than the wind I fancy myself in different places without any consideration of the time or distance" (p. 462). Does that mean that our fantasy ignores hypotheses? It is apparent, Varendonck suggests, that the tension between the two suppositions is active in thinking, only that in visualizing we have no means for presenting what we competently do by means of words and sentences, namely, suppositions. A visualized fantasy, very much like a dream, present, perforce, an expectation or a supposition as an actualized deed. Freud (1900) defined this feature of our dream-life as "the first of the transformations which even the undistorted dream imposes on the dream-thoughts ... We dispose of it by a reference to the conscious fantasy, the daydreams, which behaves in a similar fashion with its conceptual content" (p. 487).

It is, thus, not impossible that at least some sudden and unexplained shifts in the dream-story are of the kind described here. Indeed, Foulkes and Vogel (1965) found that some of the dreams of sleep onset they collected were characterized by a "rapid snapshot-like" sequence. Yet, the subjects reported and experienced them as a story with some continuity, "the continuity residing in the dreamer's 'understanding' rather than in his visual imagery" (p. 240). As one of these subjects put it: there was a connection through thought. The images themselves were like a series of stills, but there seemed to be unity through the thought itself. Dreams, then, sometimes, or perhaps, as Freud would have had it, usually, are a composite of visual imagery and "understood" accompaniments, which while invisible, nevertheless are integral elements of the dream. Incidentally, Foulkes and Vogel think that it was this feature of our dreams which may have given rise to the notion that dreams do not unfold in time but rather occur simultaneously. Such a notion, they think, may not be entirely wrong.

Be that as it may, one feels quite sure that the other criterion for identifying bizarreness, the violation of logic and reality testing, is not surrounded by a similar ambiguity. How shall we explain its presence? How, indeed, is it possible to quote Dostoevsky again, that a murderer turns into a woman, and this woman into a dwarf, and the dreamer accepts these metamorphoses without the slightest surprise. Surely, such a picture cannot be a re-activated experience, the memory of something the dreamer met with while awake. Yet this precisely is the question. Dreams are not perceptions, they are made of our memories; how to explain, then, the bizarreness of some of our dreams?

In what will follow here I shall suggest that it is the very nature of the organization of our memories which may be held responsible for our generating some bizarre, unlikely dreams. Generally speaking, there are two possible avenues available for anyone who would like to construct a theory in regard to the organization of our memories. One may decide in favor of an itemized or an abstract organization. While never really spelled out, an item was understood to be a subjectively delimited experience, an "idea", a *Vorstellung*, and not one particular feature of a more complex "idea". For example, even after distinguishing between an experience and its verbal representation, Freud (1915) uses the concept of "idea" in the broad sense: "What we could permissibly call the conscious idea of the object can now be split up into the idea of the word (verbal idea) and the idea of the thing (concrete idea) ... the system Unconscious contains the thing-cathexes of the objects, the first and true object-cathexes; the system Preconscious originates in a hypercathexis of this concrete idea by a linking up of it with the verbal ideas corresponding to it" (p. 201).

Such an "idea" was thought to be retained by means of some organic change in the brain, the engram. The "ideas" were interconnected, they were associated. If recalled, the "idea" was assumed to re-appear as a true replica of the original experience. Any change in what was assumed to be registered, filed, as it were, and kept unaltered in memory, should have been a distortion due to some intervention, probably during the course of recall. In accord with this view of the organization of our memories, dreams like the one described by Dostoevsky should be understood as distortions of veridical memories. The edifice built by Freud (1900) in his *Interpretation of Dreams*, was based on this theory of remembering.

The alternative view of the organization of memories contends that there is empirical evidence for assuming an abstract, indirect mode of preserving our memories. Individual "ideas" and their associations are not the material substrate of our thinking but rather memory codes which, by implementing some rules of transformation, will represent an indirect, abstract reference to the original experience.

The first evidence of the alternative view, or rather at first the evidence surfaced as a puzzle, which intrigued Lashley (1950) for years. Lashley was able to show that 80% or even more of a rat's visual cortex could be damaged without loss of the ability to recognize patterns learned prior to the damage. How can such an extensive destruction of the optic system produce so little consequence? Lashley v. is unable to find an answer to this puzzle, but he did succeed in weakening the position of the theory according to which we preserve our memories in the form of individual "ideas", as a row of separate items. It is apparent that if such were the principle of organizing memories, Lashley should have found that he destroyed the "engrams" of many memories, and this loss resulted in a failure to remember what was learned earlier. Yet he found the opposite: in spite of a destruction of the major part of the visual cortex, visual discrimination based on earlier learning was not affected at all.

Pribram (1974, 1980) contends that he has the solution to the puzzle which, in a manner of speaking, haunted Lashley throughout all his creative years. If we assume that our memories are "written" in accord with the principle of holograms, then we should expect to see what Lashley indeed found, For in a hologram every part contains information sufficient to reconstruct the complete information stored in that hologram. Let us note, constructing and not retrieving. Speaking of retrieving, one presumes that the "ideas" are kept, as it were, on shelves, and if the need arises for recalling them, all what one has to do is to find out where they are stored. Speaking of reconstruction, one indicates the belief that our memories are made of abstract signs of events and characters rather than of fully evolved representations of those events and characters.

Further evidence lending credence to this view of the organization of memories was entailed in G. Miller's (1956) study on the difference between immediate and long- term memory. While our ability to remember events immediately after their having been registered is rather restricted, we know of no limits for accumulating and preserving memories for long-term usage. How can we explain these differences in the range of our abilities? G. Miller suggested that our memories are organized in "chunks". It is due to these "chunks" that long-term memory may expand to its known dimensions. In order to be included in a chunk, an item of information must be recorded, made abstract and similar to some other information. While every experience is an individual event, it is precisely those individual features which should be lost for the sake of an encompassing formula. Although not stated explicitly by G. Miller, it follows from the conception of "chunks" of memories that to remember individual experiences means reconstructing them from their abstracted, higher-order store.

Johnson (1970, 1972) further elaborated on this suggestion. Chunks, he thinks, are not the end but rather an interim phase in preserving our memories. Chunks may be recorded and abstracted into higher-order codes. "At the highest level of the code hierarchy, the entire sequence may be represented in memory by a single code" (1970, p. 172).

Both Johnson and Pribram then felt it necessary to hypothesize a very abstract mode of registration for preserving memories, the only difference between them being the procedure they thought was applied. Unlike Johnson who left it open-ended, Pribram was in this regard specific and explicit. It may happen that one finds it difficult to agree with Pribram and assume that the brain works along the principles of holography. It is then not superfluous to point out that the conception of "chunks" and memory codes is compatible with but does not depend upon this particular principle of encoding.

How shall we now understand the process of remembering? In order to remember, first one has to activate one's memory codes. However, a code comprises much of, and a super-code even all our memories. Having then activated these codes, one is immediately confronted by the task of selecting the sought-for-information and rejecting all the other information, which though related, is not pertinent to the needs of the moment. However, information kept in a memory code is abstract hints and not fully constructed representations of the original experience. Therefore, having defined the proper direction, the next step should be what thus far has been loosely called reconstruction. By a confluence of evidence from normal behavior and neurology, we may attempt a description of this process. As will be shown, there may be a link between the process of reconstruction and bizarre dreams.

We became used to being cautious in accepting the evidence of our subjective experiences. One should then not hesitate in pointing to one more field where the evidence proffered by self-observation is not beyond doubt. Remembering is this field. Our subjective experiences may support the assumption of separate yet connected "ideas" and not that of reconstruction from highly abstract memory codes. I suppose most people, if informed about these alternatives, would prefer the first possibility over the latter. We think and speak with alacrity and speed, why should one assume that all these easy performances were preceded by an effortful process of reconstructing?

Indeed, normally we are supplied by our stored memories so smoothly as to prevent any reflections on abstract recoding; then, for whatever reason, we may get stuck. We are looking for a word or a name, but it eludes us. Not definitely, though, for we have a distinct feeling of knowing it, and if somebody would suggest a word, we would not hesitate in deciding whether or not this was the word or name we were struggling to recall. For the elusive word was on the "tip of the tongue". If, however, nobody is around to help us, and we continue our search until we arrive at our destination, we may reveal some indications in favor of the theory of memory codes.

Brown and McNeill (1966) succeed in experimentally creating a state of tip-of-the-tongue in their subjects, thus elevating the phenomenon from its anecdotal status, and suggest some conclusions which are pertinent to our discussion. Their subjects were presented with a list of rare words and their definitions. Then they were again shown the definitions and had to provide the fitting words. If the subjects could not recall the word, even though they knew that they knew it, then they were requested to say all the words that came to their mind, until the search was stopped.

Each subject then produced several words, some of which were close in meaning or in sound to the words on the tip of his tongue. Seventy percent of these words were similar in sound, but not in meaning; approximately half of the similar sounding words had the same number of syllables as the target words, but only 20% of the words similar in meaning matched the number of syllables in the target words. Also 49% of the initial letters of the words similar in sound matched the initial letters of the target words as compared with only 8% matches for the words similar in meaning.

Thus it seems the physical features of a word, like the number of its consonants and vowels and the number of its syllables, are processed separately from its meaning and are of no less help for the searching mind than the words from the same category of meaning. I find this result quite counterintuitive. Also, the abundance of similar sounding words may be understood as indicating that while evolving a word, we generate and eliminate, unbeknown to us, a relatively large number of clang-associations. Still, the finding most relevant here was the occurrence of non-lexical words. In their effort to overcome the obstacles of remembering, these students created non-existing words, and while fully aware of their exact status, verbalized them. For example, in attempting to recall the target word: sampan, some S's produced, among many other words, also: sanching and sympoon. Why? Evidently, such words were not mistakenly recalled; since non-lexical words were never registered among our memories, there is no possibility to "retrieve" them. Rather, they were created on the spot to be used as a scaffolding to help construct communicative words. An impressive indication, indeed, of the mental effort invested and of the need for this effort, a need which was created by the nature of the organization of our memories.

It is apparent that while generating words and thoughts we also generate, as interim positions, clang-associations and neologisms. Usually, however, our mental work proceeds unhampered and efficiently and we are unaware of them, but moments of tip-of-the-tongue, extreme fatigue, drowsiness, fever or, pathology make them observable to all. For under such conditions, one is unable to invest the mental effort necessary to evolve "sampan" and gets stuck, as some of Brown and McNeill' subjects indeed got stuck at "sarong" or "Siam". Sarong and Siam as substitutes for sampan will be defined as bizarre, non-communicative utterings. By now, however, to quote a sentence of mine written above, the mystery of such productions lost its otherworldliness.

Many of the readers, I presume, are acquainted with Freud's (1904) efforts to recall the name of the Italian painter, Signorelli. Touring from Dalmatia to Herzegovina in the company of a fellow traveller, he was unable to recall the name he was so well acquainted with. The names of two other Italian painters, Botticelli and Boltraffio, came to his mind, but he knew that neither of these names was the correct one. Informed by his fellow-traveller or perhaps by someone else of the sought-for-name, Freud immediately recognized and agreed with it. Immediately before failing to verbalize the name Signorelli, Freud was involved in telling anecdotes about the fatalistic surrender to death but not to impotence of the Turkish peasants of Bosnia-Herzegovina. To be precise, he related to these peasants' approach to death, but stopped before touching on the sexual aspect. Instead, he initiated a new line of conversation: the frescoes in Orvieto, only to be confronted by his inability to name the painter. Because of the temporal proximity of these two topics, it was Freud's understanding that the inhibition he exerted on the former led to his failure in the latter one. In addressing their Austrian physician, the Turkish peasants usually said; *Herr* (Sir) which in Italian is Signor; further, the initial letters of Herzegovina are Her. This is why Signorelli, an allusion to Herr, Herzegovina and impotence, was, as Freud put it, repressed.

While the connection created by the temporal contiguity is indeed suggestive, the conclusion seems tenuous. Instead of Signorelli, Freud verbalized Botticelli and Boltraffio. Now, if Signorelli was barred because of its alliteration with Herzegovina (due to the mediating Herr), then by the same token Botticelli and Boltraffio should have been occluded because of their alliteration with Bosnia (the region discussed was called Bosnia-Herzegovina). In fact, the association between Bosnia and Botticelli is stronger, and the repression should have been more imperative than in the case of Signorelli-Herzegovina. Boltraffio should have been avoided for the further reason that shortly before this conversation, while staying in Trafio, Freud was informed of the suicide of a patient of his who was suffering from an incurable sexual disease. In his relation to death and sex, this patient then seemingly replicated the Turkish peasants' approach and this precisely was the topic Freud tried to forget about. Yet, Botticelli and Boltraffio did surface, only Signorelli was kept submerged. One may counter that nature is lawful but seems capricious or, to put it differently, while the principle is simple the individual applications may be too complex to be always understood.

As against this possible suggestion, one should point out that Freud knew that the painter he intended to discuss was neither Boticelli nor Boltraffio, and when helped out, he immediately recognized the correct name. All this is very uncharacteristic of repression, otherwise Freud would not have been compelled to conceive the concepts of resistance and negation in the course of psychotherapies as proofs of the correctness of an interpretation. Then we don't know why of all possible topics Freud chose the frescoes in Orvieto. In fact, we don't know why Freud decided not to speak of sexual matters. In short, it is impossible to decide what was here a deliberate decision and what was determined by the repressed unconscious. The scant information Freud agreed to share with his readers is not enough to conjecture a role for the repressed unconscious.

The elusive word, Signorelli, seems to have been a tip-of-the-tongue phenomenon and it should be analyzed accordingly. That is to say, there is a distinct possibility that what was displayed here due to a conflict between Freud's intentions was the regular way of evolving the word "Signorelli" from its memory codes. Unfortunately, Freud uttered only two names, and he was spared further effort to evolve the correct word. We are then unable to follow up the microgenesis of "Signorelli", but we may point out that all these names are composed of four syllables, with the stress on the third one, and of course all of them are painters. Whatever the reason or reasons for Freud's failure, we may say that he experienced a tip-of-the-tongue state, and that his behavior fits the expectations aroused by the theory of abstract memory codes and recalling by means of effortful constructing and reconstructing.

I would now like to mention the pioneering works of two researchers at the beginning of this century. Based on some observations obtained in the neurology and experimental psychology of his days, Schilder (1920) suggested that "the formal characteristics of schizophrenic thinking warrants the thesis that in many schizophrenic cases such formations, which nor-

mally would be only transitory phases in thought-development, appear as the end results of thought processes. The point
of view that these formations are abortive products of thought-
development contributes considerably to this understanding"
(p. 514). Schilder then proposed that not only words, but also
thoughts, are kept in abstract codes and in order to communicate them, one has to evolve, to reconstruct them.

Finally, it is important to point out that not only in evolving
memories from their abstract codes do we have to run through
some strange preparatory phases. The encoding of a percept is
also a complex drama, far more complex than anybody trusting
the evidence of his/her subjective experience might imagine.
By presenting visual stimuli very briefly in a tachistoscope, in
dim light, in indirect view, or in extreme miniature, and then
gradually improving these unfavorable conditions, Sander
(1928, 1930) was able to show that percepts emerge as the end
product of a multi-staged process. The first stage of an evolving percept is, in a term coined by Undeutsch (1942), a fog of
light, an unstructured impression of hue. The next step is a
ground figure differentiation, although the identity of the
figure remains vague. Then the contour and inner content
become more distinct, but this configuration is very unstable
and changing. Thus a contour, which according to the actual
stimulus is interrupted, is perceived accordingly but then tends
to close again at the next movement, only to open once more.
Eventually, the finalized percept emerges.

Were it not that experimental psychology proved otherwise,
we would believe, as our subjective experience indeed leads us
to, that perception comes into existence in one immediate act.
Surely, nobody would be inclined to think that some stages of
an evolving percept distort rather than depict the environment.
Sander called this process of gradual evolving of a percept,
Aktualgenese. Werner (1959) used the term microgenesis, that
is, following up the evolving of a percept or thought in micro-
dimension. Applying this term, we may then say that the
microgenesis of perceptions and thoughts revealed so many

possible pitfalls that one wonders how one succeeds in generating correct products. The danger of stopping at a bizarre interim stage lurks everywhere. So much so, that instead of explaining how some deviation from logic and reality testing could have occurred, we might as well ponder about how we manage to conform with logic and reality testing.

Indeed, success is contingent upon our ability to invest the proper measure of mental effort. While being aware and alert, we are endowed with the means to do so and are ready to apply this effort. In sleep, however, the situation changes. Not as dramatically, though, as it is sometimes assumed. People with an analytical style of thinking, awake or asleep, are ever-ready to invest the necessary mental effort. Regarding the majority, whose style of thinking is mixed, one is reminded of Foulkes' (1962) finding that people generate both "dreams" and "thoughts". In other words, the dreams of the majority indicate that their measure of mental effort rises and falls in a cyclical manner. Individuals of global-intuitive style, if confronted by some strange dreams of theirs, will not be alerted, but rather may stop their efforts at evolving and reconstructing and feel content or even enjoy the ambiguity a d bizarreness thus created. Such bizarreness, however, let us once more emphasize, does not necessarily evidence a motivated distortion of an originally acceptable "idea". Rather, as Schilder (1920) put it: "such formations, which normally would be only transitory phases in thought-development, appear as the end results of thought processes" (p. 514).

The psychodynamics of bizarre dreams

It is high time to move beyond the preparatory steps and relate the ideas propounded in the earlier chapters to the theory that has dominated the field throughout this century, as well as my mind for so many years: Freud's understanding of the nature of dreams. This understanding, as we all know, is not condensable into one sentence, but it is possible to single out its most important feature, namely the suggestion of two kinds of psychical functioning. In his *Interpretation of Dreams*, Freud (1900) concluded: "Thus we are driven to conclude that two fundamentally different kinds of psychical processes are concerned in the formation of dreams" (p. 596). Again, somewhat later he details: "But from the moment at which the repressed thoughts are strongly cathected by the unconscious wishful impulse and, on the other hand, abandoned by the preconscious cathexis, they become subject to the primary psychical process ... the irrational processes ... are the primary ones" (p. 605).

In his *Introduction to Freud's* (1901) *Psychopathology of Everyday Life*, Strachey undertook to justify the preference Freud gave "in his expository writings" to parapraxes over dreams. After all, dreams are more complex phenomena and "lead rapidly into deep waters". Parapraxes, indeed, are simple and easily explained. Nevertheless, "it was possible for Freud to demonstrate on them what was, after all, the fundamental thesis established in the Interpretation of Dreams - the existence of two distinct modes of mental functioning, what he described as the primary and secondary processes" (p. XIII). Primary processes, Jones (1953) stated, are "unchecked by any logical contradiction, any causal association, they have no sense of either time or of external reality" (p. 397).

If dreams, containing some wish which emerged from the unconscious, are shaped along these characteristics, their otherworldliness indeed seems to be inevitable and well-explained. However, we have already seen that only a minority of dreams are in fact bizarre, and Freud's explanation, or rather, explanations, for this discrepancy between the expected and observable appearance of dreams are self-contradictory and make it difficult to work with. To begin with, in the same *Psychopathology of Everyday Life*, the Introduction to which by Strachey I have quoted from above, Freud's concluding sentences seem to differ from Strachey's resume. "The incongruities, absurdities and errors of the dream content, which result in the dream being scarcely recognized as the product of psychological activity, originate in the same way, though it is true with a freer use of the means at hand, as our common mistakes in everyday life. In both cases the appearance of an incorrect function is explained by the peculiar mutual interferences between two or several correct functions" (p. 277/8).

It is the interference between two correctly functioning processes which is responsible for the absurdities and incongruities both in dreams and parapraxes. But then what place was left here for warranting the assumption of primary processes? Speaking of two correct functions in itself should preclude relating to one of them in the way described by Jones and of course by Freud.

Yet, Freud held both of these contradictory views. Earlier, I have quoted him stating that the repressed thought, abandoned by the preconscious cathexes, becomes subject to the irrational primary process. Then, in his *Note on the Unconscious*, Freud (1912/c) wrote that the latent thought of the dream, "by entering into connections with the unconscious tendencies during the night, ... have become assimilated to the latter, degraded as it were to the condition of unconscious thoughts, and subjected to the laws by which unconscious activity is governed" (p. 265) – Here the absurdities and incongruities of a dream are explained by the peculiarity of the laws which govern unconscious activity. However, in the *Psychopathology of Everyday Life* we were told that a peculiarity of the interference between two correct functions is the reason for these absurdities.

Not only in the *Psychopathology of Everyday Life*, but in *The Interpretation of Dreams* itself, there are statements which would derive the existence of primary processes from the absurdities of dreams, and other statements which collide with such a conclusion. I have quoted above from p. 605 in support of the possibility of primary process. But we also read there the following resume: "Thus we are driven to conclude that two fundamentally different kinds of psychical processes are concerned in the formation of dreams. One of these produces perfectly rational dream-thoughts of no less validity than normal thinking; while the other treats these thoughts in a manner which is in the highest degree bewildering and irrational. We have already ... segregated this second psychical process as being the dream-work proper" (p. 597).

Again, more succinctly: "At bottom, dreams are nothing other than a particular form of thinking ... It is the dream-work which creates that form, and it alone is the essence of dreaming – the explanation of its peculiar nature" (p. 506/7).

Some of Freud's readers became aware of this inconsistency in his thinking and tried to remedy this weakness in one of the main pillars of his theory of behavior. Reeves (1966) observed that "Freud contrived ... to stress both the 'rationality' of latent dream-thoughts and the irrationality of unconscious processes of which ... dream-thoughts are sometimes treated as one class. One can unravel this apparent contradiction in several ways. For instance, one may substitute functional intelligibility for 'rationality' in the first clause and illogicality in the second" (p. 159). In her understanding, such a choice of terms would be enough to make viable what seems to be an impasse.

Edelson (1973) stated the problem in a non-hesitant manner: "The need for interpretation suggests either that the system of processes generating such symbolic forms as dreams (unlike language perhaps) is not in any symbolic major way used in communication, and therefore is not primarily governed by or adapted to the exigencies and requirements of communicative interaction, or that the system of processes generating such symbolic forms as dreams is responsive to communicative requisites and so does operate, in fact, to obstruct the communication of meaning. Freud seems to have held both views (1900, Ch. VI, but also footnote 2 added in 1925, p. 506)" (p. 221).

Having thus stated the problem clearly, Edelson nevertheless puts the blame on Freud's readers: "It is still not generally understood that the view presented by Freud is that the thoughts ... underlying both dreams and psychopathological symptomatology are the same as the thoughts of normal, waking consciousness. Only the transformational processes operating upon these thoughts ... - e.g., a phonological representation in language or a memory-image representation in dreams – ... are different" (p. 235).

Since Edelson made it clear that Freud held two incompatible views with regard to dream-thoughts, one wonders what could have justified his speaking afterwards of "the" view of Freud. In all fairness, though, one has to point out that Edelson is not the only one who would like to straighten out what was uneven in Freud's thinking by disregarding one of his contradictory statements.

In a similar vein Foulkes (1978) wrote: "What of the underlying dream-thoughts? Are they to be identified with interpretive constructs such as unconscious impulses, or are they simply the verbal thought-elements achieved through the free-association method? In Chapter VI, the answer clearly is the latter. Speaking of 'the essential dream-thoughts' Freud remarks that 'these usually emerge as a complex of thoughts and memories of the most intricate possible structure, with all the attributes, of the trains of thought familiar to us in waking life' (1900, pp. 311/12). These thoughts stand 'in the most manifold logical relations to one another' (1900, p. 312) ... 'The dream-thoughts are entirely rational' (1900. p. 506) ... It is clear that Freud here is considering his points of origin as linguistic and propositional in form, rather than as members of some underlying domain of impulses which is devoid of logic" (p. 61).

By defining the unconscious as linguistic and propositional

in form, one rules out any possibility of invoking the primary process as an explanation of the peculiarities of some dreams, or the other way round, of proving the existence of primary process by means of deviations from logic in dreams. For a propositional and linguistic unconscious would not necessitate suggesting the concept of primary process, nor could such an unconscious justify this suggestion. Could Freud have agreed with such an understanding of his intentions? To put it differently, was it by mistake that Strachey defined the assumption of primary and secondary processes as "the fundamental thesis established in *The Interpretation of Dreams*", or that Jones (1953) saw in the "proposition that there are two fundamentally different kinds of mental processes, which he termed primary and secondary respectively, together with his description of them" (p. 397) Freud's most revolutionary contribution to psychology?

Lacan, an intellectual hero in the eyes of many, was the first to maintain that "the unconscious is structured in the most radical way like a language" (1977, p. 234). This was his understanding Freud's "essential message". As against this interpretation, Jones thought that "the laws applicable to the two groups are so widely different that any description of the earlier one must call up a picture of the more bizarre type of insanity" (p. 397). While language was called into existence with the purpose of communicating between wakeful human beings, the primary process, by definition, generates idiosyncratic products and does not allow communicative messages to be conveyed; which of these was Freud's view of the unconscious? As we have seen, Freud expressed both views, and Jones and Strachey chose one of these contradictory statements, and Lacan, Edelson, and Foulkes the other one, and proclaimed it the true message. The truth, however, expects us not to gently close one eye and overlook the complexity of the matter.

I have quoted here extensively because when discussing an issue so dear and emotionally laden to many, as ours is, it is preferable to reiterate the original wordings rather than paraphrase them. Once more, I shall quote a few sentences of Freud, which while they could have been narrated will, for the reasons indicated, be given in Freud's own words. These sentences, being Freud's last formulations of his views, may indicate that, although he did not repudiate the other, contradictory, assumption, his belief in the irrationality of the unconscious was nevertheless stronger.

In his remarks on the theory and practice of dream-interpretation, Freud (1932) suggested differentiating between dreams from "below" and dreams from "above". This might have sounded as an indication that Freud had changed his mind and agreed that dreams from above, from the Ego, are logical while dreams from below, from the Id, are bizarre. However, in the *Outline of Psychoanalysis*, Freud (1940) removed all such doubts. His formulations have shown him to believe in the stereotype of dreams as firmly as he did 40 years before.

"In short", he wrote there, "dreams may arise either from the Id or from the ego. The mechanism of dream-formation is in both cases the same and so also is the necessary dynamic precondition" (p. 166). "But what makes dreams so invaluable in giving us insight is the circumstance that, when the unconscious material makes its way into the ego, it brings its own modes of working along with it. This means that the preconscious thoughts in which the unconscious material has found its expression are handled in the course of the dream-work as though they were unconscious portions of the id; and in the case of the alternative method of dream-formation, the preconscious thoughts which have obtained reinforcement from an unconscious drive-impulse are brought down to the unconscious state. It is only in this way that we learn the laws which govern the passage of events in the unconscious and the respects in which they differ from the rules that are familiar to us in waking thought" (p. 167).

Here there is everything needed to vindicate Jones' and Strachey's interpretation: the unconscious material brings its mode of working into the ego; it is only in this way that we learn of the respects in which they differ from waking thought; and, finally, it is because of this insight that dreams are important to us. Also, it was made clear that, whether it originates from below or from above, a dream is different from our waking thought, in both cases "they are handled as though they were unconscious portions of the id", that is, "are brought down to the unconscious state". Furthermore, this long quotation above is followed in the original by one more sentence pertinent to our discussion: "It is, however, an unmistakable fact that the outcome of the dream-work is a compromise. The ego organization is not yet paralyzed and its influence is to be seen in the distortion imposed on the unconscious material and in what are often very ineffective attempts at giving the total result a form not too unacceptable to the ego" (p. 167).

Nobody has ever seen or heard a dream before it came to exist. What it looked like at the beginning of its inception is a matter of speculation. What was proved here was Freud's belief in the stereotype of dreams. All dreams are bizarre, and if they are not, then originally they were and only later on some external force gave them "a form not too unacceptable" to logic and reality testing. "When viewing the form of any dream", Grinstein (1983) states in his book of Freud's rules of dream interpretation, "the therapist should not be put off by its sensible, logical, or intellectual character [for] Freud (1916/17) stresses the fact that even if a dream 'has an apparently sensible exterior, we know that this has only come about through dream-distortion and can have ... little organic relation to the internal content of the dream'" (p. 18).

If Freud would have been correct in stating that dreams are different from our waking thought because their kernel, the repressed wish, is organized and expressed in accord with the bizarre ways the id functions, then one should have questioned the reasons for conceiving the construct of censorship. If someone who speaks and understands only English would listen to utterings verbalized in an exotic language, how would he know when and why to become alerted. The concept of censorship is only justifiable if the repressed wish appears in a way which is understandable to a logical-thinking Ego. Thus, either the id works along the rules of primary process, and since it infiltrates the sleeping ego, dreams are necessarily and inevitably bizarre (but then the censorship and the whole metastructure built on it become questionable), or the ego and id obey the same logic and the distinction between primary and secondary processes was a mistake. In this case the need for censorship is conceivable. However, we will have to assume that no dream is originally bizarre and if eventually they are bizarre, then they become so later on, due to an interference by this censorship.

Freud held both of these incompatible views; although one of these views was closer to his heart, he did not drop either of them and the self-contradiction prevails. It is then understandable that people who would like to follow Freud have to choose one of these non-compatible views. Only I would object to the attempt to declare their preferred view as the "true" Freudian understanding. The true Freudian view was the one which they felt obliged to abandon. Be that as it may, Lacan, Edelson, and Foulkes were impressed by the fact that Freud sometimes thought of the unconscious in propositional and linguistic terms. "A central hypothesis", as Edelson (1973) put it, "in Freud's theory of dreams, already delineated in the first chapter, is that the thinking of the dreamer (or some kinds of psychotic individuals) is not different from the thinking of the non-psychotic individual in the waking state, where 'thinking' refers to the most basic, probably universal categories" (p. 237).

Indeed, in the *Psychopathology of Everyday Life*, already quoted earlier, Freud expressed himself in precisely such a way by stating that the absurdities and incongruities of the dream content should be "explained by the peculiar mutual interferences between two or several correct functions" (p. 278). To put it differently, any violation of logic and reality testing which may occur in a dream should, in accord with this view, be interpreted as the result of a peculiar interaction between a logical Ego and a logical repressed Unconscious. Let us repeat here that by so deciding, one agrees that if not in their contents then in their way of mental functioning, there are no differences between the Ego and Id and, consequently, there is no justification for speaking of the irrationality of the Unconscious. Primary process, Freud's fundamental thesis, also lost thereby its right to exist.

Now as to the interference between two correct mental functions, let us substitute the better-known censorship or resistance for interference and see whether it will explain the bizarreness of some dreams. It was by employing the same method of "analysis", free associations, for interpreting dreams and parapraxes that Freud found their "mechanism" to correspond in its most essential points. The value of the method of free associations is a function of the value of the assumption regarding psychical determinism, to be precise, unconscious psychical determinism. Freud was convinced that our subjective experience misleads us; there is no free will at all. The feeling of free will attests only to a lack of conscious motivation. "But what is thus left free by the one side receives its motivation from the other side, from the unconscious" (1901, p. 254).

For example, while reading the proofs of *The Interpretation of Dreams*, Freud wrote a letter to Fliess and vowed that he would make no more changes in the work "even if it contains 2467 mistakes." Subsequently, he wrote down his associations to this unintentionally chosen number. He was 24 years old when he met someone about whose retirement he had read in a newspaper. Now he was 43 years old. 24 and 43 are 67, the year of retirement. Freud, then, "was celebrating a kind of triumph over [the other one's] career being at an end, while I still have everything before me. So one can say with justice that not even the number 2467 which I threw out unthinkingly was without its determinants from the unconscious" (1901, p. 243). These determinants, let us add, were displayed by applying the method of free associations.

The unconsciously condensed meaning of 2467, then, was

that he still has 24 years of work and achievement before him (43+24=67). An imaginative solution and a possible one. But can we be sure that things indeed evolved in that way? Freud's answer to such an objection was indicated in his "saying with justice". He felt justified and his method proven. Still, one is allowed to wonder whether Freud felt as sure as was indicated here. For a few pages later, he mentions "Herr Rudolf Schneider [who] has raised an interesting objection to the conclusiveness of such analyses of numbers". Schneider opened a history book and began to associate to the first number he came across, or he presented someone else with a number he had chosen and asked for his/her associations. "In one instance which he relates that concerned himself, the associations provided determinants just as abundant and full of meaning as in our analyses of numbers that have arisen spontaneously, whereas the number in Schneider's experiment, having been presented from outside, called for no determinant" (p. 250, n).

Schneider concluded, therefore, that the emergence of determining associations to numbers that occur to the mind spontaneously cannot prove that these numbers originated from the thoughts discovered by means of free associations. Freud's answer was remarkably cautious. He conceded that spontaneously emerging ideas "may be undetermined, or may have been determined by the thoughts that come out in the analysis, or by other thoughts not disclosed in the analysis.... In analytic practice we proceed on the presupposition that the second of the possibilities mentioned above meets the facts and that in the majority of instances use can be made of it" (p. 251, n).

As against the strong statement in the text: "Nothing in the mind is ... undetermined" (p. 242), here he admits that spontaneously emerging ideas may be undetermined. In contrast to the confidence demonstrated in interpreting parapraxes, here he agrees to such far-reaching qualifications as a "presupposition" and "in the majority of cases", which means that in fact those interpretations are possible but only possible solutions. Even though these concessions were agreed to in a footnote, there is nothing in this placing to detract from their importance. Both the main text and its footnotes were conceived and written by Freud, and one is left perplexed and wondering how he could have remained content with such a glaring self-contradiction.

Freud, however, did not seem to have found it curious or objectionable that he had committed himself simultaneously to two contradictory declarations, for in his *Introductory Lectures* (1916) he did it again. He wrote there that he is "very much inclined" to believe that slips of the tongue have their origin in repressed thoughts because every time one investigates an instance of a "slip" an explanation of this kind is forthcoming. He then added: "But it is also true, that there is no way of proving that a 'slip of the tongue' cannot occur without this mechanism" (pp.44-45).

It is apparent that Freud could not have been correct both in conjecturing an all-pervasive and mainly unconscious determination of psychic acts, and in conceding that psychic acts are either determined or chance occurrences. It is also apparent, I think, that his awareness of this contradiction notwithstanding, he behaved as if his thesis of a full determination, indeed, was proved, and as if it was not he himself who had admitted its falsity.

Freud held contradictory views both in regard to the nature of the repressed unconscious and to the determination of psychic acts. If one accepts his suggestions, one should agree that the bizarreness of some dreams is a reflection of the bizarre laws prevailing in the Id, but at the same time is also the result of a clash between a logically formulated unconscious need and a similarly logical determination to repress. In both cases his hesitation in regard to mental determinism may be detrimental to the promise that the method of free associations infallibly displays the hidden meaning of an apparently meaningless dream, for the method of associations may be fruitful only if psychic acts are always determined.

Finally, I would like to remind the reader of what was

already established here in the previous chapters: the facts of the heterogeneity of dreams and cognitive styles. Only a minority of dreams comprise violations of logic and reality testing, and these violations are causally related to one's cognitive style. Cognitive styles and microgenesis seem to explain the nature of dreams in a more simple and a more testable way than either the theory of primary process or the construct of mental censorship.

The heterogeneity of dreams and its correlation with styles of thinking is a proven fact. The differences in cooperation of these styles with the process of reconstructing our memories from their codes is a presupposition. And so is the idea that associations with a dream are determined by its underlying latent dream-thoughts. In such a situation everybody may avail himself according to his own preference. My preference followed from the principle of continuity of the modes of mental functioning through the different states of mind. The explanation which fits the clang-associations and neologisms of the state of tip-of-the-tongue in full awareness and the peculiarities of thinking of some schizophrenics is also the proper explanation for the bizarreness of some of our dreams.

What dreams teach us

While it was not clearly stated thus far, the reader may have sensed that the view suggested here leads to a reevaluation of the importance attached to dreams. Although Freud and Jung succeeded in setting dreams on a lofty pedestal and many experts as well as countless enthusiastic dreamers agree with them, nonetheless their suggestions seem to me questionable. "... I would look for the theoretical value of the study of dreams", Freud (1900) stated, "in the contributions it makes to psychological knowledge and in the ... light it throws on the problems of the psycho-neuroses. Who can guess the importance of the results which might be obtained from a thorough understanding of the structure and functions of the mental apparatus ..." (p. 619). For Freud, then, dreams were important because they were the royal road for learning of the mental apparatus. As to the question whether dreams contribute "towards a revelation of the hidden characteristics of individual men?", he did not feel justified in answering these questions. "I have not considered this side of the problem of dreams further" (p. 620).

From the beginning to the very end, such was his understanding of the contribution of dreams. In his last essay, very much like in *The Interpretation of Dreams*, Freud (1940) praised dreams as "invaluable" not because they subserve some of the practical applications of psychoanalysis, but rather because it is only through them "that we learn the laws which govern the passage of events in the unconscious and the respects in which they differ from the rules that are familiar to us in waking thought" (p. 167).

In fact, however, dreams cannot teach us of the existence of an alogical system of thinking because, to begin with, Freud's statements as to whether or not there is such a system were equivocal and Lacan, as quoted earlier, went so far as to contend that the conception of a linguistic, that is, logical and communicative unconscious was Freud's real purpose and contribution. Whatever the outcome of the different exegetical attempts to establish Freud's "true" intentions will be, we will have to agree with Lacan – for different reasons though – that the repressed unconscious is indeed governed by the self-same rules as are our conscious mentations.

The thesis about the unconscious, that is to say that mental life is not a synonym for consciousness, was well known and, as Freud (1900) put it, "forcibly" presented by many authors before him, the last of them being Lipps (1897) whom Freud (1900, pp. 611/4) extensively quoted. "The problem of the unconscious in psychology", Lipps wrote, "is less a psychological problem than *the* problem of psychology". The unconscious is the true psychical reality; everything conscious has an unconscious preliminary stage. Du Prel (1885), another author quoted by Freud, stated that dreams "show that the concept of the mind is a wider one than that of consciousness, in the same kind of way in which the gravitational force of heavenly bodies extends beyond its range of luminosity" (p. 47). A few years earlier, Galton (1879) observed: "The more I have examined the working of my mind ... the less respect I feel for the part played by consciousness ... The unconscious operations of the mind frequently far transcend the conscious ones in intellectual importance ... conscious actions are motivated, and motives can make themselves attended to, whether consciousness be present or not".

Maudsley (1867) put it even stronger, if possible: "It is a truth which cannot be too distinctly borne in mind, that consciousness is not co-extensive with mind ... the preconscious action of the mind, as certain metaphysical psychologists in Germany have called it, and the unconscious action of the mind, which is now established beyond all rational doubt, are assuredly facts of which the most ardent psychologist must admit that self-consciousness can give us no account" (p. 15). The last, in fact the first one to be mentioned here is the "metaphysical psychologist in Germany" himself, Herbart (1824), to whom we owe the concept of the threshold of consciousness and the thesis that mental life is bifurcated into two realms, those above and those below "the threshold". Incidentally, Freud learned psychology from a Herbartian textbook (Jones, 1953, p. 374).

All this is true, as is the fact that "our" unconscious, according to Freud (1900, p. 614) is quite unlike the unconscious of these authors. The thesis which they dispute "with so much heat and defend with so much energy" is the thesis that apart from conscious, there are also unconscious psychical processes. "But it is not in order to establish this thesis that we have summoned up the phenomena of dreams and of the formation of hysterical symptoms ... The new discovery [consists of the thesis that] there are two kinds of unconscious, which have not been distinguished by psychologists. Both of them are unconscious in the sense used by psychology; but in our sense one of them, which we term the Ucs, is also inadmissible to consciousness ..." (p. 614).

Freud here overstated his point, for this precisely was one of Herbart's basic tenets, and Freud's biographer, Jones (1953), agreed with this criticism: "Herbart actually describes an idea as 'verdrangt' [repressed] when it is unable to reach consciousness because of some opposing idea or when it has been driven out of consciousness by one! He conceives of two thresholds in the mind, which correspond topographically with the position of Freud's two censorships" (p. 372).

Thus, the originality of Freud's conception is more equivocal than he believed it to be. The impact of Herbart was tremendous, and it would have been quite remarkable if Freud had not been influenced by him. As Katz (1951) observed: "The majority of the professional psychologists on German speaking territories were ... [Herbart's] followers" (p. 47). His former students established a *Journal for Exact Philosophy* for propagating Herbart's ideas, and the Ministry of Education in Vienna recommended the use of Herbart's books in the universities all over the Austro-Hungarian empire. Thus, the psychology of Herbart became known by a wide circle of teachers, "and inevitably a kind of intellectual atmosphere was created due to which the concepts of Herbart became quite self-evident. This was the case not only with concepts which were already known but with the new ones, too, (Consciousness, Span of consciousness, Inhibitions and Repressions, Sinking of ideas below the threshold and their reappearance in consciousness, Mergers, Complexes, Conscious, Dimly conscious, and Unconscious). One may assume that Freud, too, created his concepts of similar names out of this intellectual atmosphere, without being in need of going back to the historical source" (p. 48). In fact, as we have seen, Freud learned psychology from a Herbartian textbook.

And yet, with all these remarkable influences of Herbart, directly or through Fechner, Freud's conception of "the laws which govern the passage of events in the Unconscious" was original with him. Rapaport (1959) put it succinctly: "Per se, this thesis [i.e., that the crucial determinants of behaviors are unconscious] is not alien to any psychology ... The psychoanalytic thesis of unconscious determination, however, differs from these [in asserting] that the rules governing the noticed are different from those governing the unnoticed, and that unnoticed can be inferred by considering the deviations of the noticed from its usual patterns" (p. 88).

Already we have seen the paradoxical ambiguity surrounding the concept of primary processes which led some psychoanalysts, like Jones and Strachey, to maintain that the laws of mental functioning in the repressed Unconscious are irrational, and some others, like Lacan and Edelson, to believe that, on the contrary, this Unconscious is propositional and linguistic. There are also others, like Rapaport, who, while agreeing that such a peculiar set of laws does exist, suggest that its allocation to the repressed Unconscious only is a mistake. It is their opinion that, though to a lesser extent, Ego functions too are governed by the rules of primary processes.

As indicated above, the position of Edelson and Lacan seems to be the correct one because infancy research – a subject matter which did not exist at the time Freud constructed his theory –

disproved the assumption according to which the early phases of ontogenesis (and by implication of phylogenesis) are governed by the rules of primary processes. We think and behave logically and adaptively from the very first days of life and if, as conceived by Freud, our Unconscious preserves the mode of existence prevailing at the beginning of onto-and phylogenesis, then the Unconscious indeed must be communicative, that is propositional and linguistic.

The present-day understanding of infancy may be indicated by the following quotations: "from his earlier days, every infant is an active, perceiving, learning, and information-organizing individual" (Stone, Smith, Murphy, 1974, p. 4); "From birth on, there appears to be a central tendency to form and test hypotheses about what is occurring in the world" (Stern, 1985, p. 42). Only a generation ago, one should have quoted appraisals like this: Behavior observable during the first weeks of life consists wholly of different types of reflexes or, like the following one: The human infant at birth and for a varying period of time thereafter, has been seen as functionally decorticated, since the cortex does not exhibit its full functioning until later. If such descriptions would have been correct and the infant, indeed, would have behaved in a manner fitting decorticated organisms which have at their disposal reflexes only – then it would make good sense to suggest that at the beginning mental life is characterised by a void of logic and reasoning. Behavior controlled by logic and reality testing should then be later developments, preceded by a period of a-logic, or as some put it, by a pre-logical phase.

Modern infancy-research, however, left us no doubt that these speculations were unfounded, for the infant is not alogical and does not behave in accord with the principles of primary processes. Human beings of whatever age are programmed to think logically and only logically. Take, for example, the Kalnins and Bruner (1974) experiment on voluntary control of behavior in the five-week-old infant. Their infant subjects were shown a movie depicting Eskimo family life. The infants were sitting in a specially designed chair, sucking on their pacifiers. By a special arrangement, the rate of sucking rotated the wheel of the film from full capacity to full blur. Usually babies suck at a rate of about two per second; these infants, however, "who sucked for clarity", as Kalnins and Bruner put it, that is to say, who discerned and understood the connection between their behavior and the sharpness of pictures, "steadily learned to increase their rate of sucking" (p. 710). Clearly, these infants and, by implication, infants in general, are able to anticipate the outcome of their behavior and to implement such behavior as needed for this outcome. Their control of their own behavior is guided by hypotheses and adapted to reality.

One should also point out that those hypotheses and adaptations are mediated by conceptualizations of a higher order than was assumed earlier. An observation of Piaget (1951) may suffice to substantiate this claim. When Piaget opened and closed his eyes several times, his 9-month-old son, in an effort to imitate his father, opened and closed his hands, then opened and closed his mouth. The next day, when Piaget resumed the same experiment, the child again began by opening and closing his mouth, then stopped for a moment and suddenly began to blink (obs. 31). It is apparent that the opening and closing of hands and mouth, as well as the blinking, were but variations of one theme, of the concept of opening and closing. This 9 months old child then was able to elaborate on the meaning of his father's behavior and abstract it into a higher-order concept. To put it differently, "the infant, from the earliest days of life, forms and acts upon abstract representations of qualities or perception ... And the need and ability to form abstract representations of primary qualities of perception and act upon them starts at the beginning of mental life; it is not the culmination or developmental landmark reached in the second year or life" (Stern, 1985, pp. 51-52).

It was perhaps to be expected that such an upheaval in our views of mental development would have an impact on our understanding of the early stages of self-consciousness. Here, too, one experiment may represent much more related evidence, all pointing to the surprising conclusion: "the infant is highly differentiated and begins to differentiate objects from day one. We need only to postulate a separate self that does so" (Klein, 1981, p. 102). An infant which differentiates between self and environment has to have the ability to observe itself as it does external objects. The assumption of a differentiated self which is conscious of its being and behaving, from the earliest days of life, is a truly revolutionary development, and it may take time before all its ramifications will become known, let alone agreed upon.

It is because of these considerations that a statement of this kind should be supported by some telling evidence. A pair of rare "Siamese twins" happened to proffer, if one may say so, such evidence (Harper et al., 1980). These twins were connected on the ventral surface between the umbilicus and the bottom of the sternum, so that they always faced one another. About one week before they were surgically separated at four months of age, Stern became acquainted with them and had an opportunity to observe that the twins sucked on their own fingers, but from time to time Alice sucked on Betty's finger, and vice versa. When Alice was sucking on her own fingers and the experimenter gently pulled the hand away from her mouth, Alice's arm resisted the interruption of sucking but her head did not strain forward. Conversely, when Alice was sucking on her sister's fingers and the sister's arm was gently pulled from Alice's mouth, Alice's arms showed no resistance but her head did strain forward. Such a difference in the means employed for continuing sucking – arms resisting being pulled away or head straining forward – clearly indicates that these four-month-old infants were able to distinguish whether or not one's own mouth sucking a finger and this finger make a coherent self.

Infancy, characterized by self-consciousness and feats of cognitive performance, is the antithesis of what the construct of primary processes led us to expect. If the charm and importance of dreams were contingent on this expectation, namely on the hope that dreams are the proof of and instrument for displaying a colorful but irrational stratum in our mental life, then one cannot but agree that our interest in dreams has lost one of its reasons.

The second reason for the great, sometimes even exceptional, interest in dreams, the hope to learn by means of dreams of the lost memories and hidden motives of the dreamer, also rests on premises which are less firm than they seemed to be. In fact, I would contend that the rules of dream-interpretation suggested by Freud hamper rather than help attempts to reconstruct a patient's life history. The hallmark of dream analysis is the use of the method of free associations. These associations to the elements of a dream should lead to the unconscious wishes, which are the hidden meaning of this dream. Recalling, however, that in his reply to Schneider's arguments, Freud (1901) admitted that spontaneously emerging ideas "may be undetermined, or may have been determined by the thoughts that come out in the analysis, or by other thoughts not disclosed in the analysis" (p. 251, n), one may doubt whether reconstructions prompted by those associations are, indeed, reconstructions or rather, constructions.

Freud, though, seems to have related to this important statement of his as if it did not belong to the "main text". For some years later, in his *Introductory Lectures to Psychoanalysis* (1916/17) he declared as follows: "Our dream-intrepretations are made on the basis of the premises ... that dreams in general have a sense, that it is legitimate to carry across from hypnotic to normnal sleep the fact of the existence of mental processes which are at the time unconscious, and that everything that occurs to the mind is determined" (p. 143). As in the case of the propositional/irrational Id, here too Freud held two incompatible views. Here, however, all his followers, as if acquiescing with Freud in forgetting his discussion of Schneider's objections, contend that all associations are determined. This, however, is the crux of the matter, for if the associations are not, or not always, determined then clearly any interpretation and every display of the unconscious meaning of a dream is in danger of being an unvalidated subjective construction. Freud may have been correct in contending that associations are always unconsciously determined and wrong in agreeing with Schneider that associations cannot always lead us to some disguised motives. Considering, however, the importance of such a decision, which in fact touches on the very roots of the conception of a dynamic psychology, one would expect to be informed of the reasons for preferring statement one (i.e., associations are always determined) over statement two (i.e., some associations are determined).

In the absence of such reasons, one cannot but relate to the interpretation of dreams by means of associations as not validated subjective constructions. Actually, even if one were to agree, for the sake of discussion, that the lack of convincing reasons notwithstanding, associations with a dream are always determined and infallibly lead us to thoughts which have instigated the dream, our difficulties in displaying this latent dream would only begin: "It is true that in carrying out the interpretation in the waking state we follow a path which leads back from the elements of the dream to the dream-thoughts and that the dream-work followed one in the contrary direction. But it is highly improbably that these paths are passable both ways" (Freud, 1900, p. 532). First, the visions and events of life intrude into these associations, but also "the increase in resistance that has set in since the night makes new and more devious detours necessary" (p. 532). Can then such associations lead us to the meaning of the dreams? Freud thought that despite these allowances "the number and nature of the collaterals that we spin in this way during the day is of no psychological importance whatever, so long as they lead us to the dream-thoughts of which we are in search" (p. 532).

Which of the thoughts associated now participated in the construction of dreams and which association is a recent "collateral" one, how can one distinguish between them and decide which direction to follow up and which one to bypass as irrelevant - these crucial questions were not even considered as a task to be dealt with. Thus, every interpreter of a dream decides for himself, to his own satisfaction, what is relevant and what is collateral. There is no certainty that another interpreter will, or indeed, should decide similarly.

The interpretation of symbols in dreams proceeds in a similarly uncontrolled way. To begin with, Freud suggested no criteria for defining symbols: "We must restrict ourselves here to remarking that representation by symbol is among the indirect methods of representation, but that all kinds of indications warn us against lumping it in with other forms of indirect representation without being able to form any clear conceptual picture of their distinguishing features" (p. 351). Are we now sure that symbols, as a special category of indirect representation, indeed exist? Are "all kinds of indications", not specified here, enough to allow the undefined symbols to enjoy a prominent place? Since we have no criteria for identifying them, I wonder what entitles us nevertheless to speak of them as if they were identified not intuitively or arbitrarily but by means of a publicly known definition.

And now, a second problem: symbols "frequently" have more than one meaning. "The ambiguity of the symbols links up with the characteristic of dreams for admitting of 'overinterpretation' – for representing in a single piece of content thoughts, and wishes which are often widely divergent in their nature" (p. 353). Despite his inability to define them and thereby give them a conceptual existence, Freud did not hesitate to assume that he knew their many meanings, and the only question to be dealt with was the meaning expressed in this particular dream. Here is his advice: "the current interpretation can only be arrived at on each occasion from the context" (p. 353).

This advice grants the interpreter all the freedom he would like to have, for the context of a dream is no better defined than symbols are. Can, indeed, an undefined context help to eluic- idate the meaning of an undefined symbol? Incidentally, in regard to the value of context in interpreting dreams, Jung was of one mind with Freud. No sixth sense is needed to under- stand dreams, Jung (1945) stated. "Stereotyped interpretation of dream-motifs is to be avoided; the only justifiable interpreta- tions are those reached through a painstaking examination of the context" (p. 287). Considering the differences between the approaches and interpretations of Freud and Jung, one may be sceptical in regard to the value of such advice. Was it the contexts that led Freud and Jung to their divergent views, or was it their views which helped them to find the fitting con- texts?

If by relying on the context, the possibility of a public control was not made difficult enough, Freud added here, in passing, "Often enough a symbol has to be interpreted in its proper meaning and not symbolically" (p. 352). When to interpret symbolically which meaning of a symbol to prefer and when to decide that a symbol now is not symbolic, and of course what is a symbol and how many symbols we have - it is the sovereign right of the interpreter to answer all these questions. Can we relate to information attained by such methods as facts?

Not only symbols are ambiguous. Dreams, in general, Freud thinks, "show a particular preference for combining contraries into a unity or for representing them as one and the same thing ... so that there is no way of deciding at first glance whether any element that admits of a contrary is present in the dream- thoughts as a positive or as a negative" (p. 318). Therefore, he suggests, "if a dream obstinately declines to reveal its meaning, it is always worthwhile to see the effects of reversing some particular elements in its manifest content, after which the whole situation often becomes immediately clear" (p. 372). Again, it is the interpreter who decides when to regard and when to disregard what he hears, when to agree that the dream revealed its meaning, or to decide that it did not and that therefore the reversal of an arbitrarily chosen element is now justified.

Finally, dreams are ambiguous because of the condensation which takes place at the moment of their construction. Compared with the unending line of associations, the dream is always brief and laconic. If we assume that all these associations (minus the collaterals) participated in the construction of the dreams, one may speak here of condensation. Due to this condensation, "it is in fact never possible to be sure that a dream has been completely interpreted. Even if the solution seems satisfactory and without gaps, the possibility always remains that the dream may yet have another meaning" (p. 279). In view of such an all-pervading ambiguity, it would not be surprising if Freud had concluded that either the subject matter or his method of proving, or both, do not allow simple factual statements. But he did not.

Spence (1982) called it ironic that the importance of ambiguity in the analytic process was never acknowledged in its theory. "Freud would agree with respect to dream fragments or symptomatic acts, but he was unwilling to extend the claim to cover the analyst's understanding. This was somehow exempt - more than that, it was eventually unambiguous ..." (p. 268). In fact, however, "once we assume that meanings are multiple, we can hardly assume that the one we discover is necessarily the most significant" (p. 261). Rather, an interpretation is "a claim to a belief in the proposition and nothing more" (p. 273).

One may then doubt whether the art of interpreting dreams is as important for learning about the dreamer and especially his unconscious motives as many people would contend. Indeed, Ornstein (1979) observed that "contemporary psychoanalysts ... are somewhat divided on this issue. There are those who still consider the dream the royal road ... whereas others view it as one of many accessible and perhaps equally important roads leading ... to the complex inner life of man" (p. 95). As an example of the latter view, one may quote a panel of the

Kris Study Group (Joseph, 1967) which concluded that there are no reasons for preferring dreams over the other means of communications between a patient and his/her therapist. One should also mention that Erikson (1954), from his ego-psychology vantage point, could not agree with this particular commitment of dream-analysis to display some unconscious motives of the dreamer: "Unofficially, we often interpret dreams entirely or in parts on the basis of their manifest approach. Officially, we hurry at every confrontation with a dream to crack its manifest appearance as if it were a useless shell and to hasten to discard this shell in favor of what seems to be the more worthwhile core" (p. 140). His distinction between the approaches to dreams publicly and privately may indicate that the approach suggested by the Kris Study Group "officially" is the approach of many experts "unofficially".

Psychotherapists who find themselves caught on the horns of dilemma between their sincere attachment to an ideology and their own experience which contradicts this ideology may consider that an attention to surface, in Erikson's words, should not be mistaken for superficiality, especially, I would like to add, if the equipment for diving into the depths is of the quality of free association.

Jung would have agreed with this statement, one may suppose, for in *Psychology and Religion* (1938) he wrote: "Much as I admire the boldness of [Freud's] attempt, I cannot agree with his method or with its results. He explains the dream as a mere facade behind which something has been carefully hidden ... I doubt whether we can assume that a dream is something other than what it appears to be. I am rather inclined to quote another Jewish authority, the Talmud, which says: 'The dream is its own interpretation'. In other words I take the dream for what it is" (p. 491).

Erikson's (1954) criticism and the conclusions of the Kris Study Group (Joseph, 1967) may seem to echo this statement. Yet, a closer look will show that controversies over many issues notwithstanding, both Freud and Jung valued dreams because of their role in teaching us about the unconscious. It is the task of dreams, Jung (1933) suggested, to subserve a most fundamental function of the psyche, that of self-regulation. The psyche, he contended, is a self-regulatory system that maintains itself in equilibrium "as the body does". Every process that disturbs this equilibrium calls forth a compensatory activity. Since the relation between conscious and unconscious is compensatory, "it is always helpful when we set out to interpret a dream, to ask: what conscious attitude does it compensate?" (p. 17). These compensating unconscious processes appearing in dreams may be "not consciously recognized personal motives ... or the meanings of daily situations which we have overlooked, or conclusions we have failed to draw, or affects we have not permitted, or criticisms we have spared ourselves" (Jung, 1928, p. 148).

The reasons for and conditions of the compensatory activities detailed here may seem to point to the Freudian preconscious as the source of these messages rather than to the repressed or collective unconscious. We must, however, realize that "even though dreams refer to a definite attitude of consciousness and a definite psychic situation, their roots lie deep in the infathomably dark recesses of the conscious mind. For want of a more descriptive term we call this unknown background, the unconscious ... dreams ... provide the bulk of the material for its investigation" (Jung, 1945, p. 369).

Here is an example demonstrating the practical application of this principle. A seventeen-year-old girl dreamed that she was coming home at night. Everything was as quiet as death. The door into the living room was half open, and she saw her mother hanging from the chandelier, swinging to and fro in the cold wind that blew in through the open windows.

"The way in which [this] dream alludes to death is enough to give one pause", Jung (1933, p. 23) observes, and one will readily agree with him. Still, the dreamer, a frightened young person afflicted by a progressive atrophy of the muscles, did not reflect on death in general but on the death of her mother.

"But the mother symbol", Jung explained, "points to a darker meaning which eludes conceptual formulation and can only be vaguely apprehended as the hidden, nature-bound life of the body. Yet even this expression is too narrow, and excludes too many pertinent side-meanings. The psychic reality which underlies this symbol is so inconceivably complex that we can only discern it from far off, and then but very dimly. It is such realities that call for symbolic expression" (pp. 24-25).

To Jung the figure of the suicidal mother represented not herself, the mother of the dreamer, but rather served as a symbol for the unconscious. "If we apply our findings to the dream, its meaning will be: the unconscious life destroys itself. That's the dream's message to the conscious mind of the dreamer and to everyone who has ears to hear" (p. 25). It is apparent that Jung, very much like Freud, easily shifted his interpretations from the level of the concrete to the symbolic representations and vice versa. Why should her own mother stand for a vague concept, and why at another time may she represent herself, and how can we know when to relate to a mother in a dream as one's own parent and when as a symbol of the unconscious? Jung did not seem to have felt the need for any explanation.

Also, one cannot but take note that Jung did not try to prove here that the roots of this dream indeed lie in the unfathomable recesses of the conscious mind. This, however, is the crucial issue for a psychology of dreaming. Paraphasing Lipps (1897), I would say that this is not a question but *the* question of the psychology of dreaming. A functioning brain, i.e., mental activity, is one of life's defining features; its absence indicates death. Although mental activity never ceases, the conditions of living do change in a cyclic manner. While aware, one perceives and relates to the environment; in sleep, however, these interactions are feeble and very dim. Shall we, therefore, assume that the mental activity of sleep, the dream, is motivated by needs and nurtured by stimuli which are different from those prevailing in wakefulness or rather suggest that in spite of the "introversion" characteristic of sleep, mental functioning, by and large, remained unaltered? These are the questions a psychology of dreaming is expected to solve. *Ex cathedra* statements may only strengthen the doubt as to whether one has to conjecture a repressed or collective unconscious behind every dream.

Rather, we may conclude that the suggestions of the Kris Study Group seem to have been well-conceived. Dreams may teach important but also trivial lessons. In both cases, dreams are not the sole representatives of these communications. Our behavior by daylight may provide the self-same information. We do not need to be taught by an ambiguously speaking (collective) unconscious that a poor girl, frightened to death by a series of medical examinations, a worried family, and her deteriorating condition, cannot but think of her inevitable fate. In her dream, however, she visualized these fears - if these indeed were the instigators of this dream - by letting her mother commit suicide. Since we were left uninformed in regard to the dreamer's relationship with her mother, but also about the ways her mother reacted to her illness, (like, for example, blaming herself for what happened to her daughter, or expressing herself in a way which may have indicated that she will not survive her daughter), any suggestion as to the meaning of this dream is possible and none of them provable.

If such dreams do impart a lesson, then in fact, this lesson supports those who think that the topics, ways of reasoning, and functions of dreams are no different from those of our cognition by daylight. This conclusion notwithstanding, I would not want to discourage anybody who is inclined to consult dreams from doing so, I would only warn them not to expect extraordinary illumination from an ordinary light.

Interpretation of dreams: promise and fulfillment

Since for so many years I did expect an extraordinary illumination from dreams, I do not need – to use this expression again – an extraordinary measure of empathy to predict the reaction of many readers to my concluding remarks in the previous chapter. I shall try here, therefore, to prove that the panel of the Kris Study Group (Joseph, 1967) was correct in suggesting that dreams related in the course of psychotherapy are communications the content of which is also conveyed by other means, and that dreams are not especially useful in eliciting memories of early childhood.

Although usually Freud's Irma-dream is regarded as the dream-specimen of psychoanalysis, in fact, despite the wealth of associations, its interpretation remained vague and close to the surface. The wish, which was identified as the dream-instigator, was a so-called "day-residue" rather than a wish emerging from the repressed unconscious. Conversely, the case-history of the Wolf-man, and his dream as its centerpiece, was thoroughly and psychodynamically analyzed. Freud's biographer, Jones (1955) calls "From the History of an Infantile Neurosis" (1918) the best of his case-histories. "Freud was then at the very height of his powers, a confident master of his method, and the technique he displays in the synthesis of the incredibly complex material must win every reader's admiration ... It illustrated how infantile memories can be recovered through an analysis in adult life ..." (vol. 2, p. 274). If is for these and for one further reason, which will become apparent later on, that this one deserves to be appreciated as paradigmatic of Freud's method of interpreting dreams.

Here is the dream the Wolf-man dreamt as a child of four and recalled in his analysis with Freud as a grown-up. "I dreamt that it was night and that I was lying in my bed. (My bed stood, with its foot towards the window; in front of the windows there was a row of old walnut trees. I knew it was winter when I had the dream, and nighttime.) Suddenly the window opened of its own accord, and I was terrified to see that some white wolves were sitting on the big walnut tree in front of the window. There were six or seven of them. The wolves were quite white, and looked more like foxes or sheep-dogs, for they had big tails, like foxes and they had their ears pricked like dogs when they pay attention to something. In great terror, evidently of being eaten up by the wolves, I screamed and woke up. My nurse hurried to my bed to see what had happened to me. It took quite a long while before I was convinced that it had only been a dream; I had had such a clear and life-like picture of the window opening and the wolves sitting on the tree. At last I grew quieter, felt as though I had escaped from some danger, and went to sleep again."

As the starting point for his interpretations, Freud (1918) chose the lasting sense of reality which the dream left behind. The sense of reality "assures us that some part of the latent dream is claiming in the dreamer's memory to possess the quality of reality, that is, that the dream relates to an occurrence that really took place and was not merely imagined" (p. 33). The dream, Freud suggests, points to an occurrence the reality of which is strongly emphasized as being in marked contrast to the unreality of the fairy tales, which emerged in the associations. Further, Freud states, "if it was to be assumed that behind the content of the dream there lay some such unknown scene ... then it must have taken place very early" (p. 33). The most salient features of the manifest content of the dream are the attentive appearance and motionlessness of the wolves; therefore, they must lead to the content of this scene. "We must naturally expect to find", Freud continues, "that this material reproduces the unknown material of the scene in its distorted form, perhaps even distorted into its opposite" (p. 34).

Thus far we have heard of Freud's reflection only. Here is then a contribution of the Wolf-man to the effort of interpreting this dream. "One day the patient began to continue with the interpretation of the dream" (p. 34), he thought that the part of the dream which said that "suddenly the windows opened of its own accord" must mean: My eyes suddenly opened, I woke up and saw the tree with the wolves. Here Freud comments: the attentive look, then, which in the dream was ascribed to the wolves, should rather be shifted on to him. But then perhaps should the immobility of the wolves also be reversed to their opposite? That is to say, the dreamer suddenly woke up and saw in front of him a scene of violent movement at which he looked with strained attention. He saw his parents making love.

His knowledge of the Wolf-man's sexual development enabled him, Freud thought, to state that of all the wishes concerned in the formation of the dream, the most powerful must have been the wish for homosexual love from his father. This wish instigated the dream but also revived the memory of a scene in which, at the age of 1 1/2 years, he saw his parents performing coitus a tergo, and therefore, could observe the sexual organs of both parties. Now during the dreaming he understood the lesson of this scene, namely that his wish means castration, "and the result was terror, horror of the fulfillment of the wish, the repression of the impulse, and consequently a flight from his father to his less dangerous nurse" (p. 36).

One should still mention that while in the dream there were "six or seven" wolves, in the illustration to the dream prepared by the Wolf-man one sees five wolves, and the parents of course were only two persons. "The fact that the number two in the primal scene is replaced by a larger number, which would be absurd in the primal scene, is welcomed by the resistance as a means of distortion. In the illustration to the dream, the dreamer brings forward the number five, which is probably meant to correct the statement 'It was night'" (p. 43, n.).

The pivotal point in this construction is the primal scene. The remembrance of this scene turned the dream, which had begun with high hopes, into an anxiety dream; it also became a turning point in the psychosexual development of the Wolf-man. It is because of its "extraordinary significance", as Freud put it, that one would like to know how this information (the primal scene at the age of 1 1/2 years) was obtained? "Let us assume as an uncontradicted premise that a primal scene of this kind has been correctly educed technically ... Then, in view of its content, it is impossible that it can be anything else than the reproduction of a reality experienced by the child. For a child, like an adult, can produce phantasies only from material which has been acquired from some source or other" (p. 55).

If the existence of the memory of a primal scene was correctly deduced, then this memory must refer to a real and not imagined experience. There is here, in this sentence, a premise and a conclusion; our question above related to the premise. Freud's answer may be regarded as the very heart of the philosophy of dream interpretation: "... scenes, like this one in my present patient's case, which dates from such an early period ... are as a rule not reproduced as recollections, but have to be divined – constructed – gradually and laboriously from an aggregate of indications" (p. 51). This method of arriving at early memories, though, may seem less than convincing. "I am not of the opinion, however, that such scenes must necessarily be phantasies because they do not reappear in the shape of recollections. It seems to me absolutely equivalent to a recollection, if the memories are replaced (as in the present case) by dreams, the analysis of which invariably leads back to the same scene ..." (p. 51).

The key, then, is the interpretation of a dream and not the dream itself. Indeed, in the case-history of the Wolf-man, Freud had an opportunity to demonstrate this priority of the interpretation over the dream. The Wolf-man recollected that while he was still very small, his sister had seduced him into sexual plays. However, the Wolf-man also had some dreams in which he was aggressive towards his sister, had tried to undress her, and was punished for his behavior. Unhesitatingly, Freud concluded that "his seduction by his sister was certainly not a phantasy" (p. 21). On the other hand, the dreams could have been only phantasies, "which the dreamer had made ... probably at the age of puberty ..." (p. 19). In his decision, Freud relied first, on the fact that a cousin of the Wolf-man, ten years older than him, told him once that his sister (who in the meantime had committed suicide) was "a sensual little thing". The "credibility", as Freud put it, of the memory of being seduced by the sister was increased by this information. And second, those dreams "gave an impression of always working over the same material in various different ways" (p. 164), and, therefore, these "ostensible" reminiscences, in fact, were phantasies.

These two arguments, though, are not without their problems. In regard to the value of information like that supplied by the cousin, only a few pages earlier Freud explained why one should not succumb to the temptation and fill the gaps in a patient's memory, by making enquiries of the older members of his family: "... I cannot advise too strongly against such a technique ... One invariably regrets having made oneself dependent upon such information" (p. 14, n.). As to the dreams, which represented the same material in various different ways, this argument too is questionable for in precisely this way also the other dreams were recalled: "... in the course of the treatment the first dream [with the wolves] returned in innumerable variations and new editions, in connection with which the analysis produced the information that was required" (p. 36). The information, as one may recall, was that the dream relates to a real experience and not to a phantasy.

The inconsistency and arbitrariness displayed here speak for themselves, and need no further elaboration. Rather, I shall return to what was earlier defined as the pivotal issue: the reality of the primal scene observed at the age of 1 1/2 years. Or was it real? A few years after composing the first report of this case-history, Freud seemed ready to reconsider his stance: "There remains the possibility of taking yet another view of the primal scene underlying the dream ... It is true that we cannot dispense with the assumption that the child observed a copulation, the sight of which gave him a conviction that castration might be more than an empty threat ... But there is another factor which is not so irreplaceable and which may be dropped. Perhaps what the child observed was not copulation between his parents but copulation between animals, which he then displaced on to his parents, as though he had inferred that his parents did things in the same way" (p. 57).

At the time he composed his first report on the Wolf-man, Freud was "still freshly under the impression of the twisted re-interpretations" (p. 7) by Jung and Adler of the findings of psychoanalysis, and this case-history was meant to prove Freud's understanding. The polemic was over the importance of the early years in the aetiology of neuroses. The view Freud tried to refute was that the causes of psychoneuroses are to be found in the conflicts of later life. Neurotics, Jung and Adler maintained, may express their present problems in reminiscences and symbols from the remote past, however, the conflicts themselves are of the mature years. The gap between their respective views, Freud felt, was unbridgeable; he and his colleagues are the embodiments of the proverbial whale and polar bear which cannot wage war on each other, for since each is confined to his own element they cannot meet (p. 48).

Twenty years later, Freud (1939) still related to this polemic in a rather combatant mood. The genesis of neuroses, he wrote in his "Moses and Monotheism", "invariably" goes back to very early experiences in childhood. Then, in a footnote he added: "this therefore makes it nonsensible to say that one is practising psychoanalysis if one excluded from examination and consideration precisely these earliest periods – as happens in some quarters" (p. 73). And yet, in the case of the Wolf-man, as we have seen, he did agree to a certain modification of his position and renounced his earlier belief in the reality of the primal scene at the age of 1 1/2 years. Freud (1918) was not unaware of the possible effects of his change of mind: "I can well believe that I have now laid myself open to grave aspersions on the part of the readers of this case-history ... how could I possible have taken it on myself to begin by advocating [an argument] which seemed so absurd? ... I intend on this occasion to close the discussion of the reality of the primal scene with a non liquet" (p. 60).

While Freud's evasiveness here in regard to an issue as important for his theory of neuroses as the very early traumatic experiences is not without interest, in what follows here, I shall restrict the discussion to the impact on the interpretation of dreams of this reconsideration of his position. At the beginning, Freud was firmly convinced of the reality of the primal scene observed by the Wolf-man at the tender age of 1 1/2 years and of the power of dream-interpretations for substantiating such claims: "Let us assume as an uncontradicted premise that a primal scene of this kind has been correctly educed technically". Further: "It seems to me to be absolutely equivalent to a recollection, if the memories are replaced by dreams, the analysis of which invariably leads back to the same scene". Now that the belief in the reality of the primal scene, for reasons not disclosed, has lost its "uncontradicted" character, what shall we think of the interpretations of the dream which were the proof for the reality of the primal scene? Was the interpretation of the dream incorrect technically, so that some improvements in the technique may still reestablish the reality of the primal scene? Or shall we conclude that it was precisely the method of interpretation which failed the interpreter?

Regrettably, Freud did not tackle these issues. Yet, without saying it in so many words, he gave us to understand that the proof of the reality of the primal scene obtained by his method of interpreting dreams was not really a proof, for otherwise he would not have changed his mind. In contradiction to his earlier confidence, now Freud seems to have admitted that interpretations of dreams are not helpful in (re)constructing forgotten past events; in fact, they may even be misleading. Although, as already pointed out, he did not clarify what was wrong with the method of interpretation, he did clarify that in spite of what his own dream-interpretation established, he had some more important reasons which led him to abandon his belief in the reality of the primal scene. It is this demonstration by Freud himself of the real value of dream-interpretations for replacing recollections which was hinted at in the beginning of this chapter, as the further reason for discussing the Wolf-man's dream. In the opinion of Jones, though, one of the merits of this case-history was in Freud's demonstrating how to recover infantile memories through an analysis in adult life. But is it possible to agree with this understanding in view of Freud's change of mind regarding the primal scene?

Incidentally, in another, not lesser known moment in the history of psychoanalysis, Freud behaved in precisely the same way, that is to say, he left unanswered, actually untackled, this issue of justifying his method of interpretation. At the beginning, Freud (1896) believed that hysteria is caused by some early traumatic sexual experiences. Before they come for analysis "the patients know nothing about these scenes ... Only the strongest compulsion of the treatment can induce them to embark on a reproduction of them ... [and even then] they still attempt to withhold beliefs from them, by emphasizing the fact that unlike what happens in the case of other forgotten material, they have no feeling of remembering the scenes" (p. 204). This behavior of his patients, Freud argued, rather than weakening seems to conclusively prove his thesis: "Why should patients assure me so emphatically of their unbelief, if what they want to discredit is something which – from whatever motive – they have themselves invented" (p. 204). Yet, as in the case of the observation by the Wolf-man of his parents' coitus a tergo here, too, Freud changed his mind and agreed with what he had earlier definitely rejected. Soon, because of the "weight of its improbability", as he (1914) put it, Freud abandoned the seduction theory and propounded a new theory, that of unconscious sexual fantasies. Here Freud observed: "Analysis had led back to these infantile sexual traumas by the right path, and yet they were not true" (p. 17). One wonders how to reconcile the two parts of this sentence. If the method of interpreting is proper and correct, how could the results not have been true, and vice versa, if the end result was an error, how was it proven that the method of analysis was correct?

As in the case of the primal scene discussed above, here too, Freud seems to have separated between the method and the finding this method led to. The value of the method is independent of its merits; whether it results in facts or errors, it is praised and believed in. Yet, at the same time the results of interpretation are not binding. Although produced by the interpreter, he may shove them aside, and decide on an understanding which opposes the one supported by the interpretation. The seduction theory broke down under the weight of its improbability, nevertheless the method of interpreting, which was the pillar supporting this disproved theory, was "the right path". It is apparent, I think, that such a distinction between a method of proof and its results is unacceptable, and it is not without significance that it was Freud himself who demonstrated the unreliability of his own method of interpretation.

Freud was ready to drop the claim to reality for his construction of the primal scene; yet he would not let fall the other construction regarding the threat of castration: "we cannot dispense with the assumption that the child observed a copulation a tergo", the sight of which convinced him of the possibility of "castration". Incidentally, this kind of formulation: "we cannot dispense", perforce causes one to ponder about the ways this interpretation was produced. Did Freud arrive at the observation of a primal scene in the first interpretation, and of a coitus between animals in the revised one inadvertently, that is to say, because the method of interpretation led to it, or because he was in need of a reason which might explain the Wolf-man's "flight from his father to his nurse"? At any rate, not even for this purpose must we assume the observation of a coitus a tergo. The Wolf-man did not need inferential evidence, he knew from first-hand experience what homosexual love means.

During his collaboration with Eissler in the Freud Archives, Masson (1984) had access to some unpublished material concerning the Wolf-man, which Muriel Gardiner, a psychoanalyst well-acquainted with the Wolf-man, had in her home. Some years after his analysis with Freud, the Wolf-man again asked for his help. At that time, however, because of his poor health, Freud was unable to accept him, and the Wolf-man was referred to Ruth Mack Brunswick. She (1928) reported on this treatment in a psychoanalytic periodical. To his surprise, Masson found in the material kept by Muriel Gardiner some notes by Ruth Mack Brunswick for a paper she never published. "At Freud's request, she had re-analyzed the Wolf-man and was astonished to learn that as a child he had been anally seduced by a member of his family -and that Freud did not know this. She never told him" (Masson, 1984, p. XIX).

She never told him, but left a message to posterity. It is an intriguing question, and we may never know why she did not inform Freud of what she had heard from the Wolf-man. Considering that this information would have profoundly affected the whole case-history as constructed by Freud, one may perhaps if not justify, at least understand her silence. Nevertheless, one is mystified by the behavior of the Wolf-man, of Freud, and after all, also of Ruth Mack Brunswick. I wonder how to explain that the Wolf-man revealed his secret to Ruth Mack Brunswick in a few months, but kept it (out of cooperation?) for so many years from Freud. Or did he tell him and Freud did not listen? Ruth Mack Brunswick, fully aware of these questions, seems to have accepted her role in this play of mystery and did not disperse the fog. Be that as it may, now that we know of the anal seduction, it seems quite clear that interpretations of dreams are not equivalent to recollections. Freud's analysis of the Wolf-man's dream did not disclose this fact.

One is here reminded of Steele and Jacobsen (1977) for these authors, in contradistinction to Freud, maintain that interpretations do not replace recollections because they cannot. In Freudian theory, they say "one moves from the observed to its replacement, an interpretation of an event. Continually, though, one sees in Freudian theory the problematic assumption that the interpreted event is the same as some original event; that once an observed or reported event has been fully interpreted, the latent meaning has been restored and an original event which preceded the observed or reported has been found" (p. 393). These, indeed, were Freud's assumptions when he undertook to interpret the dream of the Wolf-man. We have seen the results of his endeavour. Freud's analysis of the dreams produced a result that fitted his expectations but not the recollections of the Wolf-man. What Steele and Jacobson called the problematic assumption might as well be called the disproved assumption of Freud.

Steele and Jacobsen observe that Freud listens to the reported, the so-called manifest dream, elicits associations to it and constructs an interpretation "which he calls the latent dream. He asserts that this latent dream existed prior to the manifest dream" (p. 394). Indeed, Freud (1900) illustrated his distinction between the latent and manifest dreams with an analogy to a rebus (pp. 277/8). Just as the rebus is a pictographic description of some original phrase, the manifest dream is a systematic distortion of the original latent dream. A phrase is translated into a puzzling picture by the rebus maker and the latent dream is transformed into the manifest content by the dream work. "In solving the rebus", Steele and Jacobsen (1977) comment, "we can check our solution against the original phrase, but, and this is where Freud's analogy leads us astray, there is no original text independent of interpretation to which we can compare our dream solution ... there is a confusion between an actual meaningful explanation, the dream interpretation, and a hypothetical original event, the latent dream" (p. 394).

I would like to add here that such meaningful explanations may indeed be arrived at by means of dream-interpretations. One should, however, carefully distinguish between true causes of behavior on the one hand, and meaningful explanations, narrations, in the definition of Sherwood (1969), on the other hand. Both Freudian and Jungian analysts, Sherwood stated, "may produce evocative and perceptive, but radically different, views of the same subject matter that are each self-consistent, coherent and comprehensive. It might even be said that psychoanalysis, particularly in its clinical and therapeutic setting, functions essentially in this way, by presenting new and varied perspectives to patients of their own behavior, rather than by telling them the true causes of their behavior" (p. 294). Indeed, the dream-interpretation of Jung quoted above may demonstrate the cogency of Sherwood's statement. The analysis of his patient's dream, in the context of what we know about her, makes sense, that is to say, is meaningful. But can we be sure that it was also the "true cause" of her dream, and by the same token, may we contend that early memories re-covered by means of dream-interpretations are indeed recon-structions of real pieces of one's forgotten past?

Consider the interpretation by Aristander of a dream of Alexander the Great. Freud (1900) praised it as "the nicest instance of a dream-interpretation which has reached us from ancient times ..." (p. 99, n.). Alexander was besieging Tyre (Tyros in Greek); however, the brave and skillful defenders of the city frustrated his hopes for an easy victory. Troubled and impatient, he went to sleep and dreamt of a satyr (satyros, in Greek) dancing on his shield. Aristander, who was with his king, offered an interpretation which fitted the circumstances perfectly. The satyros in your dream, he suggested, was a message from the gods: if you divide satyros into sa (thine) and tyros (the city), then, you may understand that the gods pro-mise you the capture of Tyros. Encouraged by this interpreta-tion, Alexander eventually conquered the recalcitrant city, and did not forget to savagely punish its inhabitants for their auda-ciousness in resisting him.

We would be less sure, I suppose, than Alexander was regarding the basis of his interpretation, that is, that gods communicate with mankind by means of ambiguous messages wrapped in dreams. As to the cause of dreams, then, Aristander sounds less convincing today than in his day.

However, as to the meaningfulness of interpretation, he was as sage as anyone else. His decision to divide the word satyros into two parts was as possible or impossible as Freud's decision to revert the motionlessness of six or seven wolves into violent movements of two parents or, "It was night" in the dream into: it was 5 o'clock in the afternoon, in the interpretation. At any rate, Freud, Jung, and Aristander suggested "coherent and comprehensive views of the dreams" they interpreted, but none of them seems to have had the right to contend that he had discovered the true causes of those dreams. "In solving the rebus", to quote Steele and Jacobsen once more, "we can check our solution against the original phrase, but ... there is no original text independent of interpretation to which we can compare our dream solution." We should not forget the difference between a meaningful interpretation which fits the known circumstances of the dreamer well, and a hypothetical substrate to this dream.

As one may understand, these considerations also apply to interpretations which intend to elucidate the unconscious meaning of parapraxes. In his *Psychopathology of Everyday Life*, Freud (1901) recalls a conversation he had with a young Austrian Jew, who bitterly complained of the discriminations against Jews in Austria-Hungary, and concluded with the line that the Roman poet, Virgil put in the mouth of Dido when abandoned by Aeneas and on the point of suicide: *Exoriare aliquis nostris ex ossibus ultor* (Let someone arise from my bones as an Avenger, or: Arise from my bones, O Avenger). However, he quoted the curse of Dido incorrectly: *exoriare ex nostris ossibus ultor;* he omitted *aliquis* and inverted *nostris ex*. Freud interpreted the omission of aliquis only. The first association of the young man was to divide *aliquis* into two words, *a liquis,* and the further associations were connected with that first hint. He had a love affair with a woman in Italy and now was anxiously awaiting her message to know whether or not she was pregnant. It was Freud's understanding that while the young man intended to borrow Dido's words to express his hope to revenge the injustices inflicted upon his people, unbeknown to himself, he became aware that his hope meant to have children; but this was precisely what he at that moment did not want. No, no children, even if the hoped for revenge would demand their existence. The word *aliquis* had then to be omitted.

In a study of psycho-analysis and textual criticism, Timpanaro (1974) took issue with this interpretation and suggested instead, a "pedestrian (but true) "explanation of this incomplete quotation. To begin with, the construction *exoriare aliquis ... ultor* is highly anomalous, for it is not clear whether *aliquis* is to be understood as subject and *ultor* as its predicate: Let someone arise from my bones as an Avenger, or whether *ultor* is to be understood as subject and *aliquis* as its attribute: Let some Avenger arise from my bones. "The anomaly consists in the coexistence in the line of the second person singular with the indefinite pronoun aliquis: Dido uses the familiar tu form of address to the future Avenger, as if she saw him standing in front of her ... while at the same time she expresses with the aliquis ... his indeterminate identity" (p. 32). In German, Timpanaro observes, such a construction is virtually untranslatable literally. Wilhelm von Hertzberg, a philologist and translator in the 19th century chose the first solution: *Mog aus meinem Gebein sich einst ein Racher erheben* (Let someone arise from my bones as an avenger). In contrast Johann Heinrich Voss, a poet and translator, opted for the second solution, suppressing the *aliquis* altogether. *Aufstehn mogest du doch aus unser Asche, du Racher* (Arise from our ashes, O Avenger).

"But while philologists and translators, in direct contact with the text, were aware of the untranslatability of this expression from Virgil, a young Austrian of average culture, for whom Dido's words were no doubt little more than a distant memory from grammar school, was led ... to assimilate it to his own linguistic sensibility ... exoriare ex nostris ossibus ultor is a sentence which can be transposed perfectly into German without any need to strain the order of words ... It was no accident that the young Austrian's simplified quotation corresponded to the rendering given by Voss" (p. 33-34). *Aliquis*, then, was omitted because of the "tendency to banalize a highly irregular syntactic structure" (p. 39).

Both the interpretations of Freud and Timpanaro are meaningful, coherent and comprehensive, and both are possible. As an afterthought, though, I would like to point out that Freud's interpretation assumes that the young man identified himself with Dido. Yet, it is not impossible that to the contrary, he identified himself with Aeneas who left poor Dido in the lurch, and it was to this chain of thoughts and to the possible revenge against him by the as yet unborn child that he had to drop *aliquis*. While this solution is not impossible, I do not contend that in precisely this way and only this way the omission of *aliquis* was effected. Possibilities mean tolerance and coexistence; any pretension of displaying hard facts with the help of such a soft method would be self-defeating.

I shall conclude this discussion with a reference to Codignola (1974). In his *Essay on the Logical Structure of Psychoanalytic Interpretation*, an enthusiastic presentation of the thesis that psychoanalysis "has the right to claim a position sui generis, so to speak, among scientific theories" (p. 341), one reads: "Thus, in reality, interpretation is the most coherent instrument of observation at the disposal of the analyst and, at the same time, the analyst's therapeutic agent par excellence" (p. 342). Let us note that Codignola here identified interpretation with observation. Somewhat later, he put it explicitly thus: "It is noteworthy ... that Anna Freud (1965, p. 22) makes a point of distinguishing among the ego functions some that she finds assessable ... also through objective observations, thereby confirming that these cases are in some way exceptions to the general rule of analytic observation. At present there are but a few analysts who still insist in the use of 'direct observation' of the child to confirm their hypothesis ... And if this were not so, after all, psychoanalysis would become a science of objective truth in psychology – something, that is, which since Freud and ever after it has never sought to be" (p. 342).

While I have some doubts about whether Freud would have agreed with the statement that psychoanalysis is not a science of objective truth, I agree with Codignola that interpretations of dreams or parapraxes and behavior in general, obtained by the method of free associations, do not and cannot lead to "raw" data.

The remembrance of dreams

In one of his parables, entitled Inferno, I, 32, Borges (1962) told of a leopard, which "from the twilight of day till the twilight of evening, in the last years of the thirteenth century", would see some wooden planks, some vertical iron bars, and a few men and women. In a dream God explained to him: You live and will die in this prison so that a certain man may see you from time to time and remember to place your figure and symbol in a poem. The leopard understood the reasons for his suffering and accepted his destiny. But, "when he awoke there was in him only an obscure resignation, a valorous ignorance, for the machinery of the world is much too complex for the simplicity of a beast". Years later, Dante was dying in Ravenna, "as unjustified and as lonely as any other man". He, too, had a dream of revelation. God explained to him the reasons for the bitterness of his life. Alas, upon waking, Dante, not unlike the leopard, "felt that he had received and lost an infinite thing, something he would not be able to recuperate or even glimpse, for the machinery of the world is much too complex for the simplicity of man".

Dante of Borges' parable had the remembrance of a content-less dream, as we became used to calling it. He knew that he dreamt of something important, but the content of the dream eluded him; by the best of his efforts he could not recall it. Some dreams, in fact most of them, disappear even before leaving an ambiguous sign of existence. Since whether awake or asleep, mentation never ceases, our sleeping hours uninterruptedly generate dreams. And since by recalling a dream, we are more, and certainly not less, explicit than we were by experiencing it, to recall all that went through our mind while asleep would need at least as much, and very probably more, than the hours of sleeping and dreaming. To the chagrin of the lovers of dream-life, all that we are able to recall is a story of the length of a few minutes, at best. How can we understand this disso-ciation of the dreaming from the waking existence?

The results of an experiment of Evans and associates (1970) seem to indicate a possible answer. Their subjects slept in a sleep laboratory for two consecutive nights. Whenever a subject entered a REM period of sleep, the experimenter entered the experimental room and administered a few suggestions in a slow, quiet voice, like: If I say the word "itch", your nose will feel itchy until you scratch it. Soon, during the same REM period, the specific word for that suggestion (e.g., "itch") was spoken softly. During the next REM period, the specific word alone was said again. In 21 percent of all the specific words administered, subjects behaved as suggested. These communicative responses were obtained while the subjects remained asleep. In fact, the authors concluded that for those subjects who responded most frequently, "alpha evoked by a cue was similar in frequency to the lower spontaneous alpha during stage 1 sleep rather than to waking alpha frequency. In contrast, for those subjects who responded only occasionally, the evoked alpha was similar in frequency to waking alpha" (p. 185).

In the morning, the subjects were tested by means of an interview and, interspersed with the words used in the experiments, a word association test. The results have shown that subjects responded to sleep-administered suggestions while they were asleep, but apparently they could recall neither responding nor the specific words themselves upon awakening. "Any memory obtained was, at best, fragmentary" (p. 181). Yet, during the second night, these self-same subjects behaved again as they did during the first night; the responders performed what they were expected to, and the non-responders, too, behaved in their characteristic manner. "When subjects returned to sleep the next night, or even five months later, the mere repetition of the relevant cue word, (without repetition of the suggestion itself), was sufficient to elicit the appropriate response" (p. 186).

Evans and associates think that what was demonstrated here was not forgetting, but rather amnesia, similar to posthypnotic

amnesia. In post-hypnotic amnesia some information is dissociated, not available for recall, while one is fully self-controlled,
but will be retrievable if the state of mind of the original
learning is re-established.

The construct of state-dependent learning produced by
drugs, as Overton (1978) put it, "has excited considerable interest during the last 40 years" (p. 283). Animals, if drugged, for
example, by sodium pentobarbital, will be able to recall and use
what they learned earlier under the influence of the same drug,
but will fail to demonstrate such adaptive responses in the
intervening sober period. And contrarywise, if they learned
something useful while sober, they will be able to recall it
during their next sober period, but not if under the influence of
drugs. These animals, of course, did not receive any post-hypnotic suggestion to forget, nor does it seem justified to assume
here a repression due to a conflict between motives. Rather,
their behavior indicates that we have more than one stream of
consciousness, more than one state of mind, and these states of
mind seem to be dissociated from one another.

Dreams, then, belonging to a state of mind which is different
from that of the waking existence, are dissociated, that is, not
or only fragmentarily retrievable while awake. The behavior
of the subjects in the Evans et al., experiment may be seen as
paradigmatic for dream recall, and one may conclude that a
dissociation between the dreaming and waking existence is one
of the reasons for the difficulty in recalling dreams.

To be precise though, one has to point out that, as indicated
by some results of Holloway and Wansley (1973), waking itself
is a complexity of states of mind. In the experiment of these
authors, rats were electroshocked when entering a darkened
chamber. Independent groups of rats were then tested immediately after training, or at successive 6-hour intervals. Recall
of the earlier learning (indicated by longer step-through laten-
cies before the same darkened chamber) was best immediately
after training or when testing occurred at the same time of day
as training. Second best results were obtained at successive 12

hour intervals from the occasion of training, but was poor six hours after training or a multiple of 12 hours from this 6-hour post-training point.

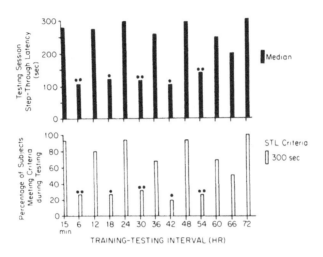

One may feel mystified by the pecularities of these ultradian rhythmic processes which determine what and when is available for recall. Holloway and Wansley were unable to identify the factor responsible for this "multiphasic" presence and absence in consciousness of past experiences. Winfree (1984) quotes Einstein as having said: "Everything should be made as simple as possible ... but not simpler". The process of recalling seems to be in need of such a sentence of self-justification. At any rate, it seems clear that this repetitive pattern of high then low performances of recall is a state-dependent phenomenon, without the interference of any motives or clash beteen motives.

Weingartner (1978) pointed out a feature particular to man in "disparate-state" availability, as he called it, of past experiences. It is verbal rather than visual information that is most likely to be dissociated in learning while intoxicated, sleep-deprived, or in patients with focal brain lesions associated with long histories of alcoholism and poor diet.

Applying these findings to dream recall, one may expect that visual dreams have more chances of being recalled than dreams which mainly consist of thoughts and dialogues. One explanation for the well-known difficulty of recalling NREM-generated dreams as compared with the relatively easier recall of REM-dreams may be in this inhomogeneity of state-dependent dissociations. A finding of Cohen and MacNeilage (1974) may complement and buttress this speculation.

These authors reported that on a baseline night during which their subjects were allowed to sleep and waken spontaneously, five of seven frequent recallers awakened from REM sleep while five of seven infrequent recallers awakened from NREM sleep. Dreams generated during NREM sleep are indeed less available for recall during daytime than dreams generated during REM sleep because the change in state of mind seems to dissociate verbal learning more than visual information, and people who habitually waken from NREM sleep are subject to this stricter dissociation.

A further reason for the preference in recall of REM dreams was indicated in the study of Cory, Orniston, Simmel, and Dainoff (1975). Cory and associates found a positive correlation between frequency of dream recall and performances on tests for visual memory (short-term, long-term, as well as incidental). Thus people who habitually waken from a REM period of sleep and are endowed by a relatively strong visual memory have good chances to be labelled as frequent recallers of dreams because, compared with people who usually waken from a NREM period of sleep and whose visual memory is less efficient, they will be able to recall more dreams. But let us not forget that the frequent recallers, too, do no more than, to quote Borges again, recuperate a faint glimpse of the vast unknown continent of the sleeping existence. In spite of their not unimportant differences, both the frequent and infrequent recallers are only well-acquainted with the curtain of dissociation which separates between the sleeping and waking existence.

Freud (1900), as we all know, had a different explanation for the forgetting of dreams. Dreams, he suggested, are "invariably wish-fulfillments," (p. 568), and these wishes are the products of the system Ucs., whose activity knows no other aim than the fulfillment of wishes. These wishes, however, are resisted by a mental force which sees to it that those wishful impulses are pushed beyond the perimeter of self-controlled consciousness. Dreams expressing, as they do, repressed wishes, are only possible because "*sleep ... reduces the power of the endopsychic censorship*" (p. 526, emphasis in the original). In this account of the conditions for generating dreams, Freud thought, one also got the conditions for the forgetting of dreams. During the night the resistance against the repressed wishes loses some, but not all, of its power. During the daytime, however, the full control of wakefulness is re-established, and the concessions granted to the repressed impulses are cancelled; the resisted wishes are repressed again, and thus dreams are bound to be forgotten. "... having regained its full strength at the moment of waking, [resistance] at once proceeds to get rid of what it was obliged to permit while it was weak" (p. 526).

I have some objections to this theory of dreams. The first, and because of its consequences, the most important one, relates to Freud's understanding that one must find a particular reason which should explain why we dream at all. Freud's construct hinges upon the fate of this underlying assumption, namely, that sleep and mental functioning are contradictory terms: "As regards the embittered and apparently irreconcilable dispute as to whether the mind sleeps at night or is as much in command of all its faculties as it is by day ... it is imperative to assume that there is such a thing as a sleeping state of mind" (p. 590). Or: "this abandonment of interest in thought-processes during the night has a purpose: thinking is to come to a standstill, for the Pcs. requires sleep" (p. 575). Again, he expressed the same view by stating that dreams interrupt sleep: "Experience shows that dreaming is compatible with sleeping, even if it interrupts sleep several times during the night. One wakes up for an instant and then falls asleep again at once" (p. 575). Likewise, in his *Introductory Lectures*, Freud (1915/16) stated: "In our opinion, too, a dreamless sleep is the best, the only proper one. There ought to be no mental activity at all" (p. 89).

Dreaming interrupts sleep, that is, sleep is not compatible with mental functioning; thinking has to come to a standstill in order for sleep to be established. To agree with this characterization of "the sleeping state of mind", one should agree that the brain ceases to function for hours, and yet the organism is well and alive. In fact, however, where thinking came to a standstill for hours, we have to speak of death and not of sleep. Whether awake or asleep, we think ceaselessly, and only death may interrupt it. It follows, then, that we do not dream one or five short dreams during seven or eight hours of sleep but rather, we dream continuously for seven or eight hours and the few dreams we are able to recall are but faint reflections of an immense stream of thought, small islands in a great ocean. Dreaming is inevitable for, mental activity and life are synonyms. There is no need, then, to construct some specific conditions due to which dreams may come to exist and, consequently, no alterations in this presumed condition can explain forgetting.

Incidentally, Freud also expressed himself in a way which may be understood as though in contradiction to his formulations quoted above, he did agree that sleep does not obliterate mental functioning: "I am driven to conclude that *throughout our whole sleeping state we know just as certainly that we are dreaming as we know that we are sleeping*" (p. 57, emphasis in original). Such an ability to reflect upon ourselves while asleep, granted not to the few capable of lucid dreaming but to everybody is indeed a far cry from the other statements according to which thinking has to come to a standstill for otherwise sleep is impossible. To know that one is sleeping and dreaming is not just an evidence of thinking. Rather, it attests to a quality of thinking, reflective self-consciousness, which some would doubt that the sleeping state of mind is capable of. This self-contradiction, together with the other self-contradictions regarding the full/partial determinism of psychic acts and the rational/irrational unconscious, are intriguing enough, for the moment, however, it may suffice to point out that Freud's theory of dreams is shaped in accord with the assumption of the "abandonment" of thinking in sleep. This assumption seems untenable.

The second objection to Freud's explanation of why we usually are unable to recall our dreams relates to his suggestions of a conflict between some repressed wishes and resistance to them. Already we have seen the analysis of young Wolfman's dream by Freud. The lesson of this analysis, which is regarded as a classic of psychodynamic dream-interpretations, was that Freud's method for interpreting dreams, free associations, is not dependable and the conclusions they lead to are not binding. But even if one would agree that the method of free association may help in elucidating unconscious conflicts, one should emphasize that Freud's assertion that only such conflicts may generate dreams, and that otherwise sleep would go on "undisturbed" by any mental activity for hours is, as I have just said, untenable.

Unconscious conflicts, as a class of our ever-active mental functioning, do contribute to dreaming. That much is evident and logically necessary. Nonetheless, any statements intending to specify the nature of the assumed wishes and their possibilities for shaping our behavior are subject to the accepted norms of proving and validating. Freud's method of proving, the association of a patient interpreted by a therapist, does not seem to comply with these demands. By contrast, the concept of dissociation between the different states of mind as an explanation of the forgetting of dreams is empirically testifiable.

Consider, for example, the study of Cohen and Wolfe (1973). These authors asked volunteer subjects to call the weather number immediately upon awakening and write down the temperature for the day before reporting their dream. A control group was requested to fill out a dream diary sheet immediately upon awakening. 33% of the experimental reports had content, 43% were contentless, and 24% were dreamless. Conversely, 63% of the control group's reports had content, 18% were contentless, and 20% were dreamless. The two groups were comparable with regard to the total failure to recall dreams. It was the contentless dreams which differentiated between the groups and this difference in contentless dreams seems to be the result of interposing a minor task between awakening and reporting the dream. As regards the re-awakening of mental resistance to the repressed wishes, the two groups should have shown no differences, and one sees no possibilities to explain the rise of contentless dreams in the experimental group by the construct of psychodynamic conflicts.

The results of this experiment remind me of an old adage according to which if you would like to remember your dream, try to awaken motionlessly. Even if this advice may help to recall one dream only and certainly not all that went through our mind in the course of sleep, it is a remarkable fact that some unimportant performance or even some random movements accompanying our transition from one state of mind to another are enough to eradicate from our waking memory the content of an otherwise recallable dream.

Perhaps, if Dante (or Borges) had been instructed not to move during awakening, the illumination he received while dreaming would not have faded away, tantalizingly as it did, at the moment of arousal.

Dreaming like waking

Popper-Lynkeus (1899) in Vienna wrote a story, entitled Dreaming like Waking, "about a man who [had] the remarkable attribute of never dreaming nonsense." "This splendid gift of yours," his friend explained to him, "for dreaming as though you were waking, is a consequence of your virtues, of your kindness, your sense of justice, and your love of truth." The hero of the story, however, would not agree: "But when I think the matter over properly, I almost believe that everyone is made like me, and that no one at all ever dreams nonsense ..., any dream, that is to say, which is not a fever-dream, must always make sense, and it cannot possibly be otherwise." The friend then concluded: "In you other people, there seems always to be something unchaste in a special and higher sense, a certain secret quality in your being, which it is hard to follow. And that is why your dreams so often seem to be without meaning or even to be nonsense. But in the deepest sense this is not in the least so; indeed it cannot be so at all - for it is always the same man, whether he is awake or dreaming."

Freud (1900) was impressed by this analysis of Popper-Lynkeus: "I may say that the kernel of my theory of dreams lies in my derivation of dream-distortion from the censorship" (p. 308, n), and, this, precisely was the reason given by Popper-Lynkeus for the seeming meaninglessness or even nonsensicality of many dreams. Years later, Freud (1923) again had an opportunity to express his appreciation of Popper-Lynkeus: "I started out from the strange, confused and senseless character of so many dreams, and hit upon the notion that dreams were bound to become like this because something was struggling for expression in them which was opposed by a resistance from other mental forces ... The dreamer was thus ashamed of these impulses, turned away from them and refused to acknowledge them in day-time, and if during the night he could not withhold expression of some kind from them, he submitted them to a 'dream-distortion' which made the content of the dream appear confused and senseless ... Precisely this essential part of my theory of dreams was, however, discovered by Popper-Lynkeus independently" (p. 261/2). Dreams seem senseless because they are the distorted expressions of some objectionable wishes. The mental force responsible for this distortion is called censorship or resistance, and the result of this collision between the wish and resistance: repression. The repression, being a function of the ego, is stiff while the person is awake, somewhat relaxed in periods of day-dreaming, and loose during the hours of sleep. The wish is active continuously and since the ego must sleep from time to time, the wish may take advantage of its declining vigilance and try to achieve fulfillment. Sleepy, though it may be, it is not paralysed, and thus the ego usually succeeds in frustrating the wish. Nonetheless, unlike in well-guarded wakefulness, in dreams, the wish does succeed in getting expression, but only distortedly, under disguise, as if out of place.

Richardson and Moore (1963) thought it possible to add to this continuum of ever weaker defence against the repressed wish: awake - daydreaming - dreaming, one further step. They reasoned that since while awake, the schizophrenic patients' egos are less efficient than that of the normals, their dreams, too, are less defended than the dreams of normals. The dreams of schizophrenic patients, then, should reflect the repressed wishes in their original form, or at least very close to it.

Richardson and Moore expected to find openly revealed incestuous and aggressive fantasies in the manifest dreams of schizophrenic patients. In fact, however, their comparison of these dreams with those of a control group of nonschizophrenics had shown that undisguised aggression and undistorted incestuous fantasies occurred no more frequently in the schizophrenics than in the nonschizophrenics. "Repression (i.e., censorship)" they had to conclude not without surprise, "appeared to be approximately as effective in the dream of the schizophrenic as in the non-schizophrenic" (p. 293.). Richardson and Moore did not elaborate on the implications of their findings, but they have indicated them by questioning: "Does the dream serve a different function in the schizophrenic than the wish-fulfillment function?" (p. 300). These authors, then, indicated that to their understanding, the dreams of schizophrenics contradict the expectations aroused by Freud's theory of dreams.

Reformulating Richardson and Moore's question, one may ask: is the sleeping ego of schizophrenic patients more successful in repressing than their waking ego? If so, then, the construct of a continuum of defence and with it, Freud's theory of dreams, are in jeopardy. "The kernel" of this theory is the suggestion that, as compared with the waking ego, the sleeping ego is only capable of a lesser "censorship".

This kernel seems to be endangered for a second, not less unexpected reason, too. Kramer, Winget and Whitman (1971) compared dreams with early memories of the same subject. They found slightly more covert than overt hostility in early memories; in dreams, however, covert hostility was four times as common as overt hostility. "Any notion that the dream reports reflect the unbridled expression of feelings is dispelled, we believe, by an examination of hostility in the protocols .... In dream reports, the indirect rather than the direct expression of hostility is clearly the preferred mode" (pp. 1353-1354). An indirect expression of hostility in dreams as against a (fourfold) stronger freedom to experience it in fantasy is the antipode of what the continuum of defence would lead us to expect. Why should dreams restrict the expression of these wishes if one is allowed to be aware of them in daylight?

These comparisons of fantasies with dreams leave not much room for doubt: the construct of a continuum of defence is less than perfect. But Freud's theory for explaining the bizarreness of some dreams stands or falls with the existence of such a continuum, the weakest phase of which is during dreaming and not during fantasizing while one is awake. My understanding of the bizarreness of some dreams is different from that of Freud and Popper-Lynkeus. Nonetheless, I, too, found an idea worthy of praise in this story about a man who had the "splendid gift" for dreaming as though he were awake. I agree with Popper-Lynkeus that "in the deepest sense, dreams are not nonsensical. Indeed, it cannot be at all for it is always the same man, whether he is awake or dreaming" or, as the title of the story put it: Dreaming like waking.

Is, indeed, dreaming like waking? The experts are divided on this question, and in what will follow here I shall try to prove that Popper-Lynkeus was correct in supposing an essential similarity between dreaming and waking existence.

Descartes, in his often quoted first meditation, propounded a view similar to that of Popper-Lynkeus. At this moment, he wrote there, it does indeed seem to me that it is with eyes awake that I am looking at this paper; that this head which I move is not asleep, that it is deliberately and of set purpose that I extend my hand and perceive it. "But in thinking of it carefully, I recall being often deceived during sleep by similar illusions and in pausing at that thought, I see very clearly that there are no certain indications by which it is possible to distinguish clearly the wakeful from the sleeping state...".

Sartre (1940), however, thinks that there is a sophism in this passage of Descartes for there is an essential difference between the waking and dreaming existence. Descartes took for granted that the man who perceives is conscious of perceiving, and since dreamers have a similar certainty on their part, he was lost as to how to differentiate between them. However, Sartre suggests, "the position of existence of the dreamer cannot be likened to that of the person who is awake, because the reflective consciousness, in the one case, destroys the dream, by the very fact that it presents for what it is, whereas in the case of perception reflective consciousness confirms and reinforces the perception itself ... what produces [the dream] and what saves it is that most often this reflective consciousness does not appear" (pp. 233-234).

I find it interesting that this strong statement which began as though stating that the dreaming existence, by definition, is unable to reflect upon itself, ended on a conciliatory note by proposing that reflective consciousness is "most often" absent in dreams. I shall soon return to this issue and elaborate on its implications, but first I would like to relate to a similar analysis of Rechtschaffen.

In an influential paper, Rechtschaffen (1978) states that the most noted properties of dreams, their bizarreness and their meaningfulness, are neither unique to nor even distinctive of dreaming. In fact relatively few dreams are bizarre and "most waking thought or behavior can be interpreted, correctly or incorrectly, as having a significance beyond immediate appearances" (p. 97). Rather, Rechtschaffen suggests, let us pay attention to another, truly distinctive feature of dreams: their single-mindedness. In dreams we may discern a "strong tendency for a single train of related thoughts and images to persist over extended periods without disruption or competition from other simultaneous thoughts and images" (p. 97).

The main features of this single-mindedness are (1) non-reflectiveness, (2) lack of imagination, (3) dream isolation. To be reflective or self-conscious means that while doing or thinking something we are aware of being engaged in such an activity, and while performing we are able to observe ourselves and judge the quality and value of our productions. In dreaming, we are usually unaware of the circumstances, namely, that we are lying and sleeping, and of the fact that our experience, the dream, is a creation of our mind and not an occurrence of the external world. For example, in a laboratory study, Zimmerman (1970) wakened subjects from REM periods and asked whether they had been aware that they were sleeping and dreaming. In approximately 90% of the cases, subjects related non-reflectively to their dreams.

It is the opinion of Rechtschaffen that even these figures overestimated reflectiveness in dreams, "In fact, I can think of no other single state short of severe and chronic psychosis in which there is such a persistent, massive, regular loss of reflectiveness. Herein may lie the most distinctive psychological characteristic of dreaming ... it is only during dreaming that most of us regularly lose so completely, the road map of our own consciousness" (p. 100).

Reflective consciousness is dependent upon our ability to generate simultaneously two parallel ongoing and not necessarily interdependent mentations. It is a common experience that while performing one act, our mind is able to "wander," to allocate the energy needed for attending simultaneously to two tasks. While driving and properly handling the demands put by a tumultuous and crowded street, our parallel ongoing thoughts may take us to another place and another atmosphere. However, Rechtschaffen contends, dreams lack this ability of dividing attention; they are single-minded. He experimentally investigated this dimension of the sleeping mind and was able to show that of 168 dreams recalled at interrupted REM periods by two subjects only, 22 (13%) reports indicated thinking something "above and beyond" an immediate perception of the dream events.

Both of these very interesting observations of Rechtschaffen indicate that we are dealing here with a continuum and not with absolute differences. "Most of us" dream without being aware of dreaming, and most of us (87% in this experiment) are unable to divide our attention while dreaming. Rechtschaffen and Sartre succeeded, indeed, in defining an important and rather neglected attribute of our dreaming existence, but also made salient the fact of individual differences. Dreamers usually are single-minded, but some individuals are able to divide their attention and reflect upon themselves also in sleeping and dreaming. In these days of lively interest in lucid dreams there is no need to prove what seems rather obvious. Lucid dreamers are aware of being asleep and dreaming; moreover, they are able to influence the unfolding of their dreams and turn a frightening experience into a pleasant one. Dreamers of lucid dreams, in the felicitous term of Laberge and Gackenbach (1986), are participant-observers; their ability to observe themselves does not obliterate their sleep, and we may conclude, as indicated by Sartre and Rechtschaffen, that dreaming does not preclude the possibility of reflective consciousness.

McCarley and Hoffman (1981), though, are more reserved in this respect. They collected 104 dreams from 14 subjects. Seventy dreams contained at least one element of bizarreness. In 17 dreams, the dreamer was puzzled by some oddity. In 15 of these dreams, the dreamer merely registered the presence of an oddity; in one dream, action was held up while the dreamer puzzled about the oddity, in only one dream did the dreamer become conscious that he was dreaming. "What appears unusual about the dream situation", commented McCarley and Hoffman, "in contrast to waking, is that oddity is not more frequently and more strongly registered. This absence of reflective self-consciousness may be related to dreams being primarily generated as a result of activation from lower, brainstem centers, in contrast to the control of waking behavior that is directed by higher brain centers" (p. 911).

It seems to me that these data allow one to arrive at a different conclusion. To begin with, I would question their statement that violations of logic are "strongly" registered in waking. Apart from the facts of repression and denial, one has to be reminded of the global-intuitive style of cognition. Intuitive individuals are rather "tolerant" in their relation to contradictions and other violations of logic, that is to say, there are differences in this respect between normal persons in waking and in dreaming too; *we have to confront styles of cognition rather than states of consciousness.*

Some relevant studies of Orne (1972) and Josephine Hilgard (1972) may demonstrate the validity of this contention. Some, but not all, deeply hypnotized individuals are able to integrate a suggested hallucination with a conflicting veridical perception into one experience, and the resulting incongruity, as Orne put it, "does not seem to unduly trouble" them. For example, a subject who was told to hallucinate someone sitting in a chair, described his experience as follows: "You know, it is the strangest thing, I see X sitting there and smiling in the chair.

He is there and yet I can see the outline of the chair through him." Strange though it is, the subject would nevertheless not doubt that he sees Mr. X sitting in a chair. Yet, such an acquiescence in face of a blatant self-contradiction is not characteristic of all hypnotized subjects. Josephine Hilgard (1972) reports on a female subject who was instructed to awake from hypnosis and find that she has no hands, but this would not bother her. Then her "absent" hands were given a quite strong electric shock. Although no suggestion was given regarding analgesia, the subject reported that she felt nothing. Here the hypnotized subject, on her own initiative, prevented the genesis of a possible self-contradiction: since she has no hands, as it were, quite logically she should feel no pain in her hands.

It is apparent that it is not the hypnosis but their different styles of cognition, which prevail through all the states of consciousness, that are responsible for the difference in their behavior. Thus, the one subject of McCarley and Hoffman, who was puzzled by the absurdity of what he experienced in his dream and had to conclude that he must be asleep and dreaming, indeed was a true participant-observant. His case may demonstrate that reflective consciousness does not necessarily destroy sleep. The other dreamers, those who registered the oddities but succumbed to them and those who accepted them without any protest, only behaved in accord with their respective styles of cognition. Their behavior neither proves nor disproves the possibility of reflective consciousness in dreaming.

The second evidence for reflective consciousness in dreaming, apart from the lucid dreams, is proffered by sleep-talking. In his encyclopedic treatment of sleep-talking, Arkin (1979) noted "the not infrequent occurrence of the subject uttering in sleep a self-correction of an overt error, or an apparently 'unintended' sequence" (p. 345). For example, the dreamer (sleep stage 4) says: "I wanna take a net - a note ..." (p. 345); the dreamer seems to have been aware of the discrepancy between his intention and performance and behaved not unlike he would have done while awake. Or, to take another example (sleep stage 2): "... it seemed rather expensive type things - mbl - was on the left and that was the youngest of the lead - leak - after leaft - least active hum ..." (p. 346). The dreamer, Arkin observed, seems to have been dissatisfied with his utterance, and persists, tries again, until his thought is properly reflected in the word emitted. In dreams as in waking, words are used for purposes of communication, and this demands agreed-upon constructs rather than idiosyncratic creations. Although sleeping, this subject was self-observant enough to be able to judge whether or not his verbalizations were communicative.

Some dreamers, then, but not the majority, are participant-observers. One may, therefore, argue, as did Sartre and Rechtschaffen, that the absence of reflective consciousness is a distinguishing feature of the dreaming existence, but one may also contend, as I did, that there are individual differences in this respect too, and, therefore, one has to agree that sleep and reflective consciousness are not contradictory terms. Furthermore, I would like to suggest that these individual differences are continuously active throughout the different states of consciousness. Two studies of Foulkes and associates may be recalled here in support of this proposition.

In their study on mental activity at sleep onset, Foulkes and Vogel (1965) were able to separate three features of change in the period of transition from waking to sleeping. Their subjects were awakened separately during the following four sequential changes in EEG and EOG variables as wakefulness passes into sleep; alpha EEG with one or more REM's a few seconds prior to the awakening; alpha EEG with pronounced SEM (slow eye movements which lack fixation and are sometimes binocularly asymmetrical); descending Stage 1; descending Stage 2. The subjects had to judge whether they were controlling their thoughts, whether they were aware that they were in the laboratory, and whether they knew that they were observing the contents of their mind. The result showed that five (of the nine) subjects had completely lost their control and reality-orientation during Stages 1 and 2, but 3 subjects retained a relatively high degree of control and reality-orientation during alpha stages and only later, during descending Stages 1 and 2, demonstrated a comparable reduction in these functions. During descending Stage 2, then, which is the last station of what one may yet define as belonging to the hypnagogic period, some subjects were still able to evidence a relatively functioning reflective consciousness.

Regarding the other end of this continuum, fantasizing while awake, we shall now turn to the study of Foulkes and Fleisher (1975). They instructed their S's to relax but stay awake. This they did in a moderately illuminated room, the experimenters sitting in another room of the laboratory. At randomly selected times, the subjects were interviewed about what was going through their minds before being interrupted, whether they believed in the external reality of these occurrences, whether they were aware of being in a laboratory, etc.

68% of the reports were of visually experienced fantasies. 27% of these day-dreams were non-reflective or hallucinatory, that is, the subject was not aware of his/her place of dwelling and related to the content of the imagery as if it occurred "out there". Foulkes and Fleisher also found that 22% of their subjects were "lost in thought". These subjects were not aware of the room and the laboratory in general, yet their mentations were non-hallucinatory. They were halfway non-reflective; with one leg already in non-reflectiveness, while the other still stood where reality-testing does prevail. The halfway and fully non-reflective mentations obtained from waking subjects add up to almost half of the reports.

Zimmerman (1970), as one may recall, found that 90% of his subjects behaved in a non-reflective manner in sleep. Dreams, then, usually are non-reflective but to a surprisingly high degree, so are our day-dreams. Dreams appear here to be on a continuum and may be defined, among things, by their position on this continuum. La Berge and associates (1986) found a consistent correlation between lucid dreaming ability and field-independence. Field-independence is also correlated with more realistic dreams and daydreams than field-dependence, and we discussed earlier this finding of Starker (1973, 1974). We may then suppose that individuals whose style of cognition is analytic and whose dreams are logical, are able to maintain varying degrees of reflective consciousness while fantasizing and dreaming. Intuitive individuals easily lose or perhaps give up their control over their fantasies and dreams, and experience them fully hallucinating. And as usual, between these two extremes is posited the majority, which is once closer to the analytic and at another time closer to the intuitives.

Incidentally, this disinterest of the intuitives in a participant-observant approach exposes them to the threat of terrifying dreams. Being deeply absorbed by this one track of negative thoughts the truthfulness of which they do not doubt, there is nothing around to help the dreamer construct a relativising perspective. The threat seems absolute and overwhelming.

Earlier, I have suggested that sleep and reflective consciousness are not contradictory terms. But I have to agree that the belief in their incompatibility seems to be well supported. Sleep, by its very definition, means isolation from the "wear and tear" of daily life. If there is any empirical foundation for solipsism, that is, for the belief that the human mind has no valid ground for accepting the existence of anything but itself, then sleep seems to be this foundation. And yet, at a closer look, the evidence, to borrow a term used by Halasz, Pal, and Rajna (1985) in their study of K complex, is Janus-faced.

K complex, first decribed by Loomis, Harvey, and Hobart (1936), is generated spontaneously by the brain in sleep, but is also elicited by different sensory stimuli. This is why Halasz and his associates called it Janus-faced.

Loomis and his associates suggested that the K complex is a "forerunner of the high voltage slow potential of deep sleep." Likewise, Koella (1967) considered the K complex to be an "anti-arousal" mechanism since, he argued, there is no actual awakening at the time of the K complexes, but strong stimuli which do interrupt the sleep do not elicit K complexes. The K complex, then, indicates an activity, a kind of vigilance amidst somnolence. The function which generates the K complexes is that of guardianship, the task of which is to secure the continuance of the sleep. Clearly, the guardian must be sensitive enough to decide when to persist in defending the sleep and when to interrupt it, and thus we arrived at the paradox of sleep: it is as much isolation as it is contact. Oswald, Taylor and Treisman (1960) read a long series of names to sleeping individuals. The subject's own name elicited a K response in two-thirds of the instances, but the name immediately preceding it, in one-third of the instances only. Moreover, the K complexes in response to personally important names were bigger and better. It is apparent that the sentinel function, indicated by the K complexes, does what guardians in a watchtower are expected to do: to be alert so that the others may sleep. Sleep, indeed, is Janus-faced.

Berger (1963) was able to show that meaningful spoken names were incorporated into the dreams ongoing at that moment. This, then, indicates an even greater opennes during sleep than the study of Oswald et al. On the other hand, Rechtschaffen and Foulkes (1965) have shown that in sleep we are functionally blind. Their subjects, "good sleepers", slept with their eyes taped open. (Three narrow strips of tape were secured to each eye and pulled upward to open the eye.) The experimenter held different stimuli, illuminated with a small light, in front of the subject's eyes. Each stimulus was presented twice, once during a REM period and once during a NREM period. A few seconds after the stimulus light was turned off, the subject was awakened and asked: "Was anything going through your mind just before I called you?" None of the 30 experimental trials yielded a direct, undistorted perception of the stimulus object. In only one of about 20 trials in pilot studies was there any hint of a possible incorporation. Four of the 30 reports included images of bright lights, which could have represented incorporation of the light that was used to illuminate the stimulus object. Again, the difference in open-ness between the visual and auditory modalities is a further demonstration of the Janus-faced sleep.

One may then argue, as indeed Rechtschaffen (1978) did, that external stimuli impinging on the dreamer do not clearly in-fluence dreams. Indeed, only about one-third of the dreams generated in laboratories contain indications of this unnatural environment. Sprays of cold water during REMs were incor-porated in only 47% of subsequent dream reports. A spray of cold water, Rechtschaffen observes, would certainly enter the consciousness of aware subjects. But one may also point out that absent-minded individuals may or may not become aware of such an event. People in the heat of battle may not even immediately take notice of having been wounded, and subjects in hypnotic rapport may exclude from their consciousness even more intrusive stimuli. Some may even endure surgical opera-tions without anaesthesia.

Further, the findings of Perky (1910) and Joelson Segal (1972) show that in this regard too, fantasizing while awake and dreaming are quite close to each other. Perky asked her sub-jects to relax in a darkened room and imagine, for example, a banana. While the subjects were describing their imagery, a yellow-colored form shaped like a banana oscillated briefly before their gaze. All her subjects described the banana of their imagery as being on end, yet none of them were aware of and could report on the external stimulus which influenced their imagery. Joelson Segal replicated this experiment and con-firmed Perky's findings. Individuals engaged in active imagin-ing, that is attempting to visualize some object and see it before them, as in a dream, do assimilate external stimuli without being consciously aware of those stimuli. However, in contrast to Perky, Joelson Segal was able to show that the assimilation is rather limited, as the mean effect ranged from 4 to 18% above chance and usually were about 10-15% over chance. The find-ings then on the assimilation of external stimuli to dreams, rather than attesting to an encapsulation of dreams, show them to be positioned on a continuum. Both fantasies in waking and dreams in sleep demonstrate a paradoxical blend of spontaneous mentations and some measure of openness to environmental influences.

A second thought warns me not to close this discussion of the continuity between waking and dreaming existence yet. Thus far, I have related to sleep in a unitary manner, but we know that sleep is not unitary. With regard to the isolation one should, perhaps, differentiate between the different stages of sleep and put special emphasis on Stages 3 and 4 (also called slow-wave sleep, SWS). It is more difficult to awaken subjects from SWS than from REM sleep or Stage 1. By this measure of arousability, then, SWS is the deep sleep. Perhaps what was said of the isolation of sleep applies to SWS? Indeed, Evans et al. (1966) were able to show that sleeping subjects react to verbal reactions given in REM sleep, and Ullman and Krippner (1978) provided evidence that some subjects are able to receive telepathic messages in their REM sleep and incorporate them in their dreams. REM sleep then appears to be relatively open to environmental influences. In contrast, "SWS reflects a unique form of cerebral shutdown not found in other sleep stages" (Horne, 1985, p. 38). Indications that the human cerebrum enters a peculiar state of isolation during SWS, Horne states, come from a variety of studies. A report on the evocation of epilepsy during sleep concluded that during SWS there was a "functional disconnection of the cortex", not found in other sleep states (Sato, Dreifuss, and Penry, 1975). Another study, on evoked potentials during sleep, found that the blocking effect of SWS was unique (Velasco, Velasco, Cepeda, and Munoz, 1980), and recently it has been shown that SWS reflects a partial disconnection between the hemispheres (Banquet, 1983).

SWS, then, seems to be sealed off almost hermetically; it may serve, indeed, as the modernized rendition of the earlier notion of the isolatedness of sleep and dreaming existence. And since it is more isolated than the other stages of sleep, we will have to pay special attention in our theorizing to the fact that dreams from NREM stages of sleep are simple and logical or, as Foulkes (1962) called them, "thoughts". Whether one interacts with the environment or retreats to one's inner self, one's thinking remains the same. Indeed, dreaming like waking.

A THEORY OF PSYCHOTHERAPY

Breuer–Freud–Ferenczi

In his short *Account of Psychoanalysis*, Freud (1924) reminded us that "as may well be supposed, it did not drop from the skies ready-made. It had its starting point in older ideas, which it developed further; it sprang from earlier suggestions, which it elaborated" (p. 191). The phenomena of hypnotism, Freud wrote, were among the decisive influences shaping psychoanalysis. "It is not easy to over-estimate the importance of the part played by hypnotism in the history of the origin of psycho-analysis. From a theoretical as well as from a therapeutic point of view, psycho-analysis has at its command a legacy which it has inherited from hypnotism" (p. 192). Hypnosis has proved first, that striking somatic changes can be brought about by mental influences and second, that unconscious mental processes are "tangible and subject to experiment". Moreover, Pierre Janet, a pupil of Charcot, was able to show with the help of hypnosis that the symptoms of hysteria were caused by certain unconscious thoughts *(idees fixes)*.

Such similarity of conceptions notwithstanding, psychoanalysis was not based on Janet's, but rather on Breuer's research. In 1881, "independently of any outside influence", Breuer treated a young girl who, while she was nursing her father, developed several hysteric symptoms. "This case of Breuer's retains its unique significance for our understanding of the neuroses to this day ... Breuer was able to establish that all her symptoms were related to this period of nursing and could be explained by it. Thus it had, for the first time, become possible to obtain a complete view of a case of this puzzling neurosis, and all its symptoms had turned out to have a meaning" (p. 193). Remarkably, these traumatic precipitating causes were lost to the patient's memory. "Here, therefore, we had a fresh proof of the existence of mental processes which were unconscious but for that very reason especially powerful ..." (p. 194). Breuer induced the patient, under hypnosis, to remember the forgotten traumas and to react to them with powerful expressions of effect. "The cathartic method [purging, setting free of a strangulated effect] was the immediate precursor of psycho-analysis, and in spite of every extension of experience and of every modification of theory, is still contained within it as its nucleus" (p. 194).

Nevertheless, modifications, as Freud modestly put it, did seem necessary. Freud was not particularly apt in handling hypnosis, and the results of hypnotherapy, while striking, were of short duration. Despite these shortcomings, hypnosis succeeded in turning unconscious memories into conscious ones. And so, having decided against the further use of hypnosis, and in search of a method which, like hypnosis, could restore "to the patient's memory what he had forgotten ... the idea occurred to Freud of substituting for [hypnosis] the method of 'free association'" (p. 195). In substituting "free" association for hypnosis, Freud was led by an expectation that the so-called "free" association would prove in fact to be unfree, "since, when all conscious intellectual purposes had been suppressed, the ideas that emerged would be seen to be determined by the unconscious material. This expectation was justified by experience" (p. 195).

In fact, not only was Freud substituting free association for hypnosis to explore the unconscious, he also substituted the *Ucs.* for the unconscious he had dealt with up until then, with the consequence that in contradiction to the experiences unearthed by hypnosis, free association "did not bring up what had actually been forgotten, but ... with the help of a certain amount of supplementing and interpreting, the doctor was able to guess (to reconstruct) the forgotten material from it. Thus, the free association together with the act of interpretation performed the same function as had previously been performed by hypnotism" (p. 196). The replacement of hypnosis by free association made evident the mechanism of resistance, which in its turn made salient the existence of a conflict between two groups of mental trends. Not because of the use of free association though, Freud "also came upon another purely empirical finding in the discovery [of] ... infantile sexuality" (p. 197).

The turning point in this process of transmutation was the adoption of the method of free association. "After hypnosis was replaced by the technique of free association", Freud (1924) observed, "Breuer's cathartic procedure turned into psychoanalysis" (p. 197). Ferenczi, for several years a friend and close collaborator of Freud, seems to have regretted this development at the end of his life. In his last paper entitled: "The Confusion of Tongues", read before a psychoanalytic Congress, he stated that trauma, specifically sexual trauma, "cannot be stressed enough" as a pathogenic factor. In an earlier paper, Ferenczi (1930) paid tribute to Breuer (and challenged Freud) by saying that "Breuer's remarkable contribution was this: not only did he pursue the method indicated by the patient but he had faith in the *reality* of the memories which emerged and did not, as was customary, dismiss them out of hand, as the fantastic inventions of a mentally abnormal patient" (p. 429; emphasis in the original). In the same paper, Ferenczi also made it known that he "constantly" found himself impinging on one or another of Freud's injunctions in his *Recommendations on Technique*.

Yet, in none of these papers did he mention the construct of *Ucs*. The logic of his views though would lead us to expect him to do so, for during the years of their cooperation, Breuer and Freud were not required to implement an art of interpretation. They listened to "memories of aetiological importance which dated back from fifteen to twenty-five years [and yet] were found to be astonishingly intact and to possess remarkable sensory force ..." (Breuer and Freud, 1893-95, pp. 9-10). Their findings, very much like those relating to the then much discussed peculiarities of double personalities, made conspicuous the existence of an unconscious realm in human mental life, a realm which, while "dissociated" from the dominant personality, once made visible - by the help of hypnosis - appeared in its original form. It is only when speaking of "repression" that we assume a forever ongoing process of disguise, displacement, and derivatives of the original experience. This is why Breuer and Freud had to listen and record only, whereas Freud and Freudians, by definition, supplement and interpret what they perceive to be hints from the repressed unconscious.

Since Ferenczi saw that trauma and external agencies, and not fantasy, were at the roots of psychopathology, and since he knew that the treatment of badly hurt persons must be different from one conceived for people who suffer from the predicament of their fantasy, and finally, since traumas may but need not be unconscious, and in any case, the memories are direct and reliable, what could have justified his working with the concept of repressed unconscious and the commitment to interpret a forever veiled wish? It is a matter of speculation whether, if he had been granted a few more years of life, Ferenczi would have become aware of this issue and would have been ready to conclude in the spirit of his other decisions? Agreeing with Ferenczi on the question he dealt with, in what will follow here I completed what he left unfinished. I shall suggest: (a) critically reconsidering the heart of Freud's theory of behavior, the concept of *Ucs.*, (b) adopting trauma as the main reason for developing psychoneuroses and, consequently, a theory of real meeting - in contrast to the construct of transference and opaque mirror - for conducting psychotherapy.

On the unconscious determination of behavior

There is a fundamental distinction between normality and neurosis, Kubie (1954) stated: "No moment of behavior can be looked upon as neurotic unless the processes that have set it in motion predetermine its automatic repetition irrespective of its suitability to the immediate situation or its immediate or remote consequences" (p. 185). This, he emphasized, may be the most basic lesson about human conduct that has been learned from psychoanalysis.

Likewise, Meissner (1981) defined the thesis that all neurotic phenomena have an unconscious meaning, "Freud's unique contribution and the basis for all psychoanalytic understanding" (p. 943). Above, I have quoted Freud (1924) praising Breuer, who "independently of any outside influence" was the first to establish that all his patients' symptoms had a meaning. Earlier, in his *Introductory Lectures on Psychoanalysis*, Freud (1915/16) told his audience that "it was discovered one day that the pathological symptoms of certain neurotic patients have a sense". In a footnote he added: "By Joseph Breuer in the years of 1880-1881". He then continued: "On this discovery the psycho-analytic method of treatment was founded" (p. 85). Freud, then, would have agreed that the assumption concerning the unconsciously determined meaning of neurotic symptoms is, indeed, the very basis of psychoanalysis, but he also left no reason for doubting who was the real discoverer of this novelty. And yet, in our "collective consciousness" it was Freud who discovered the new continent. Why is that so?

While such stories and questions are interesting in themselves and may illuminate some aspects of human history, they may also serve to introduce our topic here, the puzzling ambiguities surrounding this most basic concept of Freud's psychopathology: the unconscious determination of behavior.

I shall quote here a few statements in the order in which they appear in Freud (1901), *Psychopathology of Everyday Life*: "*By the side of simple cases where proper names are forgotten there is a type of forgetting which is motivated by repression"* (p. 7, emphasis in original) - "Among the 'slips of the tongue' that I have collected myself ... I *almost invariably* discover [a] disturbing influence ... that has remained unconscious ... and which can often be brought to consciousness only by means of searching analysis" (p. 61, emphasis added). A few pages later: "... there is nothing, on the other hand, to prevent me at the same time from allowing that, in situations where speaking is hurried and attention is to some extent diverted, the conditions governing 'slips of the tongue' may easily be confined within the limits defined by Meringer and Mayer" (p. 81). Strachey added here a footnote: "i.e., may be confined to phonetic factors".

Some "slips of the tongue" then, but not all, are unconsciously determined. But he also found, "almost invariably", that all of them are unconsciously determined. What a well-chosen characterization this is of the confusion created here. There are a few more places where Freud dealt with this question but, unfortunately, they do not disambiguate the ambiguity we are facing here. In his *Introductory Lectures on Psychoanalysis*, Freud (1915/16) succeeded in putting into one sentence the conflicting statements of the *Psychopathology of Everyday Life:* "Let me insist once again that I am not asserting – and for our purposes there is no need to do so – that every single parapraxis that occurs has a sense, even though I regard that as probably the case" (p. 60).

Indeed, Freud allowed Brill (1938) to insert into his translation of the *Psychology of Everyday Life* the following story: "Those were the pioneer days of Freud among psychiatrists and we observed and studied and noted whatever was done or said about us with unfailing patience and untiring interest and zeal. We made no scruples, for instance, of asking a man at table why he did not use his spoon in the proper way, or why he did such and such a thing in such and such a manner. It was impossible for one to show any degree of hesitation or make some abrupt pause in speaking without being at once called to account" (p. 57). Was it not Brill himself who, a few pages before this anecdote, translated Freud as saying: "We shall represent [the] state of affairs carefully enough if we assert that *besides the simple forgetting of proper names, there is another forgetting which is motivated by repression*" (p. 40, emphasis in original)? It is apparent that Brill, and all the others who behaved like him, should have felt that his written statements notwithstanding, Freud believed that parapraxes, dreams, neurotic behavior, and behavior in general, are "invariably" determined by the repressed unconscious. The fact that Freud admitted the existence of "simple" forgetting, that is, a behavior not determined by the motives of the repressed unconscious, seems to have been gallantly overlooked by Brill, and curiously enough, by Freud himself.

Bettelheim (1976) put this sweeping interpretation of Freud's intentions succinctly: "Psychoanalysis indicates that *whatever* the rational causes of an action, they also have an unconscious meaning" (p. 50, emphasis added). Brill's story reflects the same understanding, and Freud's agreement to let him print it in his book vindicates him as well as Bettelheim. Here only the reader who respects the text more than the presumed contradictory intentions of the author is perplexed. His perplexity may become even more acute by realizing that such all-embracing formulations of the unconscious determination notwithstanding, Freud was also pondering the possibility of chance occurrences in mental life, conscious and unconscious.

In his *Psychopathology of Everyday Life*, Freud (1901) agreed that "... *spontaneous ideas (words or numbers) may be undetermined, or may have been determined* by the thoughts that come out in the analysis, or by any other thoughts, not disclosed in the analysis ... In analytic practice we proceed on the presupposition that the second of the possibilities mentioned above meets the facts ..." (p. 251, n, emphasis added). However, in sharp contradiction to what he conceded here, namely, that mental determinism is as possible as the lack of it, in his *Introductory Lectures* Freud (1915/16) was again the hard-liner: "Our dream-interpretations are made on the basis of the premises ... that dreams in general have a sense, that it is legitimate to carry across from hypnotic to normal sleep the fact of the existence of mental processes which are at the time unconscious, and that *everything* that occurs to the mind is determined" (p. 143, emphasis added).

Thus, Freud believed both in total mental determinism, which should have also comprised the motives of the repressed unconscious, and in the possibility that mental acts may be undetermined chance occurrences. This is a self-contradiction in a topic, the importance of which should not allow it to be overlooked or disregarded. For, psychodynamic interpretations and, in fact, dynamic psychology, are only possible if dreams, parapraxes, and behavior in general are determined. Curiously enough, precisely here, regarding the (unconscious) determination of behavior, Freud left the issue in limbo, without supplying arguments for preferring one view over the other. Freud had opportunity enough to nullify this statement and perhaps also to explain why he thought it possible in the first place. One cannot admit that "In the analytic practice we proceed on the *presupposition* that the second of the possibilities mentioned above [i.e., spontaneous ideas are determined by the thoughts revealed in the analysis] meets the facts and that in the *majority* of circumstances use can be made of it" (1901, p. 251, n. emphasis added), and at the same time agree with Brill. Since, however, he did not explain himself, neither did he disprove the reasons which led him to conceive such a possibility, one has to conclude that despite his strong statements to the contrary, Freud was (also) skeptical in regard to the psychic determinism. Such skepticism, as one may understand, is incompatible with the concept of dynamic psychology.

Finally, I should point out a disturbing laxity in the use of the concept of unconscious. In his programmatic statement in *The Interpretation of Dreams*, Freud (1900) distinguished between the concepts of the philosophers and of his own: "... there are two kinds of unconscious, which have not yet been distinguished by psychologists ... One of them, which we term the *Ucs.* is also *inadmissible to consciousness,* while we term the other the *Pcs.* because its excitations ... are able to reach consciousness" (pp. 614-615, emphasis in original). Reading some of the examples provided by Freud in *The Interpretation of Dreams* and in *The Psychopathology of Everyday Life,* one cannot but wonder whether they were meant to demonstrate Freud's or perhaps the philosophers' conception of consciousness.

Take for example number 13 of the slips of the tongue. A young man addressed a lady in the street by saying to her: If you will permit me, madam, I should like to *begleit-digen* you. "It was obvious," Freud (1901) commented, "what his thoughts were: he would like to *begleiten* (accompany) her, but was afraid his offer would *beleidigen* [insult] her. But while he attempted to conceal this from her, his unconscious played a trick on him by betraying his real intention" (p. 68). If this young man was aware that his offer to *begleiten* is an offer to *beleidigen,* then his slip of the tongue was the outcome of a conflict between two conscious thoughts. If so, the conflict, as described by Freud, does not justify speaking here of the influence of the (repressed) unconscious. The young man knew of his impulses, so much so that "he attempted to conceal" them from the young lady. Such a situation, of course, has nothing to do with conflicts which unbeknown to oneself, influence one's behavior.

Likewise, in example 14, Stekel recalls once having said to a patient of his: If, as I hope, you will not leave your bed soon. He, of course, intended to express his hopes that soon she will be able to leave her bed, but "due to an egoistic motive in the unconscious, namely that I should be able to continue treating this well-to-do patient some time longer" (p. 68), his tongue slipped. Is this egoistic motive a repressed wish like, for example, the Wolfman's oedipal wish? Or rather, like the young man in example 13, Stekel was fully aware both of his disinterested devotion to the welfare of his patients and his financial needs, and the conflictive "not" played an embarrassing trick on him but did not reveal anything he did not know of?

And, one may continue, is the meaning suggested by Freud

(1900) to his "Irma-dream" a repressed wish? Freud defined this dream as a "specimen-dream", and the date of its interpretation in 1895 as the date when "the secret of dreams was revealed" (p. 121) to him. The meaning of this dream was as follows: "I became aware of an intention which was carried into effect by the dream and which must have been my motive for dreaming it. The dream fulfilled certain wishes which were started in me by the events of the previous evening ... the conclusion of the dream, that is to say, was that I was not responsible for the persistence of Irma's pains, but that Otto was. ... *Thus its content was the fulfillment of a wish and its motive was a wish*" (pp. 118-119, emphasis in original). Was this conflict between Otto who accused Freud and Freud who accused Otto of being responsible for Irma's poor condition, a conflict Freud was unaware of? Was his wish to justify himself a repressed motive?

In another dream of his, Freud (1900) dreamt that his friend R. was his uncle. Freud had a great feeling of affection for him (p. 137). Analyzing this dream, Freud concluded that one of its motives was his wish to be appointed to a professorship (p. 192). Yet, he was dissatisfied. "If it was indeed true that my craving to be addressed with a different title was as strong as all that, it showed a pathological ambition which I did not recognize in myself and which I believed was alien to me ... What, then, could have been the origin of the ambitiousness which produced the dream in me?" (p. 192). Eventually, he found the agreeable solution. Further associations led him to the conclusion that in the latent substrate of this dream he put himself in the place of the Minister who prevented his nomination to professorship. "Turning the tables on his Excellency with a vengeance! He had refused to appoint me *professor extraordinarius* and I had retaliated in the dream by stepping into his shoes" (p. 193).

While the difference between the two interpretations is not immediately apparent, after all Freud expressly identifies the reason of his vengeance: the Minister refused to appoint him, and thus one may assume that Freud, like all of us, did want to be addressed by a "different title". The main point for us here is this: was Freud unconscious of his conflict with the Minister of Education? Freud did not say so, and in any case, it would be difficult to agree with such an assertion. The wish, then, which according to Freud, instigated his dream, was a conscious one.

I shall close this series of perplexing inconsistencies and self-contradictions by a definition of the "mechanism" of the slips of the tongue suggested by Freud (1916/17) in his *Introductory Lectures:* "The speaker *decides not to put it* [the disturbing purpose] *into words, and after that the slip of the tongue occurs: after that, that is to say, the purpose which has been forced back is put into words against the speaker's will, either by altering the expression of the intention which he has permitted, as by mingling with it, or by actually taking its place. This, then, is the mechanism of a slip of the tongue"* (p. 65, emphasis in original). If parapraxes are the result of a clash between two conscious intentions, between a conscious "will" not to say and a conscious "purpose" nonetheless to say it, what can they contribute for establishing a psychodynamic theory of behavior?

Freud, then, spoke two languages: 1) Everything in mental life is determined, and yet spontaneously emerging ideas may be chance occurrences; 2) Every act is unconsciously determined (and yet) besides the forgetting motivated by the repressed unconscious, there is also a "simple" forgetting; 3) Dreams, parapraxes, and behavior in general, are influenced by the repressed unconscious - the examples given for proving this assertion would hardly be enough for convincing one of the participation of the *Pcs.,* and certainly not of the *Ucs.* His followers, unperturbed by such ambiguities, interpret Freud's statements in a one-sided, sweeping manner which puts in relief the "Freudian" aspect of these statements, while relating to his contradictory views as if they were but "airy nothings". In the following chapters, I shall try to show that Freud spoke in two languages in regard to the pathogenic factor and the theory of psychotherapy as well, and that his disciples, here too, did their best to "Freudianize" what Freud left double-faced. In contrast to these authors, I found in these ambiguities of Freud's an indirect support for a revival of the original stance of Breuer and Freud.

Trauma or fantasy?

The heart and reason of discussions is the understanding that the matter considered can be decided by proofs, and that both parties will respect their verdict. Reason and not authority is the parole of debates and yet, we all know that deeply ingrained beliefs die hard and, in fact, continue to thrive even if convincing arguments are proffered in favor of their discontinuance. I may exaggerate, perhaps, but not seriously, I think, by stating that the concept of the repressed unconscious and its power for influencing behavior became such a deeply ingrained conviction. Except for behaviorists, most psychotherapists regard it as a foundation stone, and while any other part of a building may be altered or renewed, foundation stones usually are revered and left untouched. Thus, I am well aware that my discussion of Freud's presentation of this concept will have to be more practical or rather more clinical, in order to have a chance of being listened to and, perhaps, changing the mind of the readers.

It is because of the repressed wishes, and especially of the Oedipal one, that psychotherapists have such an outstanding interest in the repressed unconscious. In his *Three Essays on Sexuality*, Freud (1905/b) called this wish a shibboleth: "It has justly been said that the Oedipus complex is the nuclear complex of the neuroses, and constitutes the essential part of their content ... [Its] recognition has become the Shibboleth which distinguishes the adherents of psychoanalysis from its opponents" (p. 226, n), and in his posthumous *Outline of Psychoanalysis* Freud (1940) stated that "the discovery of the repressed Oedipus complex ... alone would give it a claim to be included among the precious new acquisitions of mankind" (p. 193). This shibboleth, as we know, was preceded by a rather different concept of aetiology. I shall here reconstruct both of these etiological approaches, trauma and fantasy, and try to prove that traumata and not fantasy are at the basis of neuroses, and that for conceptualizing these traumata and their effects one does not need the construct of repressed unconscious.

In his lecture on the aetiology of hysteria before the Society for Psychiatry and Neurology in Vienna, Freud (1896) suggested to "take our start from Josef Breuer's momentous discovery: *the symptoms of hysteria (apart from the stigmata) are determined by certain experiences of the patients' which have operated in a traumatic fashion and which are being reproduced in his psychical life in the form of mnemonic symbols*" (p. 253, emphasis in original). But, Freud emphasized, the most important finding that is arrived at if an analysis is consistently pursued is this: Whatever case and whatever symptom we take as our point of departure, *"in the end we infallibly come to the field of sexual experience"* (p. 259, emphasis in original). It was, however, known and Freud was ready to acknowledge that there are numerous people who have a very clear recollection of infantile sexual experiences, and who nevertheless do not suffer from hysteria. "This objection has no weight ... with our patients, those memories are never conscious; but we cure them of their hysteria by transforming their unconscious memories of the infantile scenes into conscious ones" (p. 272). From this one may understand, Freud concluded that for evolving hysteria, it is not enough to have had sexual experiences; the experiences must be preserved as unconscious memories. "But what decides whether those experiences produce conscious or unconscious memories ... that is a fresh problem, which we shall prudently avoid" (p. 272).

The period of earliest childhood is "a period before the development of sexual life; and thus would seem to involve the abandonment of a sexual aetiology" (p. 262). But have we not a right to assume, Freud countered, "that even the age of childhood is not wanting in slight sexual excitations, that later sexual development may perhaps be decisively influenced by childhood experiences?" (p. 262). Nonetheless, "The foundation for a neurosis would ... always be laid in childhood by adults ..." (p. 269). A further component of this theory was the assumption of a postponed action of the trauma. "Our view then is that infantile sexual experiences are the fundamental precondition for hysteria ... but [they] remain without effect to begin with and only exercise a pathogenic action later, when they have been aroused after puberty in the form of unconscious memories" (p. 272).

In a nutshell, then, this is Freud's first theory of neuroses. It suggested some solutions and left others unanswered. To begin with, why of all the possible traumatic experiences and abuses a child may be subjected to, only sexual traumata may cause neurotic behavior? Then it was left unexplained what decides whether the early sexual experience will be recalled consciously or not, and connected with this question: does the definition of trauma include the condition of an inability to consciously recall the experience? For example, in regard to melancholy, Freud did not suggest that in addition to the trauma of loss its memory should be unconscious. A further question relates to the delayed action of the early sexual experience. In general, traumata are understood to exert their influence close to their occurrence, what explains this particular feature of the early sexual trauma? Finally, Freud mentioned but did not deal with the possible contribution of sociological factors: "... I do not myself regard this etiological series as complete; nor does it solve the riddle of why hysteria is not more common among the lower classes" (Freud, 1896, p. 271).

As it happened, Freud's lecture met with criticism but not for the reasons mentioned above. The chairman of the session, Krafft-Ebing, author of the extremely popular *Psychopathia Sexualis* and numerous related publications, called it a scientific fairy-tale. Krafft-Ebing was one of the two professors who recommended Freud's promotion. Thus, his reaction was not derogatory or belittling, but rather an indication of his reaction to the possibility that adults, and relatives at that, are capable of sexually attacking children and, consequently, turning them into hysterics. This is a fairy-tale, a fantasy characteristic of these patients, and physicians should not be gullible and relate to these fantasies as recollections of facts. Even Breuer joined the rank of those who believed Freud was losing his grip on reality, as we see from an unpublished passage in a letter from Freud to Fliess of March 1, 1896, in which he writes: "According to him [Breuer], I would daily have to ask myself whether I am suffering from moral insanity or paranoia scientifica. The medical community was offended by Freud. Breuer had now abandoned him. Lowenfeld, who had initially shown some interest, certainly more than other psychiatrists, seems to have attempted to persuade Freud to abandon the seduction hypothesis. As long as he held to the seduction theory, Freud was alone" (Masson, 1984, p. 135-6).

A year and a few months after his lecture at the Viennese Society, Freud informed Fliess that he had turned about; he agreed that his patients told him fantasies and not facts. Fantasy and not trauma are at the roots of neurotic phenomena. In his letter of September 21, 1897, to Fliess, Freud mentioned four reasons for abandoning his theory of early sexual trauma as the etiological factor of hysteria. First, "The continual disappointment in my efforts to bring any analysis to a real conclusion ... the absence of the complete successes on which I had counted" (Masson's [1984] translation, p. 108). Then, the necessity to accuse in all cases, not excluding his own, the father of being perverse. Third, the possibility that there are no indications of reality in the unconscious, so that one cannot distinguish between truth and fiction. Finally, the fact that in the most deep-reaching psychosis the unconscious memory does not break through, which may mean that there were no such experiences. "If one thus sees that the unconscious never overcomes the resistance of the conscious, the expectation that in treatment the opposite is bound to happen ... also diminishes" (Masson, p. 109).

An impartial reader may find Freud's reasons for abandoning his theory of trauma less convincing than Freud was inclined to believe. I say inclined, since for quite a while he continued wavering until he felt sure about his second theory of psychoneuroses. The first reason, the lack of success in treatments, is of mixed value. The theory of psychopathology, which guides the thinking of a therapist, is important but as psychotherapists of different convictions may attest, there are also other factors, no less important, which share the responsibility for the success or failure of a therapy.

Forty years later Freud (1937/a) expressed a similar dissatisfaction, this time concerning the psychoanalytic therapy: "... one ought not to be surprised", he wrote in his Analysis terminable and interminable, "if it should turn out in the end that the difference between a person who has not been analyzed and the behavior of a person after he has been analyzed is not so thorough-going as we aim at making it and as we expect and maintain it to be" (p. 228). These are clear and strong words. Moreover, the editor of the Standard Edition of his works added a note of his own here to the effect that Freud's doubts extend to the prospects of preventing not merely the occurrence of a fresh and different neurosis, but even the return of a neurosis that has already been treated. Since Freud did not disclose the reasons for his resignation, we cannot be sure whether he thought something should have been done and was not done or, to the contrary, what was done was not to the point. Perhaps Freud had no explanation and could not understand why he was unable to realize his hopes. At any rate, had he been consistent, then in 1937, he should have reached the same conclusion about the Oedipus construct as he had in 1897 about the "seduction theory". In both cases he was dissatisfied with the results of the respective treatments, but only in one of them did he claim that the theory was responsible for the failure.

As to the impossibility of accusing the fathers of hysteric patients: this indeed was the essence of controversy between Freud and his colleagues. Here he said what others like Krafft-Ebing maintained all the time. Nevertheless, one would like to be informed as to why it is impossible. Why was it possible a year ago, but impossible now? As it stands, this enigmatic sentence does not improve but rather, I am afraid, detracts from the value of Freud's arguments for dropping the trauma theory.

Both the first and second arguments, then, are not relevant for they neither prove nor disprove the theory of early sexual trauma. The third argument, too, leaves the matter undecided, for if there are no indications of reality in the unconscious, how shall we know whether we listened to the memory of a real occurrence or to a fantasy of a wished-for occurrence? Under such circumstances one guess is as possible and as good as another. One does not see why this argument should have caused Freud to change his mind.

In contrast, the fourth argument sounds convincing. If neither the loss of control in psychoses nor the taming – as Freud put it in his letter – of the unconscious by the conscious allow the early sexual trauma to appear, then one may, indeed one should conclude that there were no such experiences. Agreeable as this conclusion may seem, it cannot but arouse some uneasy feelings. In his lecture in Vienna, Freud (1896) stated that in order to be pathogenic, the early sexual trauma must be forgotten. "With our patients, those memories are never conscious, but we cure them of their hysteria by transforming their unconscious memories of the infantile scenes into conscious ones" (p. 172). In contrast to the confessions in the letter, namely that neither psychosis nor his treatment succeeded in making the memory of trauma conscious, here Freud proclaimed something to the contrary.

In addition to the incompatibility between the information given in the lecture and the letter, one may mention here a finding of Richardson and Moore (1963). These authors compared dreams of schizophrenic patients with those of a control group. They expected to find openly expressed incestuous and aggressive wishes in the dreams of schizophrenics. The results, however, told a different story. Such themes occurred no more frequently in schizophrenics than in the nonschizophrenic sample. Since schizophrenic patients disappointed the theoretically justifiable expectation, namely that due to their weak ego and ability to repress, their incestuous wishes would be displayed in their original form, should we now conclude, as did Freud (1897) concerning the pathogenic sexual traumata, that such wishes do not exist? I wonder whether Freud would have agreed to apply this argument against the Oedipus construct.

We may then conclude that Freud changed his mind; he defined the Oedipus construct and the construct of repression, in fact of the repressed unconscious, as the two cornerstones of psychoanalysis, the acceptance of which distinguished between psychoanalysts and all the others. Yet, the reasons Freud gave for this reversal are not convincing. While we may trust that he did not behave capriciously, we must point out that his reasons seem less than satisfying. Perhaps he had other reasons, too, which he did not make public. For the reader, however, who can only relate to what was meant to be known, these four arguments do not make the trauma theory obsolete.

Nor do such considerations make the Oedipus construct obsolete. This construct is supported by positive proofs, and we shall now turn to them. A comparison between the proofs available may help us to decide in favor of one of these competing theories.

The unspoken motive

While there is a certain contradiction between the promise of positive proofs, indicated at the end of the third chapter, and the title of this chapter, borrowed from Kaplan and Kloss' (1913) book, both statements are correct. Rather than try to explain, I may illustrate this contention by quoting a reply by Ornstein (1983) in a discussion with Kernberg. Kernberg asked how was it possible that self-psychologists did not see the Oedipus complex in the narcisstic disorders, which were on a higher developmental level, when he saw it in borderline conditions which were on a lower developmental level. Ornstein responded by saying that "neither he [Kernberg] nor we *saw* the Oedipus complex. *He* simply decided to use that clinical construct to order his data, I said, whereas *we* choose a different clinical explanatory construct to order our observations" (p. 355, emphasis in original).

Indeed, even Little Hans did not express such a wish, it was Freud (1909) who interpreted the child's behavior as if Little Hans had such intentions:

"The instinctive impulse which underwent repression in 'Little Hans' was a hostile one against his father. Proof of this was obtained in his analysis while the idea of the biting horse was followed up. He had seen a horse fall down and he had also seen a playmate, with whom he was playing horses, fall down and hurt himself. Analysis justified the inference that he had a wishful impulse that his father should fall down and hurt himself as his playmate and the horse had done ... But a wish of this sort is tantamount to the murderous impulse of the Oedipus complex" (p. 102, emphasis added).

Even at this early age, one depends on interpretations, inferences, for as Ornstein put it so well, one does not see the Oedipus complex, one constructs it, and this construction is the proof, the positive proof, of its existence. It is at such moments that I feel the need to extensively quote from Wallerstein's

Introduction to Spence's (1982) *Narrative Truth Historical Truth*, for he is among the very few psychoanalytic authors who asked that attention be paid to the least appreciated and yet the most important item of their conceptual mansion, its foundation. Representatives of warring factions, he observed, "share almost completely their guiding assumptions about the nature of the basic data ... whatever the scientific status of the overarching explanatory theory ... at least the data are 'self-evident' ... It is precisely at this point that Donald Spence's books is so disturbing ... For Spence ... remind us that our 'data' are not self-evident, their nature not at all to be taken for granted ..." (p. 10). Having put the word "data" in quotation marks, all it was necessary to say was said.

Putting it in plain words, the Oedipus construct was not a "fact", a "discovery". It was, to turn again to Ornstein, "an explanatory construct", as good as the construct of Kohut that Ornstein was referring to. In fact, some anthropologists think that the Oedipus construct does not fit the known facts. For example, Goody (1956) complained that "the whole lengthy discussion of incest has turned on the supposition that it is a type of illicit sexual intercourse which is characterized by a particular horror" (p. 294). In truth, however, "the grisly horror of incest" is not a universal characteristic of human societies. For example, among the patrilineal Tallensi, in Africa, sexual relationships between brother and sister are merely "disreputable", whereas among the matrilineal Ashanti, also in Africa, it is met with "horror" and punished by death. Clearly, the reactions to a breach vary within and between societies. "This is a fact which psychologists venturing into the cross-cultural field have often forgotten" (p. 304).

Likewise, Hopkins (1980) emphasizes as his "main point ... that it is dangerous for us to assume that other cultures share our definition of incest and our incest boundaries" (p. 306). Indeed, he was able to establish that in Roman Egypt in the first centuries after Christ, marriage between full brothers and sisters was lawful and widely practiced. Every fourteen years, between 19-20 and 257-8, the Roman governor of Egypt ordered district officials to carry out a household census of the whole population for matters of taxation. 270 of these census returns have been preserved, and based on them, Hopkins calculated that "one-third, and perhaps more, of all brothers with marriageable sisters married inside the family" (p. 304). These brother-sister marriages were fertile, and were declared openly, not only in family matters but also in business, in lawsuits, or in a petition to an official. "It seems clear that in Roman Egypt brother-sister marriages were common and were taken for granted" (p. 324). Hopkins quotes some extant wedding invitations, like: Dionysius invites you to dinner at the marriage of his own children ... tomorrow, that is the 30th at the 9th hour (p. 324). One may here also mention the Jewish philosopher in Alexandria, Philon, who in his Special Laws, 3, 23-4 wrote: "But the law-giver of the Egyptians ... gave full liberty to marry any sister of either parent or both, not only younger but also older and of the same age ... these practices our most holy Moses rejected with abhorrence." Such general statements, Hopkins observes, do not tell us how common brother-sister marriage was, but suggests that it was an established practice of considerable antiquity (p. 312).

At the beginning of the fourth century, the Emperor Constantine converted to Christianity, the Empire became Christian, and brother-sister marriages were no longer permitted in Egypt. Interestingly, though, "in early Christian writings we have no detailed attacks against brother-sister marriage in Egypt, not even in the voluminous writings of Origin and Clement of Alexandria, who both lived in Egypt and attacked other aspects of pagan morals" (p. 354).

In contrast to the Tallensi and pagan Egyptians, children raised in communal homes in Israeli kibbutzim demonstrate a spontaneous "incest-avoidance" (Shefer, 1975). Children, who from birth live together in communal children's homes, do not marry nor do they have sexual relationships with each other. This avoidance is spontaneous because the kibbutz would encourage rather than prevent marriages between the children. As to sexual relationships, the prevailing social norms do not differentiate between love-affairs in accord with the age of the participants. It is the children, who for some unknown reason, avoid their own age-group, but not the children of different age-groups. Children's homes, let us not forget, are not families. Each child has his or her parents, brothers and sisters, whom the children meet daily and are strongly attached to emotionally. Furthermore, children's homes have no fathers and mothers, it is then apparent that their spontaneous "incest-avoidance" cannot be explained along the lines of Oedipus complex. Rather, it may be understood as a point in case for the theory of Westermarck (1926). This theory stipulates that children will not be sexually attracted to persons with whom they lived together during their first years of life.

Pagan Egyptians, on the other hand, seem to contradict Westermarck's theory. How can one explain this difference between the children of kibbutzim (who in a sense regard themselves brothers and sisters) and Ashanti on the one hand, and the pagan Egyptians and Tallensi, on the other hand? While we are in want of a comprehensive theory, which would turn this cacophony of voices into a well-balanced harmony, we may state with Goody (1956) and Hopkins (1980) that what is detested and punished in one place is related to indifferently or even positively elsewhere. To put it differently, neither the wish to consummate brother-sister incestuous relationships, nor the deterrents against this wish are universal characteristics of mankind.

Conversely, the facts regarding incestuous relationships between parents and offsprings are clear and easy to summarize: there are no known human societies where sexual or marital relationships between father or mother and their children are legitimately practiced. Moreover, this precisely is the situation among animals who live in groups. As Bischof (1975) was able to summarize: "in the whole animal world with very few exceptions, no species is known in which under natural conditions inbreeding occurs to any considerable degree" (p. 42). Nature, as he puts it, systematically avoids sexual activity "inside this ready-formed game of sympathy." Viewed in this perspective, incest-avoidance in human society can hardly be celebrated as the turning point, the fountainhead of moral and culture, as some would like us to have it. Mankind is not beyond nature, but rather behaves as programmed by nature. The degree of freedom granted to man here is similar to what animals have. Incest was avoided before *homo sapiens* could have invented some reasons for its justification.

Fantasies, however, one might counter; mankind not only performs deeds but also has fantasies, and fantasies may have an even greater impact on one's fate than reality. One may then avoid incestuous behavior, and at the same time actualize in fantasy, consciously or unconsciously, what one was prevented from performing in reality. While this is a possibility, and moreover is common sense, one nevertheless has to have convincing and at least indicative evidence. At this point, and in fact in every attempt to state something concerning the mental contents of the repressed unconscious, one is confronted by the impasse created by the definition of repression and by the inevitability of interpreting rather than observing and describing. It was precisely because of this state of the art that in Viderman's (1979) understanding a psychoanalyst is more a poet than a historian. For example, after describing an interpretation of Melanie Klein, he comments that "it conforms to a model that is only one among other possible interpretations ... and it cannot have claim to any other truth than the one created for it in the analytic space by the speech which formulated it" (p. 263).

Likewise, Spence (1982) stated that an interpretation can be defined "by the claim to a belief in the proposition and nothing more" (p. 273). If the construct of Oedipus complex is a matter of belief or as Ricoeur (1974), an enthusiastic defender of Freud, put it: "Properly speaking, there are no 'facts' in psychoanalysis in the sense that experimental science understands 'facts'" (p.

186) – then one may stop here and have a second look at the theory of trauma.

Trauma revisited

Our second look at the theory of trauma should begin, necessarily with Freud himself, for his writings attest to an unceasing hesitation between his two theories of neuroses, and this hesitation is of relevance to anyone interested in these topics and especially to one who would like to reestablish the trauma theory. In his *Three Essays on the Theory of Sexuality*, Freud (1905/b) wrote: " I cannot admit that in my paper 'The aetiology of hysteria' (1896) I exaggerated the frequency or importance of that influence [seduction], though I did not then know that persons who remain normal may have had the same experiences in their childhood, and though I consequently overstated the importance of seduction in comparison with the factors of sexual constitution and development" (p. 190). Freud states here that he overrated the importance of early sexual trauma ("seduction") because at the time of writing "The aetiology of hysteria" he was unaware of the fact that such traumata may but not necessarily lead to neurotic behavior in later years. However, in "The aetiology of hysteria" one reads that "We have heard and have acknowledged that there are numerous people who have a very clear recollection of infantile sexual experiences and who nevertheless do not suffer from hysteria" (p. 272).

Here his memory failed Freud, and one may conjecture that the motive of this forgetting was not unconscious and certainly not repressed. Rather, he seems to have tried to "wash himself clean"; he was here offering a kind of apology for his earlier acceptance of Breuer's and Charcot's trauma theory. If this indeed is the correct explanation of the discrepancy between the two statements, then, one should point out that, curiously enough, even now, eight years after the letter to Fliess, in which he announced the abandonment of the "seduction" theory, Freud is still thinking in terms of more-or-less, and not in terms of either-or: "and though I consequently overrated the importance of seduction ..." To overrate the importance of early traumata is one thing, to suggest a different aetiological factor is something else.

Parallel with the *Three Essays*, Freud (1905/c) published a paper entitled "My views on the part played by sexuality in the aetiology of neuroses". He wrote there that in 1896 his "material was scanty" and by chance it included a disproportionately large number of cases in which sexual seduction "by an adult or by an older children played the chief part in the history of the patient's childhood. I thus overestimated the frequency of such events (though in other respects they were not open to doubt)" (p. 274). This then is another attempt at apology and another excuse, but here too Freud speaks of overestimating the frequency of early traumata. Moreover, he found it justified to add that "in other respects they were not open to doubt", that is, they were facts and not fantasy.

Then, in his paper on the history of the psychoanalytic movement Freud (1914) wrote: "If hysterical patients trace back their symptoms to traumas that are fictitious, then the new fact which emerges is precisely that they create such scenes in fantasy ..." (p. 17). I find this statement remarkable for two reasons. If patients are "tracing back" their difficulties to some traumas, then they are able to consciously recall those traumas. Whether those traumas were real events, as Freud suggested in 1896, or fantasized events, as he now, and his colleagues already in 1896, contended, there is no place left here for the repressed unconscious. A few lines later (Freud) concludes: "The last word on the subject of traumatic etiology was spoken later by Abraham, when he pointed out that the sexual constitution which is peculiar to children is precisely calculated to provoke sexual experiences of a particular kind - namely traumas" (p. 17). That is to say, and this is the second reason for finding Freud's statement remarkable, not fantasies but deeds done by adults, though "provoked by a readiness peculiar to children", are at the root of neuroses. Then was the trauma real or fantasized?

If, indeed, this was the last word on the traumatic aetiology of neuroses, then one may conclude that even after elaborating the theory of Oedipus complex, Freud did not, in fact, abandon the trauma theory. I do not even think that one has to invest an undue effort in demonstrating his steadfastness in this respect, for in one of his latest writings Freud (1939) wrote: "We give the name of traumas to those impressions, experienced early and later forgotten, to which we attach such great importance in the aetiology of the neuroses. *We may leave on the one side the question of whether the aetiology of the neuroses in general may be regarded as traumatic"* (p. 72, emphasis added). Sometime after writing the quoted lines, Freud nevertheless answers the question he here asked to leave open by saying: "... it is true that there are cases which are distinguished as being 'traumatic' because their effects go back unmistakably to one or more powerful impressions in these early times - ... so that one is inclined to judge that if they had not occurred the neurosis would not have come about either" (p. 73).

It is then the opinion of Freud that traumatic neuroses are a category of psychoneuroses. Historians of ideas may find here an issue worthy of consideration. Psychoanalysts, but also many experts who would deny being Freudians, did their best to widen the gap beyond any chance of contamination between "neuroses" and traumata. Traumata are responsible for some disorders of behavior, but not of "neuroses", for neuroses, as defined by Freud, are the results of an unconscious conflict between a fantasy and a resistance to this fantasy. Yet, Freud here expressly defined post-traumatic behavior disorders as neuroses. More than that, Freud was inclined to agree that "the aetiology of the neuroses in general may be regarded as traumatic".

This inclination was again made apparent when Freud (1939) stated that the traumas "relate to impressions of a sexual and aggressive nature, and no doubt also to early injuries to the ego (narcissistic mortifications) ... The predominance of the sexual factor is, of course, most striking and calls for theoretical consideration" (p. 74). While fantasies of a sexual and aggressive nature, constituting the Oedipal situation, may be suggested as spontaneous, i.e., not externally elicited fantasies, it would be difficult to imagine - if this play of words is agreeable here - a similar role for narcissistic mortifications. Surely children all over the world wish to be loved, respected, and esteemed, and are not programmed to desire being disliked and rejected. Early injuries to the self are traumata and only traumata. Clearly, Freud was suggesting here that narcissistic mortifications may cause the development of neuroses. Surprisingly enough, his suggestion becomes ambiguous precisely at the moment when he relates to the oedipal factor. Here he wrote of "impressions", a term which points to external events, and unlike spontaneous fantasies, external events may but must not occur "so that if they had not occurred the neurosis would not have come about either" (p. 73). Did Freud suggest here a trauma-theory of neuroses?

At any rate, even if one maintained that in spite of the ambiguities of formulations, Freud referred here to spontaneous Oedipal fantasies as predominant among the factors which generate neuroses, even then fantasy is at most the first, followed by trauma (sexual as well as non-sexual). From 1896 to 1939, throughout his psychoanalytic career, Freud kept faith with the trauma theory. Trauma, let us emphasize again, means that had it not occurred the neurosis would not have evolved either.

It is, then, a puzzling question why a similar suggestion of Ferenczi aroused the animosity of his colleagues, Freud included? In the last years of his life, Ferenczi seemingly returned to the early path beaten by Freud, in a series of three papers that, as Masson (1984) put it, uncannily parallel Freud's three 1896 papers, Ferenczi began to believe more and more strongly that the source of neurosis lay in sexual seductions suffered by children at the hands of those closest to them. This culminated in a paper "Confusion of tongues", his last, "that was in many respects, the twin to Freud's 'The aetiology of hysteria'" (Masson, p. 145). Among other things, one reads in this paper "that trauma, specifically sexual trauma, cannot be stressed enough as a pathogenic agent ..." (p. 288). The obvious objection, Ferenczi observed, that we are dealing with sexual fantasies of the child himself, "that is, with hysterical lies, unfortunately is weakened by the multitude of confessions of this kind, on the part of patients in analysis, to assaults on children" (p. 289).

Ferenczi planned to present this paper at the Wiesbaden Congress, but Freud wrote to Eitingon on August 29, 1932: "He must not be allowed to give the paper". Eventually, Freud agreed but demanded that Ferenczi should not publish it for a year. Ferenczi protested and Freud answered him: "I no longer believe that you will correct yourself, the way I corrected myself a generation ago." (Masson, p. 171-172). Freud's formulations quoted above could hardly justify such a reaction. Reading the sprawling character of his statements, one may question whether Freud, indeed, "corrected" himself. Ferenczi could have countered by quoting from Freud's writing, as I have done, but he did not. He too seems to have related to psychoanalysis not in accord with what follows from Freud's writings, but what follows from the sweeping re-interpretation of these writings. Also Anna Freud replied to a question of Masson (1984): "Keeping up the seduction theory would mean to abandon the Oedipus complex, and with it the whole importance of phantasy life, conscious or unconscious phantasy. In fact, I think there would have been no psycho-analysis afterwards" (p. 113).

But Freud did keep up the "seduction theory", that is the theory of trauma. In 1905/b, though he stated that the Oedipus complex, that is, genetically preprogrammed fantasies, is the nucleus of the neuroses (p. 226, n.), yet in 1939, as we have just seen, he was ready to consider "that the aetiology of the neuroses in general may be regarded as traumatic" (p. 72). This hesitation of Freud, resembling his contradictory statements concerning mental determinism and the unconscious determination of every act of behavior, was, as in those earlier instances, overlooked by his disciples and corrected/interpreted in the same one-sided, sweeping manner. Had these devoted and knowledgeable men and women allowed themselves to perceive what every unbiased reader cannot help but see, they would not have been compelled to rediscover what Freud knew and ambiguously told us.

For example, explaining the theoretical basis of Kohut's self-psychology, Ornstein and Ornstein (1980) noted that both oedipal and pre-oedipal psychopathology has long been viewed as essentially conflict-based. "This generalization had been so compelling within the mainstream of psychoanalysis as to lead us not only to maintain that *all* analyzable psycho-pathology was conflict-based, but to extend this view to the unanalyzable borderline conditions and the psychoses ... Psy-choanalytic self-psychology ... through the discovery of the self-object transferences ... provided the empirical foundation for the reconceptualization of the psychopathology based on pre-oedipal-pregenital (narcissistic) fixations, duly recogniz-ing that these were primarily deficiency-based and could no longer be fitted into the conflict-based, structural model of the neuroses" (p. 203, emphasis in original).

Freud (1939) could have agreed with these formulations, for he realized long before Kohut that the Oedipus conflict is not enough to explain human neuroses and suggested that their aetiology should include, besides this conflict, also (deficiency-based) narcissistic mortifications. Thus, Kohut followed Freud more faithfully than he - and his critics - realized. For the critics too saw in Kohut's ideas a deviation from Freud's theory of psychopathology. For example, Eagle and Wolitzky (1986) stated that "Peterfreund [1983] is proposing an etiological theory that asserts that early traumas linked to parenting rather than, say, psychosexual fixations or intra-psychic conflict, are the critical factors in generating adult pathology ... In coming to this conclusion he joins others [i.e., Kohut and Bowlby] who have diverged in a similar direction from traditional psychoan-alytic theory" (p.97). Traditional psychoanalytic theory may mean Freud's theory. Since, however, Freud had three theories, the term "traditional" turns out to be the canonized but not the true Freud.

Another unwelcome consequence of this "Freudianized" reading, as I would suggest labeling it, of Freud's writings was the virtual neglect of the existence of incestuous adults, and the impact of this fact on the theory of psychotherapy. Acknowledging what, incidentally, many psychotherapists and social workers and judges also knew from firsthand experience, would have led us to the fact that Ferenczi already knew of more than sixty years ago, in spite of Freud's presence and authority. Lately, however, for some reason which I did not succeed in identifying, these very ideas are gaining momentum again and are capturing the attention of a growing number of experts. Current research on the subject of sexual abuse indicates, Finkelhor (1979) observed, that a large number of children have "sexual encounters" with adults. "After a long period of ignoring or denying it, the problem has finally established itself on the agenda of many mental health professionals" (p. 692). Although by an ironic reversal, two psychoanalytic authors, Rascovsky and Rascovsky (1950), considered the possibility that a consummated incest diminishes the subject's chance of psychosis and allows better adjustment to the external world, for most people Freud's change of mind "rendered incest nearly invisible for decades" (p. 318).

But now, the impressive number of publications attests to an important change of direction. Finkelhor (1979) reports a prevalence rate of 1% for paternal incest alone which means, he explicates, that approximately three-quarters of a million women, 18 and over, in the United States, have had such an experience, and that another 16,000 cases are added each year from among the group of girls, age 5 to 17 (p. 88). Incest, Gelinas (1983) reports, is usually initiated when the victim is between 4 and 12 years old, with particularly high-risk periods at ages 4 and 9. It is easy to gain the compliance of a young child by misrepresenting sex as affection or caring, by threats and bribes, and by exploiting the child's loyalty, need for affection, desire to please, and especially trust of the parents. These were the very ideas of Ferenczi (1932) in his paper on the confusion of tongues, the tongue of children who hope for love and support and that of the adults who want sex. This clash between expectations easily leads to a traumatic experience with persistent negative effects.

In the consequences of consummated incest a special place is reserved, as Gelinas put it, for the knowing use and induction of dissociation by the victims. "Most commonly they would attempt to 'become part of the wall' or to 'float near the ceiling and look at what was happening' ... the tendency toward dissociation under stress continues ... often showing up in the presenting picture as 'confusion', or as dissociative behavior erroneously interpreted as psychotic" (p. 316). Former incest victims also show a profound impairment in self-esteem, for they usually feel guilty and blame themselves. "This has mystified many clinicians and prompted them to make the unfortunate judgment that the children had in fact seduced the adult and were responsible for the incest" (p. 322). Finally Goodwin and associates (1979) and Gross (1979) pointed out that hysterical seizures and absences, hysteroepilepsy, are a not uncommon sequel to the trauma of incest.

It is the "parentified" girl who is at high risk of becoming the victim of an incestuous father. In the process of parentification the child comes to function as a parent. "Because of this filial loyalty, children attempt to assist, reassure and protect their parents, often at astonishingly young ages, and under pronounced parentification a complete role reversal can occur, with the child caring for the parents" (p. 320). A very high-risk time, Gelinas warns, appears to be when the mother has gone to the hospital to give birth to another child. It follows from this role of parentification that the victim, even in later years, is "intensely loyal" to and protective of the parents. If the therapist makes an attempt to shift responsibility for the incest on the father, or attempts to elicit anger about the incest from a depressed patient without paying attention to loyalty considerations, he may increase the guilt feelings of the patient or even cause the interruption of the treatment (p. 328).

It is now important to emphasize first, that "sexual encounters" between children and adults are not, by definition, traumatic. This fact, as we have seen, was well-known to Freud and his contemporaries at the time he wrote his paper of 1896. Likewise, Bender and associates (1937, 1952) found that "atypical" sexual experiences did not harm the children they studied. Also Finkelhor (1979) and Gelinas (1983) stated that the majority of children with such experiences are not negatively affected.

Yet, there is a difference between these authors and Freud, though not between them and Breuer and Freud. Bender, Finkelhor, Gelinas, Gross, Goodwin, and their associates described sexual encounters, whether harmless or deleterious, which took place not before the fourth year of life, and usually later on. Further, these experiences were not repressed and, thus, the patients had no need to be helped out by the (re)constructions of the therapist. The present day literature, then, differs from, and actually contradicts Freud's (1896) statement that only repressed traumata are pathogenic, and that one may cure the neurotic behavior by making conscious the unconscious traumatic experiences.

A consummated incest, quite logically, indicates a certain minimal age. This is why Gelinas and all the other authors quoted have emphasized the years which are beyond the age specified by Freud, "up to almost the fifth year". Indeed, what can be the nature of a sexual experience at the age of 1 or 2? It was not by chance but rather because of the considerations indicated here that Freud emphasized the observation of primal scenes more than "the experiences on the subject's own body". Alas, the primal scene is as if deleted by the "infantile amnesia" and has to be re-established by means of the therapist's interpretations, and we are back at the impasse built into the concept of repressed unconscious. For example, concerning the assumed primal-scene experience of the Wolf-man, Freud (1918) wrote: "... scenes, like this one in my present patient's case, which dates from such an early period ... are as a rule not reproduced as recollections, but have to be derived – *constructed* – gradually and laboriously from an aggregate of indications" (p. 51, emphasis added). This, indeed, is the issue we are relating to.

Incidentally, the case-history of the Wolf-man, which was meant to prove the construct of primal scene, leaves the reader unsure as to whether he understood the message of the essay. At first, Freud (1918) interpreted the Wolf-man's dream as the equivalent of a recollection of primal scene. Soon, however, he changed his mind: "... it is true that we cannot dispense with the assumption that the child observed a copulation ... Perhaps what the child observed was not copulation between his parents but copulation between animals, which he then displaced on his parents ..." (p. 57). Then had the Wolf-man experienced the primal scene at the early age of 1 1/2 years? "I intend on this occasion to close the discussion of the reality of the primal scene with a *non-liquet*" (p. 60). The importance of the matter, however, does not allow us to leave the issue unresolved, and at the same time to behave as if his interpretations of the Wolf-man's dream decided in favor of the reality of the primal scene.

Besides, millions of children all over the world live and sleep together with their parents in one all-purpose room. They may observe their parents making love more than once; are they more prone to neurotic behaviors than our children who from birth on have a room for themselves?

One should also point out that in *The Interpretation of Dreams* Freud (1900) described the Oedipus complex as the outcome of an *interaction* between the two parties involved: "We learn from [the psychoneurotics] that a child's sexual wishes ... awaken very early, and that a girl's first affection is for her father and a boy's childish desires are for his mother ... The parents too give evidence as a rule of sexual partiality: a natural predilection sees to it that a man tends to spoil his little daughters, while his wife takes her son's part ... The child is very well aware of this partiality ..." (pp. 257-258). Due to the fascination with the spontaneity of the Oedipal wishes it was only recently that researchers and clinicians felt free to have a fresh look at the intricacies of this interaction between parents and children. Summit and Kryso (1978) pointed out that their loving care to their children may require the parents "to cope ... with erotic interest or dependency needs toward their children" (p. 240). Several mothers, these authors report, have told them of their erotic or orgasmic response to their breast feeding. Some mothers welcomed it, but there were also others who could not reconcile any erotic response with this maternal function. "She never nursed a child again" (p. 240). Mothers may touch the penis of an infant and be intrigued by the phenomenon of infantile erection. Some women report feeling very guilty about this, even years after an isolated experience (p. 240).

As children approach adolescence, parents are confronted by new challenges. The sexual development of their adolescent daughter may cause two kinds of "overreaction" by fathers. "One is withdrawal behavior, in which the father is so threatened by this potential attraction that he stops holding or touching his daughter and becomes visibly threatened by any contact with her. The other reaction is overtly seductive or self-gratifying" (p. 241). It is with the knowledge of this infor- mation, Summit and Kryso suggest, that one should listen to adolescents who come in and vaguely say, "Dad isn't the same as he used to be". It is the opinion of Searles (1965) that the aftermath of such traumatic abandonments of children by their parents is an important issue for the theory of psychotherapy: "... it seems to me clear enough, then, what this former child, now a neurotic or psychotic adult, requires from us for the successful resolution of his unresolved Oedipus complex: not such a repression of desire, ... and denial of his own worth, as he met in his relationship with his parent, but rather a maximal awareness on our part of the reciprocal feelings which we develop in response to his Oedipal strivings" (p. 303).

In the next chapter I shall come back to this point, which indeed is the very essence of this essay: a long overdue reconsideration of the theory of psychotherapy in view of a trauma-theory of psychopathology. Meanwhile I would like to emphasize first that parents do not wait until a reciprocal relationship is established. Their caring love for their children exists before their children arouse them to a reciprocal love, and we have to be aware that, as Summit and Kryso put it, there is a vague borderline between loving sensuality and abusive sexuality. Some parents are unaware of these borderlines, and some others are tensely aware of them. In any case, parents are participants as active in this drama as their children are. Both sides may have desires, as Searles formulated it, with erotic overtones. To deny this may be harmful, and for different reasons with different consequences the attempt to consummate it may also be harmful. Parent-child relations (and parent-therapist relations) are more complex than the one-dimensional construct of the Oedipus complex depicts.

Secondly, neurotic behavior may have its roots in unfulfilled conflict-arousing, sexual desires, but as Freud (1939) seems to have admitted at the end, such fantasies cannot alone carry the weight of neuroses. Life as reflected in novels, as a rule, revolves around love, real and imagined. Newspapers and history books speak of vanity and thirst for power, of wealth and poverty, of famine and violence. Life is not just this or that, but all of these. Any attempt to reduce the bewildering multitude of life phenomena to one grain of essence cannot but do injustice to the greatness of the puzzle, or shall I say: mystery that we are living and observing. Neurotic behavior attests to an impairment of the will or ability to actualize the possibilities granted within the individual confines and the joy of being involved in this unfolding. Wounds of every kind, and not only of Oedipal origin, may hamper one from accepting and performing one's role in this drama. Any experience, which by its brutal force overwhelms the individual and leaves him feeling helpless and unable to control his fate directly or by successfully appealing to benevolent external forces, is a trauma which may initiate persistent negative effects.

Trauma may but need not be unconscious; it may be of sexual origin, but it is not by definition or exclusively sexual. A killer tornado, the prolonged agony and horrors of Auschwitz, or of a war, are of sufficient force and do not need cooperation with the memory of the primal scene to make one an invalid for the rest of his life. Kubie (1954) was correct in stating that no moment of behavior can be looked upon as neurotic unless the processes that have set it in motion predetermine its automatic repetition irrespective of the situation, the utility, or the consequences of the act. However, his suggestion according to which "we are justified in calling abnormal or unhealthy or neurotic any act in the determination of which unconscious processes are dominant (whether alone or in an alliance with the preconscious) ..." (p. 185) seems unacceptable. Firstly, because statements concerning the repressed unconscious are never-provable conjectures. Secondly, because traumata, like loss of a love-object or mortifications of the self, as a rule are not repressed. Also traumatic sexual experiences are not necessarily repressed.

This understanding of the aetiology of neuroses, as the next chapters will show, may influence or rather re-shape our theory and praxis of psychotherapy.

Rapport and transference

Embarking on his venture in "Joseph and his brothers" to tell the stories of a dimly-lit past, Thomas Mann reflected thus on the perils of such an undertaking: "Very deep is the well of the past. Should we not call it bottomless ... for the unresearchable plays a kind of game with our researching ardors; it offers apparent holds and goals, behind which, when we have gained them, new reaches of the past still open out ..." (p. 3). Let us then, Thomas Mann suggests, be reconciled with some provisional origins, which, while it is understood that the depths have not actually been plumbed, may help us build a coherent story of development. I would like to suggest that Puysegur's (1774) anonymously published pamphlet on his treatment of a patient called Victor Race may be designated as the "provisional origins" of modern psychotherapy. Puysegur was a follower of Mesmer (1734-1815), a Viennese physician who was forced by his uncongenial colleagues to leave for Paris – and a firm believer in the latter's theory of animal magnetism. Mesmer suggested that a kind of ether, a subtle physical fluid, fills intergalactic space and also here on earth serves as a connecting medium between people. Diseases of different sorts are the unfortunate consequence of the unequal distribution of this fluid in the human body. His magnetic treatment was meant to restore the proper equilibrium of this fluid in the sick body. Mesmer became the hottest news in pre-revolutionary Paris, and the pressure of his would-be patients for his limited time inspired him to invent the first group-treatment. Magnetotherapy made great strides in Germany, too. "As early as 1970", Ellenberger stated, "animal magnetism had become so widespread in Germany that it was almost common practice to consult somnambulists for problems of disease and health, for practical advice, and sometimes for spiritual guidance.... Schopenhauer, who had been deeply impressed by the public performances given by the magnetizer Regazzoni in 1854, repeatedly expressed his interest in magnetism in his writings" (pp. 158-159). Indeed, in his "Parerga and Paralipomena", Schopenhauer wrote: " Although not from an economical or technical, but certainly from a philosophical point of view, Animal Magnetism is the most momentous discovery ever made, even if, for the time being, it brings more enigmas than it solves". According to a recently published book of Schiegl (1983) and its bibliography which encompasses publications from Reichenbach's (1854) "A Sensitive Person's Attitude to Od" to the present day, in Germany magnetotherapy, the transference of vital force, as Schiegl put it, did not cease to be related to and practiced as a form of alternative medicine.

In France, however, animal magnetism, by serendipidity and against Mesmer's intentions, went through a fateful metamorphosis and led to the inauguration of the era of hypnotherapy.

Inspired by philanthropic motives, Puysegur, a devoted disciple of Mesmer, treated the peasants of his estate in groups, slightly adjusting the methods of Mesmer, which were so appropriate to the salons of Paris, to the idyllic yet austere conditions prevailing in the villages. Thus it happened that he came across an atypical patient. This young peasant, who was suffering from a mild respiratory disease, when "magnetized" seemed to be asleep, yet at the same time more lucid and intelligent than he usually seemed to be. He spoke coherently and offered proper answers to questions, was very sensitive to all of Puysegur's movements and intentions, but his countenance evidenced sleep. Once returned to his usual self, the patient had no recollections of what went on during the treatment. The patient, then, behaved as if he were suffering from somnambulism. Since, however, it was provoked by the magnetic treatment, it was called artificial somnambulism. Artificial somnambulism later turned into neuro-hypnosis (Braid, 1843), and eventually into hypnosis.

Hypnosis, as we know, has no connection whatsoever with Mesmer's theory of diseases or with his method of treatment by magnetizing the patient. Apples fall near the tree, as the popular saying promises, but the apple of hypnotherapy fell to earth a great distance from magnetism, and in due time conquered the whole stage for itself, leaving no space for the magnetizers. The metaphor, "a mesmerizing effect", is the only remnant, a faint reflection of what once was a spell-binding man and a powerful movement.

First among the concepts used by the magnetizers and since then is that of "rapport". This term, Ellenberger (1970) observes, was used from the beginning by Mesmer and was handed down by generations of magnetizers and hypnotists to the beginning of the twentieth century. Mesmer himself borrowed the word from contemporary physics. For the purpose of demonstrating electricity, people formed chains by touching each other, thus transmitting to one another the electrical current originating in a machine. In such a chain people were said to be "in rapport" with each other. When magnetizing a patient, Mesmer considered himself to be a source of magnetic fluid with which the patient had to be "in rapport". It is doubtful, Ellenberger thinks, whether Mesmer realized that the rapport needed for the magnetic treatment was different from the rapport established for transmitting electricity. However, Puysegur did understand the psychological dimensions of the rapport, as did many other magnetizers, for example, Hufeland (1811), who stated that magnetic rapport is the most intimate relationship that can exist between two human beings and the only one that bears comparison with that of the fetus in the mother's womb. Also, magnetizers and especially their opponents, who quickly took advantage of such allegations, were aware of the sexual undercurrents of this rapport. This understanding and its practical consequences found its clearest expression in Janet (1896, 1897). In the initial phase of a treatment, Janet stated, the patient, freed from the pressure of some of his symptoms, feels relieved or even happy and does not think much about his/her therapist. Then comes the second phase, which Janet called that of somnambulic passion. Here the relief caused by the first encounter with the therapist and the hopes he awoke in the patient are again in danger, and the patient feels a strong need to meet the hypnotist. This need may become intense and felt as an irresistible passion. This passion, which sometimes becomes sexual, at other times, filial or maternal love, is accompanied by a need to be guided in every respect by the hypnotist. Sometimes the patient dreams of his/her therapist. Posthypnotic suggestions, Janet observed, are much less effective in this phase than at the beginning, in the period of somnambulic (hypnotic) influence.

This love and this need to be guided by the therapist, Janet suggested, should be used for the purposes of the treatment. Once the hypnotist becomes important for the patient, the therapist, who at the beginning should not object to this development, should begin "to teach" the patient to live without the presence and help of the hypnotist. Gradually widening the intervals between sessions may be instrumental in achieving this purpose. But this alone would not be enough; the patient has to be confronted by the meaning of his demands. His becoming aware of the nature of his needs will help him to overcome them.

At about the same time that Janet formulated his theory of somnambulic passion, Freud voiced his opinion in terms which differed in but one respect from that of Janet. This one respect, however, made if not all, then much of the difference between the psychotherapists of the nineteenth and twentieth centuries. "In not a few cases", Freud (1895) wrote at the period when he began to evolve his own ideas, "the patient's cooperation becomes a personal sacrifice, which must be compensated by some substitute for love. The trouble taken by the physician and his friendliness have to suffice for such a substitute" (p. 301). Here, as in Janet's work, the psychotherapist is encouraged to be kind and considerate; he has to repay – if one may say so – the patient's efforts. Of course, both Janet and Freud were interested in eventually propelling this atmosphere of attachment into a friendly detachment. Then Freud goes on to elaborate on three reasons for a possible disturbance of the cooperation necessary between the patient and therapist: 1) There is an alienation between them because of an improper behavior by the therapist toward the patient. This, however, is easy to repair. 2) The patient becomes afraid that he or she may become dependent, sexually or otherwise, on the therapist. 3) The patient transfers onto the therapist some feelings and expectations, which originally were aroused by some other person. The therapist was put into this equation by misalliance. To be a successful therapist, then, one has to properly handle the resistances originating in these three possible occurrences.

Transference by misalliance was one of the many causes of resistance which a patient may experience. In a few years' time, however, Freud would change his mind. For example, we read in his *Five Lectures on Psycho-Analysis* (1910): "In every psychoanalytic treatment of a neurotic patient the strange phenomenon that is known as 'transference' makes its appearance. The patient, that is to say, directs towards the physician a degree of affectionate feelings (mingled, often enough, with hostility) which is based on no real relation between them... Thus the part of the patient's emotional life which he can no longer recall to memory is reexperienced by him in his relation to the physician" (p. 51). In fact, Freud (1925) suggested, the scope of transference is broader than the field of psychotherapy: "It is a universal phenomenon of the human mind, it decides the success of all medical influence, and in fact dominates the whole of each person's relations to his environment. We can easily recognize it as the same dynamic factor which the hypnotists have named suggestibility, which is the agent of hypnotic rapport and whose incalculable behavior led to difficulties with the cathartic method as well" (p. 42).

The hypnotic rapport, the somnambulic passion, and transference, then, are different terms for the same phenomenon. Hypnotherapists and Freud, however, differ in the explanation they give this phenomenon and the rules they derive from it for conducting psychotherapy. Hypnotherapists agreed with their patients; they were sure that their patients' feelings toward them simply and honestly reflected what they thought and felt concerning the therapy and therapist. Freud saw in this understanding one of the pitfalls of hypnotherapy, for it located the psychotherapeutic interaction and influence in the present encounter between patient and therapist. Conversely, transference, by definition, cannot mean anything other than feelings which are out of place here, and which, in fact, are addressed to a far- away person. It was in harmony with this understanding that Freud redefined the task of the psychother- apist and likened it to that of the archeologist. Both of them have to dig up the remnants of a forgotten past.

This new understanding inevitably re-shaped the character of encounter between the patient and therapist, and in the place of a "substitute for love," suggested in 1895, now came the demand to be like an opaque mirror, present but impersonal. A demand which, together with the interpretations of uncon- scious motives and especially the Oedipal ones, turned psycho- analytic therapy into an original and unique chapter in the story of psychotherapies.

As is well-known, Freud himself was not the opaque mirror he thought one should be in a correctly conducted psycho- analysis, and not a few were puzzled by this self- contradiction. For example, the Wolf Man, his best-known and most inter- viewed patient, recalled that "Once during an analytic hour Freud told me that he had just received word that his youngest son had broken a leg skiing, but that luckily it was a mild injury with no danger of lasting damage. Freud went on to say that of his three sons the youngest was most like him in character and temperament" (Gardiner, p. 144). Further, if we are to believe the Wolf Man then, on at least one occasion, Freud spoke about another of his patients to him, then complimented him by saying that it would be good if all his pupils could grasp analysis as well as he did.

The question now is this: which Freud was correct, the practitioner or the theoretician? Let us be reminded that if

Freud the practitioner was correct than not only the concept of opaque behavior, but also its rationale: infantile neurosis and transference, became shaky. It was perhaps, in view of this possibility that in his essay on transference, Gill (1982) stated: "in practice [Freud] never gave the centrality to transference interpretation that he should have. Although his central theoretical focus is on the transference, in practice the analysis of the transference appears to have been ancillary to work with the neurosis" (p. 2). Therefore, Gill suggests, "I believe that discoverer of the transference though he was, his legacy must now be superseded" .. (p. 7).

On his understanding then, Freud, the theoretician, was correct. This decision, though, left unanswered, or rather un-tackled the question: Why did Freud not respect his own theory? Considering that in Gill's judgment "psychoanalysis as it is generally practiced is not of good quality, technically. In particular, I mean that the analysis of the transference, allegedly the heart of psychoanalytic technique, is not pursued consistently in practice" (p. 1) – we may say that both Freud and psychoanalysts, in general, believed in the concepts of infantile neurosis, transference, and opaque mirror, and yet behaved as if they did not. Why is that so?

They did so, I suggest, because Freud had two theories for explaining the rapport between patient and therapist. Al-though Freud worded it differently, namely, as a dependence, sexual or otherwise, at the beginning in the *Studies on Hysteria* (1985), he agreed with the existence of what Janet called somnambulic passion. Only he would have not agreed that that is all the rapport may comprise, for he contended that the patient may also transfer feelings on to this situation from distant times and places. This understanding did not deny the reality of the encounter and its impact on both parties involved, but alerted the therapist to be aware and look for a fantasized, not realistic component, as well. At the end of his life, Freud returned to this original view of his. In his "Analysis termi-nable and interminable", Freud (1937/a) conceded that "not every good relation between an analyst and his subject *during and after* an analysis was to be regarded as a transference; there were also friendly relations which were based on reality" (p. 222; emphasis added).

Between these two essays, for the span of 40 years, he held the view which people usually identify with Freud. Freud then had two non-concordant explanations for the meaning of rapport, and he and most of his followers behaved in accord with the first explanation, which was formulated in 1895 and again in 1937, while they believed in the second one. Belatedly, Freud harmonized between his practice and theory, alas, without solving the new problems he created thereby. For if the encounter between a therapist and a patient creates genuine attachment but also allows the transference of out-of-the-place feelings and strivings, then we need the guidance of some criteria for distinguishing between them. Clearly, no one would relate in the same way to feelings of different origins and aims like these. Yet, Freud did not even hint at the principles or characteristics which might help differentiate between the genuine and transferred attachment in rapport.

Such a situation, as we have seen with regard to the unconscious determination of every act of behavior, is inducive to Freudianized sweeping overgeneralization. Indeed, Fine (1982) did not hesitate to state that: "transference exists everywhere though this claim is hard to prove" (p. 60). Similarly, Glover (1955) instructed his readers that once the transference neurosis begins to develop "everything that takes place during the analytic session, every thought, action, gesture, every reference to external thought and action, every inhibition of thought or action, relates to the transference situation" (p. 119). Therefore, he suggests, a transference interpretation may be appropriate at any point.

We may note that Glover and Fine disregarded the correction Freud (1937/a) made in his own theory of rapport. It is, then, important to emphasize that Freud himself, in 1895 and again in 1937, differentiated between real feelings and attachments transferred on to the therapist. In-between, he held the view which we have here observed through the personal prisms of Glover and Fine. For Freud of 1937 not every good or bad relation between an analyst and his or her patient was to be regarded as a transference-phenomenon. Yet, Fein, and who knows how many others, while aware of the change in the meaning of transference in the mind of the one who conceived it, continue to equate transference with rapport. Although not self-assured in the manner of Glover, but rather by differentiating transference/a. from transference/b. Fein (1982) was perhaps the most thorough in this attempt. As befitted his wealth of experience, he proposed a whole taxonomy of transferences.

There is, he suggests, a positive (erotic) transference, a moderate positive transference, an indifferent transference, a negative transference, and a passive-dependent transference. This latter one is the most common of all transference phenomena and is characterized by requests for advice, reassurance, and an inability to leave treatment. This characterization reminds one of the "besoin de direction", the need to be directed by the hypnotherapist described by Janet (1897). The phenomenon, then, is well-known, but is it a manifestation of the infantile neurosis and, therefore, to be understood as transference?

Transference, let us not forget, prescribes that the therapist be an opaque mirror rather than a friendly stronghold which fulfills the requests for advice and assurance. Freud of 1925, who was of the opinion that transference "dominates the whole of each person's relations to his environment", should have agreed with Fine in labeling such requests as manifestations of transference. (Incidentally, according to the Wolf-Man, Freud did advise him in some important decisions.) However, Freud of 1937, who knew that "not every good relation between an analyst and his subject during and after, [and I would like to especially emphasize: after], analysis was to be regarded as a transference", may have disagreed with Fine. For, in contradistinction to Glover, Fine, and many authors not quoted here, the later Freud agreed that transference as a manifestation, a re-enactment, of the infantile neurosis was a special phenomenon among the many phenomena of rapport. "We accept more and more", Racker (1968) stated, "that in the unconscious the analyst is the centre of all the patient's love and hate, anxiety and defence, and thus we conclude that all the patient's difficulties, all his sufferings and anxieties during the treatment, have their base in the transference" (p. 57). One has then to stress that this and similar statements are not congruent with the intentions of (the later) Freud.

Although, as already indicated, Freud did not elaborate on the full consequences of his old-new approach, it is rather apparent that it implies a freedom to feel and behave accordingly for the therapist too. Earlier, when the whole of a patient's relations to the therapist were interpreted as reflections of an enactment of the infantile neurosis, it was quite logical to conclude that everything the therapist would say and do would be "distorted" by this transference, and since a reconstruction of the infantile neurosis was the heart of the therapeutic endeavour, therapists were obliged to be non-involved or, as Ferenci (1932) somewhat bitterly put it, to be reserved and cold. In a critical retrospect, Basch (1983) sensitively described the dangers an emotionally responsive therapist was presumed to bring about:

"I clearly remember how I and my fellow residents sat frightened and passive with our patients. We were passive because we felt we had to limit ourselves to encouraging patients to say what they were thinking ... We were frightened because we firmly believed that everything we might say or do had an immediate and significant sexual or aggressive implication for the patient. We really thought that to say or do anything other than interpret the genesis of the patient's problems would destroy our therapeutic, neutral stance, establishing an equivalence in the patient's unconscious between us and those earlier seductive and/or punitive figures who were responsible, we believed, for his or her problems" (p. 226).

But now, after Freud (1937) redefined his position, psychoanalysts in general and not only Kohutians, for whom Basch spoke, may reconsider whether counter-transference, as it is called, indeed threatens or enhances the prospects of a therapy. Actually, and very interestingly, some psychoanalytic writers did voice opinions which favored a relatedness to patients rather different from that depicted by Basch, even though their suggestions did not follow, but in fact, contradicted their own theoretical stance. For example, Racker (1969) agreed that "as Freud (1917) advised" analysts should actively centre their interpretations on the transference problems and, therefore, the patient's conflicts with other, extra-transference, persons should be interpreted "as conflicts between parts of his own personality or else as conflicts with the analyst. But conflicts between parts of one's personality are always related to the transference too, since one of one's own parts is always simultaneously projected (manifestly or latently) onto the analyst" (p. 57). This sounds like an echo of Freud of 1925 and yet, in contradiction to what follows from this sweeping definition of the therapeutic encounter, it was the opinion of Racker (1969) that "the concept of the 'surgeon's attitude' [prescribed by Freud] lends itself to misunderstanding and may induce a *repression of the countertransference*", and that "Freud's (1912) counsel that the analyst should be a 'mirror' has, I believe, at times also been carried to an extreme" (p. 30- 31, emphasis added).

Basch's description of his supervisor's approach may have been defined by Racker as paradigmatic of what he labelled as the "mirror"- approach carried to an extreme. In fact, however, Basch's frightened behavior was correct and commendable unless one agrees that Freud of 1925 was wrong in identifying rapport with transference, and Freud of 1937 was correct in differentiating between them. However, Racker, and many other psychotherapists as well, while promulgating the expansionist version of transference, which justifies the approach criticized by Basch, would like to free themselves from the consequences of this theory, not unlike Freud before 1937. Thus, in an attempt characteristic of one who would like to reconcile between these two incompatible views, Racker confesses: "Freud (1912/b) admonishes the analyst to withhold compassion and to adopt towards his patient an attitude similar to that of a surgeon ... many analysts now would use the perception of a feeling like the one of compassion, which is aroused by the patient to understand the underlying transference process" (p. 26). In truth, however, the version of the concept of transference subscribed to by Racker does not ask for such help but rather, strictly forbids it. The excuse made by suggesting that the transgression, namely, compassion, was made for the benefit of what should forbid such feelings, may illustrate the perplexity of therapists who accept the view of Glover or Fine on transference.

In contrast to Racker's apology, I would like to emphasize that psychotherapists should not apologize for feeling compassion. If one agrees that patients not only project but also perceive and relate realistically to their therapists, one has also to agree that therapists too should feel and behave as they are used to in other contexts. Moreover, I would like to suggest not only cautiously manoeuvering between "mirror"-type distance as the main road and compassion as a side-walk, but agreeing that psychotherapy is mainly a relationship between a therapist and a patient, and behaving accordingly.

Clearly, such a decision is contingent on a discussion of the construct of infantile neurosis, and in fact, in a way, we have already discussed this construct in the previous chapters and foreshadowed the above conclusion. In his paper, entitled "A child is being beaten", Freud (1919) stated that "infantile sexuality, which is held under repression, acts as the chief motive force in the formation of symptoms: and the essential part of its content, the Oedipus complex, is the nuclear complex of neuroses" (p. 204). Twenty years later Freud (1939) admitted that repressed infantile sexuality is but one of many pathogenic experiences. Although Freud did not elaborate on the practical consequences of this latter statement it seems quite clear that the rule of "opaque mirror", which was meant to fit the earlier theory according to which repressed infantile sexuality is "the chief motive force" in the formation of neurotic symptoms, (and as Tolpin [1970] succinctly put it: "The infantile neurosis in its strict sense is that underlying motive force" [p. 274]), it seems clear then that early mortifications of the ego do not have such repressed motive forces, nor do they demand, but in fact, forbid that the therapist be distant and opaque.

Indeed in her paper, Tolpin complains of the ambiguity surrounding the concept of infantile neurosis which, may I add, is the basis of the concept of transference and the rationale of "opaque behavior." Many psychoanalysts, she suggests, "have incorrectly designated pathological manifestations during all phases of childhood as infantile neuroses, overlooking the fact that for Freud the term was virtually synonymous with the ubiquitous oedipal conflict" (p. 276). The concept of infantile neurosis should be applied only to those adult neuroses the core-conflict of which is oedipal and which, therefore, may be defined as transference neuroses. "Narcissistic personality disorders (described by Kohut) the various character disorders associated with ... significant ego modifications; borderline disorders; psychoses, etc." (p. 277), are not transference neuroses, that is to say, their motive force is not a repressed Oedipal wish.

Tolpin's suggestion, though, is contradicted by her usage of the so well-known phrase: the ubiquitous Oedipus complex. One may then say that Tolpin's suggestion to deny the Oedipus complex its earlier position as the nucleus of neuroses, ("Psychoanalysis", she wrote, "... has progressed to further insight about symptom formation based on other models" [p. 274, n]), and her slip, which made transparent the second Freudian theory of neuroses (the first having been formulated in cooperation with Breuer in 1893 and 1895, and the third in 1939), is illustrative of the ambiguity created by Freud and not by his devoted disciples. It was Freud (1939) who spoke of mortifications of the ego as neurotogenic experiences and at the same time did not clarify whether the theory of psychotherapy could remain as it was when the theory of psychopathology was organized around the Oedipus Complex as the chief unconscious motive force in the formation of neuroses. Now that Freud himself, and as Tolpin put it, based on other models, psychoanalysis, too, have realized that life is not reducible to one essential element, one feels the time is ripe to reconsider the rules of psychotherapy conceived at a time when "the ubiquitous nuclear oedipal conflict" was thought to be the Alpha and the Omega of neuroses.

From transference to real meeting

What are transferences? "They are new editions or facsimiles of the impulses and phantasies which are aroused and made conscious during the progress of the analysis ... they replace an earlier person by the person of the physician" (Freud, 1905, p.116). Repressed fantasies of course do not become, in fact, can not become conscious, only their derivatives appear in consciousness, this is why the repressed Oedipal fantasies are transferred on to the therapist. In fact, as Freud (1910) put it, "It is only this re-experiencing in the 'transference' that convinces [the patient] of the existence and of the power of these unconscious sexual impulses" (p. 51).

Unlike the unconscious Oedipal wish, the fantasies and impulses regarding the therapist, as one may understand, are conscious. Or are they? Interestingly, or rather surprisingly, since the concept of transference is the very base of the psychoanalytic therapy, there is more than one answer available. In his encyclopedia of transference, Langs (1976) complains of the misunderstanding of "most analysts who have written about the transference neurosis", for they have assumed that "this syndrome is expressed through manifest preoccupation with and fantasies about the analyst, or their readily identified displacements. Such a viewpoint however, appears to be unduly restrictive and theoretically untenable ... one may validly consider *every communication from the patient* as having a bearing on some aspect of the unconscious transference constellations" (p. 157, emphasis added).

Everything here then is unconscious and may appear in a disguised form only. The impulses regarding the therapist become known as such because the patient's behavior was accordingly interpreted, and this interpreted fantasy now is further interpreted as an impulse belonging to some one else and transferred on to the therapist. Langs defends his understanding of the concept of transference by elaborating on Greenacre's (1955) statement that a pervasive preoccupation with the analyst is generally characteristic of more severely disturbed patients and is atypical of neurotics: "This observation suggests", Langs commented, "that the latter patient has the ego capacity to express his transference neurosis in relatively defended and disguised forms" (p. 157). In a similar manner, Gill (1979) wrote that "Many analysts believe that transference manifestations are infrequent and sporadic at the beginning of an analysis and that the patient's associations have transference meaning from the beginning and throughout. That is my opinion ..." (p. 273).

Freud seems to have been one of the authors criticized by Langs for, as Langs admits, a review of his case-histories indicates that Freud "confined his concept of transference manifestations primarily to *direct allusions* to himself and members of his family, and that he very occasionally involved the concept in cases of obvious displacements from the analyst ..." (p. 27, emphasis added).

This is a second disagreement between Freud and some psychoanalytic writers concerning transference. (The first one is over the question whether the patient - therapist relationship also contains real or only fantasized interactions.) Given the fact of opposing views, and the necessity to choose one of them, one would be interested to know the possible reason why the transference - love should be repressed and only indirectly, in a distorted and displaced manner, expressed. It is explained why the original Oedipal love cannot be felt as such now, although in its time it was experienced directly. But why should the re-enactment of this love, disconnected from its original objects, that is to say, already disguised, be further disguised and expressed in secret codes, only understandable to the initiated ones? Neither Gill, nor Langs, nor Glover, authors whom I have quoted as representatives of this view, explained it.

The third disagreement between Freud and some psychoanalytic authors relates to the question of whether or not transference phenomena are bound to appear in every psychotherapy.

Freud (1910) stated unhesitatingly: "In every psycho-analytic treatment of a neurotic patient the strange phenomenon that is known as 'transference' makes its appearance" (p. 57). Calef (1951) however suggests that there are three categories of patients with whom the transference neurosis fails to appear: those who do not respond to psychoanalytic work, those who potentially develop the neurosis but resist it, and those who do well in treatment despite the absence of a transference neurosis.

Then there are difficulties created by Freud's own contradictory statements. Is the interpretation of transference as "unreal" emotions preparatory to the analysis of the neurosis, or rather is the interpretation of the transference as a new edition of the infantile neurosis equivalent to the analysis of the neuroses? In his paper, "On beginning the treatment", Freud (1913) defined transference as a disturbance which has to be overcome in order to get on with work on the analysis of the neurosis (p. 144). However, in his *Introductory Lectures*, Freud (1916) stated that the mastery of the transference neurosis coincides with getting rid of the illness (p. 144). Gill (1979) thinks that Freud's "principal emphasis" was on equivalence. It would be equally possible to argue, I think, that, to the contrary, Freud's principal emphasis was on transference as preparatory to the analysis of the neurosis. In both cases, the term "principal emphasis" is a gesture of good-will and not a real solution. Freud suggested contradictory approaches where one would expect to hear coherent and unequivocal principles and rules.

Further, one does not know whether the transference is a resistance, or is it precisely what is rejected, resisted? In his paper on "The dynamics of transference" Freud (1912) defines the repetition of the infantile neurosis in the transference as a resistance in service of the repression, which prevents the remembering of the original Oedipal conflict. This repression, of course, is a function of the ego. But in *Beyond the Pleasure Principle*, Freud (1920) considers repetition as an id-tendency while the resistance of the ego is directed against repetition.

Earlier, I have quoted Gill; now I shall quote Racker (1968) who suggests that Freud "really" stressed the first of these views: "[Freud] advocates (even in papers subsequent to [1920]...) limiting repetition in the transference and encouraging remembering" (p. 75). Yet, Racker admitted that the matter is not as simple as that: "[Freud stated], however, that remembering the past or recovering it in dreams causes less pain than reliving it as a new experience. This admission, in my opinion, casts doubt on his previous statement that the analysand prefers repeating to remembering" (p. 75). Thus one does not know whether re-living of the repressed original Oedipal conflict, which is the explanation for the genesis of the transference, is motivated by an Ego-need for avoiding painful remembering, or by a blind Id-tendency to repeat, and resisted by the Ego, which would prefer remembering over acting out.

Finally, it is not clear whether transference, if it does emerge - for Freud stated that transference phenomena develop in every analytic treatment whereas some authors contend that this is not the case - emerges spontaneously or, to the contrary, is induced by the rules of the psychoanalytic therapy. In his autobiographical sketch, Freud (1925) wrote: "In every analytic treatment, the patient develops, without any activity on the part of the analyst, an intense affective relation to him ... It must not be assumed that analysis produces the transference ... it only unmasks it" (p. 75). Yet, in this same study Freud also wrote that transference is equivalent to the force called suggestion. Suggestion describes an act of imposition, of implantation of a foreign idea into the mind of the patient. Further, in his "History of the psychoanalytic movement", Freud (1914) wrote that the analyst must recognize that the patient's falling in love is induced by the analytic situation. Is, then, transference induced or does it develop spontaneously, influenced by the rules of the treatment?

Likewise, Glover (1931) wrote: "... and of course the induction or development of a transference neurosis during analysis is regarded as an integral part of the process." (p. 411) Macalpine (1950) comments on this statement of Glover as follows: "One is entitled, from the context, to assume that Glover commits himself to the view that some outside factors are operative which induce the transference neurosis. But it is hardly a coincidence that it is no more than a hint. The impression gained from the literature on the whole is that the spontaneity of transference is considered established and generally accepted; in fact, this opinion seems jealously guarded" (p. 518). While I know that not a few people would relate with suspicion to everything connected with Wilhelm Reich, nevertheless, I would like to mention that in his once highly respected *Character Analysis*, Reich (1933) stated that: "Clinical experience shows that only the fewest patients are capable of spontaneously establishing such a positive transference" (p. 20). With some notable exceptions, then, the literature indeed jealously guards the thesis of the spontaneously developing transference.

One mostly finds the explanation that the security, the absence of criticism, the allaying of fears and anxieties creates an atmosphere which is conducive to regression and, in consequence, to the re-enactment of the repressed Oedipal conflict. In point of fact, Macalpine contends, the security of analysis as an explanation of the regression is paradoxical. As in life, security makes for stability, whereas stress, frustration, and insecurity initiate regression. "The self-contradictory statement, that the security of analysis induces the analysand to regress is carried uncritically from one psychoanalytic publication to another" (p. 523).

In concluding this discussion, I have to point out that the most important issue is that of definition. Quite clearly, all the other questions, namely, whether transference emerges every time or only from time to time, whether it is intrapsychically preprogrammed or initiated by an interaction with the therapist, and also whether it impersonates the resistance or, in fact, is itself the phenomenon to be resisted by the Ego – all these questions are but lifeless shadows until we know what transference is. But, we don't. Freud did not provide any criteria for differentiating between "real" and "transferred" affections. "It is one of the misfortunes of the psychoanalytic literature", Langs (1976) exclaimed, and I cannot but agree with him, "that [Freud] apparently considered transference manifestations to be self-evident, and that he did not carefully establish criteria for their detection" (p. 27). And as to the authors who, unlike Freud, maintain that every thought and every inhibition of thoughts, every gesture and every reference to external reality have an unconscious transference-meaning, one should point out that this meaning exists only due to the interpretations of the therapists, and there is no irony involved if I shall now sincerely ask the question, and hope for a similar consideration: in whose mind does this special love-relationship exist? For such interpretations once more lead us back to the first issue dealt with in this essay: the nature of the repressed Unconscious, as defined by Freud, and its fateful consequences on his theory of behavior, which is mainly a psychology of the repressed Unconscious. Any statement concerning the repressed Unconscious, transference-love included, belongs to the realm of possibility; it is neither provable nor disprovable.

Surprising as it may sound, the most spoken-of concept of psychoanalytic therapy is perhaps the least understood one and the most open to subjective interpretations. Since the concept of counter-transference is but a mirror-image of transference, one may be prepared to encounter the same difficulties in the literature dealing with counter-transference. Indeed, the paper by Little (1951) on countertransference begins with the statement that different people use the term counter-transference to mean different things. "The term is used to mean any or all of the following: a) the analyst's unconscious attitude, i.e., the analyst regards the patient as he regarded his own parents; b) repressed elements ... [of] the analyst himself ... belonging to his parents or to objects of his childhood ...; c) some specific attitudes ... with which the analyst meets the patient's awareness; d) the whole of the analyst's attitudes and behavior towards his patient" (p. 32-33).

What, then, is countertransference? To put Little's technical formulations into simple words: if the therapist is emotionally aroused by the patient, and this feelings-complex is a disguised re-enactment of the therapist's repressed Oedipal wishes, one speaks of counter-transference. But also any demonstration of relatedness to the patient is countertransference. The reader now may feel that what was clear and understandable is becoming vague and difficult to follow. The specific, displaced Oedipal fantasies of the therapist, indeed, may perturb the treatment, but what about the other "attitudes and behavior"? Important as it may be, there are still areas of human interests and emotional involvements, which are independent of the Oedipus complex. Why should these latter feelings be condemned as counter-transference and avoided as a source of danger?

I am not the first one to raise this question. I already had an opportunity to point out that half a century ago, in his "Analysis terminable and interminable", Freud (1937/a) warned his readers that "not every good relation between an analyst and his subject during and after an analysis was to be regarded as a transference; there were also friendly relations which were based on reality" (p. 222). But, as we have seen, influential psychoanalytic authors disregarded this old-new approach of Freud. Regarding counter-transference, a quotation from Langs (1976) may represent this conservative mood. Commenting on a suggestion by some authors to acknowledge toward the end of an analysis a greater equality between the therapist and the patient and more openly confirm the realities of relationship between the two, Langs wrote: "My own investigations of this aspect of the analytic relationship suggest that modifications in neutrality by the analyst and shifts in the boundaries of the therapeutic relationship that are initiated by him will have far- reaching detrimental effects ..." (p. 156). From the beginning to the very end, the therapist should be

distant, neutral, and should not allow himself feelings of relatedness.

But is it possible to honestly carry through such advice?
Psychotherapists choose their profession because they are interested in people; does such advice suit their personality
make-up? Racker (1969) put this question in a rather dramatic
manner: "... the concept of the 'surgeon's' attitude lends itself
to misunderstandings and may induce a repression of the
countertransference ..." (p. 30). Because of the lack of an agreed-
upon definition for counter-transference one does not know for
sure what kind of relatedness Racker was suggesting here. At
any rate, as against the restrictiveness advocated by Langs,
Racker seems to have emphasized the character of an encounter, an interaction, between two real people and not between two actors. Lapkin and Lury (1985), who are close in
their approach to Racker, formulated it in straightforward
terms: "Some of my training had made me approach treatment
maintaining a distance form my own responsiveness to
patient's expectations. I had believed that I had to remain
neutral, albeit warm, interested, and reactive in order to analyze the 'irrational' ... It was only gradually that I learned that
this 'anti-analytic' attitude or role served as a growth-produc-
ing force similar to what normally takes place in a parent-child
relationship, a relationship in which the child's demands evoke
an appropriate response in the parent ... [and] lead to individuation, separation, and maturity, instead of leading to
what many people fear – lifelong dependency and perpetual
submission of the offspring to the patient" (p. 352).

To put it differently, a child needs and loves his parents not
only for fulfilling his presumed Oedipal wishes, and similarly,
a patient needs his or her therapist not only as an Oedipal
object. The therapist's caring interest will not necessarily be
misperceived as an Oedipal seductiveness. More often than not
it will serve as a growth-inducing factor which encourages the
patient to face life and succeed in it. Little (1951), too, thinks
that greater harm is done by the therapist's distant neutrality

than by a demonstration of his or her real emotions: "To my mind it is the question of a paranoid or phobic attitude towards the analyst's own feelings which constitutes the greatest danger and difficulty in counter-transference. The very real fear of being flooded with feeling of any kind, rage, anxiety, love, etc., in relation to one's patient and of being passive to it and at its mercy, leads to an unconscious avoidance or denial" (p. 38).

This then is an almost complete reversal. It is not the experience of the (not defined) counter-transference, the very reason for inventing the institution of training-analysis, and the behavior toward the patient in accord with it, that endangers therapy, but rather the "phobic" avoidance of it or, as Racker (1969) put it, the repression of countertransference. Searles (1965) went one, particularly significant step further beyond the authors quoted above, and with this step the turnabout from the position represented here by Gill and Langs became complete. Like Lapkin and Lury (1985), Searles also emphasizes his departure from the traditional psychoanalytic approach to therapy by saying: "My training had been predominantly such as to make me hold rather suspect any strong feelings on the part of the analyst towards his patient" (p. 285). Then, as an indication of his approach, he quotes from a paper given by Tower (1956) as follows: "It is my belief that there are inevitably, naturally, and often desirably, many countransference developments in every analysis ... I assume that erotic responses to some extent trouble nearly every analyst ... various forms of erotic fantasy and erotic countertransference phenomena of a fantasy and of an affective character are in my experience ubiquitous and presumably normal".

I called this view a complete reversal, for by now erotic fantasies towards patients are legalized, and their acknowledgement rather than their excommunication is advised. The fantasies of the patient, if he or she has any, are interpreted as "unreal" feelings – complexes transferred from the original Oedipal figures on to the therapist. Their explanation and interpretation to the patient is the essence of the psychoanalytic psychotherapy. But now, if the therapist's erotic fantasies are not interpreted as a reflection of his or her Oedipus complex, but rather are accepted as a normal reaction, why should we, how can we, deny the same right from the patient? If a patient expressed the same feeling which these authors encourage therapists to feel, why should we relate to it as commendable for the latter but as "unreal" and a sign of neurosis in the former? And if the behavior of both parties is judged by the same criteria, what will remain of the theory of psychoanalytic therapy after its praxis has been so deeply changed? I am well aware that none of the authors I have quoted intended to arrive at such a conclusion; they might even have rejected it had I an opportunity to discuss with them. Yet, their understanding of the patient-therapist relationship leads one to this conclusion.

Courageous as they have been in facing up to their daily reality, they kept untouched the philosophy which guided them into the direction they dissatisfiedly left behind. Unlike these authors, whose views I appreciate and feel encouraged by in summarizing the essence of our discussion thus far, I should state that the repressed Oedipal conflict is not the nucleus of the psychoneuroses, and that, therefore, neurotic patients do not inevitably experience transference love, the interpretation of the "disguised transference" phenomena cannot be the essence of psychotherapy, and psychotherapy is an encounter between two real people and not between a patient and an "opaque" but also interpreting mirror. Rather, as Guntrip (1974) provocatively put it: "Neither love nor insight alone cures ... What is therapeutic, when it is achieved, is the 'moment of real meeting' of two persons as a transforming experience for one of them, which as Laing (1965) said, is 'Not what happened before [i.e., transference] but what has never happened before' [i.e., an experience of relationship]" (p. 353).

Here as I promised in Chapter Five, I would like to come back to the opinion expressed by Searles (1965). "In normal personality development", he wrote, "the parent reciprocates the child's Oedipal love with greater intensity than we have recognized heretofore" (p. 285). Let us note that Searles ascribed to parents the same impulses and feelings the Oedipus complex only ascribes to children. That is to say, Searles saw a real interaction between parents and children, whereas the construct of the Oedipus complex suggests a one-directional and unreal, fantasized relatedness. This understanding of the child-parent relationship led Searles, in the context of the concept of transference, to the inevitable conclusion that patient-therapist relationships also are real relationships. The developmental Oedipal phase, Searles suggests, may lead to ego impediment primarily if the beloved parent felt threatened by his or her own feelings, and "had to repress his or her reciprocal desire for the child, chiefly through the mechanism of unconscious denial of the child's importance to the parent" (p. 302). Therefore, Searles concluded, what this former child, now a neurotic or psychotic adult, requires from us is not a similar repression of desire, "and denial of his own worth as he met in his relationship with his parent, but rather a maximal awareness on our part of the reciprocal feelings which we develop in response to his Oedipal striving" (p. 303). Not concentrating their arguments on the Oedipal construct, in fact, disregarding it, nevertheless Laing and Guntrip arrived at a similar conclusion: the essence of psychotherapy is a mutual relatedness. One should not phobically avoid being, in a gentle manner, involved in the patient's fate, but rather be aware of this relatedness and indicate it.

Some guidelines for real meeting

In the above chapters, we were pursuing two lines of reasoning which, while independent from each other, may meet in one common conclusion. The construct of unconscious transference, if one is allowed to animate abstract concepts, may boast of having generated an impressive array of contradictory statements and definitions, a sure sign of its importance, but alas, also an indication that its usefulness is questionable. What is transference? Tolpin (1970) thinks that many authors and clinicians as well mistakenly expand its use for characterizing phenomena which Freud would have defined differently. For Freud, transference meant the unconscious enactment of the infantile neurosis. It is this kind of disturbance alone which warrants speaking of transference in Freud's sense. Does transference manifest itself directly or in a disguised manner? Does it appear in every psychotherapy of neuroses or only sometimes? Is it spontaneous or does one have to induce it? Is it resistance or the pressure to be resisted? Is its handling synonymous with or rather a preliminary to treatment? The many and contradictory answers given to these questions, some by Freud and some by others, cannot fail to raise doubts as to whether this construct can serve as a reliable compass for professionals in their daily work.

One may, however, suggest that many, if not all of these uncertainties may be prevented by deciding to follow Freud. After all, he conceived this construct and he knew his ideas better than his interpreters. At this point, however, we switched to the other avenue which might be labeled: Freud *versus* Freud, or the two languages of Freud. Freud, the theoretician, as pointed out by Gill (1982), seems not to have influenced the behavior of Freud the practitioner. For example, Freud (1912/b), the theoretician, advised would-be psychoanalysts in such unequivocal terms: "I cannot recommend my colleagues emphatically enough to take as a model in psychoanalytic treatment the surgeon who puts aside his feelings, including that of human sympathy. The justification of this coldness in feeling in the analyst is that it is the condition which brings the greatest advantage to both persons involved" (p.115). Earlier I quoted the Wolfman. The Freud he met in their sessions was anything but a follower of his own rules. "Freud conducted therapy", Malcolm (1982) observed, "... *as if it were an ordinary human interaction* in which the analyst could shout at the patient, praise him, argue with him, accept flowers from him on his birthday, lend him money, and even gossip with him about other patients" (p. 37, emphasis added).

Having then decided to follow Freud, one has again to decide which one of the two to prefer. Psychoanalysts, rather predictably, have decided in favor of the (I shall use here this term for the last time) Freudianized Freud. Otherwise, Racker (1969) and Lapkin and Lury (1985) would have been aware that they were following in the footsteps of the "other" Freud and would have referred to him as their model. Instead of apologizing for their "anti-analytic" behavior and feeling guilty for the compassion they revealed toward their patients, they might have apologized for not following Freud to the extent of lending money or saying to their patients what Freud, then 77, said to Hilda Doolittle, 47: "The trouble is, I am an old man – you do not think it worth your while to love me" (Malcolm, 1982, p. 166). While uttering this sentence, Freud pounded on the back of the couch on which she was reclining.

Although Freud all along had two faces, one of them was swept away by none other than his devout followers. In contrast, I would like to suggest we first realize and acknowledge that Freud held contradictory views, one of them confessed and the other professed, on how psychotherapy should be practiced, and second, decide in favor of Freud the practitioner who, as Malcolm put it, behaved in therapy sessions as if it were an ordinary human interaction, as if it were a meeting, a real meeting, between real people. Freud's (1939) third theory of psychopathology, being a theory of trauma and the ambiguities surrounding the construct of transference, converges in a common theoretical substrate, the first by its positive contribution regarding trauma, and the latter by means of a negative proof regarding transference for explaining and justifying Freud the practitioner as opposed to, one has to emphasize, Freud the theoretician. Common sense also supports such a decision since Freud's behavior was only correct if the conception of the infantile neurosis as the nucleus of adult neuroses, and its consequence, the unconscious transfer of this neurosis onto the therapist, were not correct. If, however, these constructs were correct, then Freud's behavior was incomprehensible to an extent that one cannot relate to it by shoulder-shrugging. Rather here, as in similar cases, one may trust that his deeds revealed Freud better than his words.

The psychotherapist then, meets his/her patients as in an "ordinary human interaction". I would like to substitute for this otherwise precise description of Malcolm's, the words, the term, "real meeting". There is no difference between meeting and real meeting except that in this context the adjective "real" succinctly localizes the controversy between the unreality of the patient-therapist interaction supposed by Freud's theory and its reality demonstrated by his behavior. The adjective "real" has the further advantage of indicating that the therapist does not learn "technique" which may be implemented deftly but impersonally like a surgeon. The psychotherapist's first maxim is to be there; to meet patients as he/she meets people in his close environment.

It may sound as a greeting from a distant planet to quote here a statement by Rogers (1962) relevant to this issue, but from the moment we relate to Freud the therapist, it is impossible to overlook some commonalities between him and Rogers. "I believe", Rogers (1962) wrote, "it is the realness of the therapist in the relationship which is the most important element. Thus, our sharply different therapists achieve good results in quite different ways. For one, an impatient, no-nonsense, let's-put-the-cards-on-the-table approach is most effective, because in such an approach he is most openly being himself. For another, it may be a much more gentle and more obviously warm approach, because this is the way this therapist is. Our experience has deeply reinforced and extended my own view that the person who is able openly to be himself at that moment, as he is at the deepest levels he is able to be, is the effective therapist" (pp. 10-11). A genuine real meeting is the antithesis of the "antiseptic" techniques.

Differently worded, though, the concept of real meeting was for long espoused by the representatives of interpersonal psychoanalysis, Sullivan and Fromm. Both Sullivan and Fromm disagreed with the psychoanalytic view of the therapist as a blank screen on which the patient projected various transference manifestations. In reaction to this model, Sullivan (1940, 1953) developed the idea of the therapist as participant observer. For Sullivan, the therapist's being, his/her thoughts, feelings, actions and fantasies are as much a part of the psychotherapeutic process as those of the patient. Fromm (1960) felt that Sullivan was not explicit enough in defining his view, and therefore he recommended redefining it by saying that psychotherapists are not participant observers but rather observant participants. A therapist participates in the process unfolding rather than observing it from a safe distance "In this center to center relatedness lies one of the essential conditions for psychoanalytic understanding and care" (Fromm 1960, p. 112).

I wonder whether such a relationship between therapists and patients is indeed the essence of psychoanalytic therapy. Ferenczi (1930) seems to have been closer to the facts when he rhetorically asked: "Was it really worth while to make that enormous detour of analysis of associations and resistances, to thread the maze of the elements of ego-psychology and even to traverse the whole metapsychology in order finally to arrive at the good old 'friendly attitude' to the patient and the method of catharsis, long believed to have been discarded?" (p. 438). As is known, his answer was that this reconsideration of the theory was inevitable. Thus, while agreeing with Fromm in the essentials, I should also point out that the theory of observant participant and the theory of psychoanalysis, the ingredients of which are infantile neurosis, transference, opaque mirror and interpretation, are not the same or similar theories. It would be more correct to define them as opposing approaches.

Interpersonal psychoanalysis, Newirth (1982) states, "stresses the analyst's being affected and influenced by the patient and the analyst's expression of these reactions. This posture places the emphasis on the expression of one's understanding of how one is affected as opposed to explanation of unconscious intent [of the patient]" (p. 90). Such an unguarded self-expression by the therapist, then, is one of the meanings of "to be there". As a result, the therapist "is in a more visible and vulnerable position and can then be exposed to more criticism, hostile attacks, and loss of self-esteem" (Newirth, 1982, p. 91).

This, indeed, is one of the defining features of a real meeting. "In the old days", as Little (1951) put it, "analysts, like parents, said what they liked, as by right and patients had to take it. Now ... we ... allow them too to refuse to accept them" (p. 39). In the old days, if the patients disagreed with an interpretation offered by the therapist, this disagreement was defined as resistance and, paradoxically, the interpretation was confirmed rather than made questionable by it. But, was this practice confined to the old days, that is, to the first half of this century? I am afraid Little here proved overoptimistic. Twenty years later Langs (1972) singled out Greenson (1967) as the first analyst who would agree to extend to patients the right to agree or disagree with their therapist. Unlike Greenson, Langs observed, other "analysts [tend] to consider virtually all communications from the patient as expressions of transference fantasies that have little relationship to the reality of the analytic situation" (p. 381).

One should point out that the "other analysts" mentioned by Langs did not behave arbitrarily, but in accord with Freud's "official" theory which denied the possibility that patient and therapist may "really" meet. In parentheses, I may mention that already Ferenczi (1930) had "urged analysts to be more humble-minded in their attitude to their patients and to admit the mistakes they made" (p. 432). From Ferenczi through Little to Greenson, some experts were dissatisfied with the prevailing view that patients are puppets pulled and pushed by their repressed unconscious with no autonomy and judgment at their discretion, and that their objections to what they were taught about themselves cannot be but resistance to the truth. And yet, the mainstream analysts were justified in their behavior because that was what their ideology led them to expect. Only if we discard the theory of fantasy as the pathogenic factor and its transference as the main issue in psychotherapy and agree with the theory of trauma and real meeting, can we justify and sustain the rights of patients in psychotherapy.

These rights, in the felicitous formulation of Newirth (1982), imply that "the patient is in a position to comment on the therapist's responses just as the therapist comments on the patient's responses. Within this structure the analytic process potentially goes back and forth with both participants collaborating in the analysis of the relationship and of each other's responses and personality characteristics. This is in contrast to a structure in which the analyst interprets the patient's responses only, and the patient knows that it is he or she who is there to be analyzed and helped" (p. 85). Since we prefer democratic over authoritarian systems in politics as well as in family life, it is only natural that we should also be led by these same principles in psychotherapy.

To summarize what was said thus far, the theory of real meeting is distinguished by the change in the image of the therapist both in his own and the patient's eyes, and by the realization that the therapist not only observes but also is affected by these meetings, and further (a point to be emphasized), that he/she openly discusses it with the patients.

We may stop here and insert a qualifier: therapists may love, but from time to time, also hate their patients. Explaining this issue from the vantage point of object relations theory, Kwawer (1982) stated: "It is expected that hatred, murderous rage, and greedy destruction are always present. Object relations theory recognizes brutality of feeling and deed ... Likewise, in the countertransference, this theory does not demand a saintly or physically healing presence; *hate in the countertransference helps to make real what is happening. A model of intimacy may be extrapolated from this theory in which open acknowledgement of mutual destructiveness is accepted as a matter of course. To do otherwise is to foster the elaboration of an unintegrated internal object world. Idealized relationship based on all-sweetness-and-light reflect the infant's prospective wishes, not reality. Lovers also hate, and love can survive hatred"* (p. 60, emphasis added).

It would seem that the mainstream of psychotherapy accommodated itself to the idea of the mutual expression of anger or even hate in psychotherapy. Through the influence of Melanie Klein and object relations theory in general, this issue, metaphorically speaking, became domesticated and accepted as a regular item of the psychotherapeutic household. This was not the case with the issue of erotic fantasies, and as it seems, for good reason.

While the commitment to real meeting seems to demand a similar approach to both emotions, or rather groups of emotions, there are, in fact, some differences between them. To begin with, and this is a welcome opportunity to emphasize this, even within the context of real meeting there is a hierarchy defined by the fact that one of the participants asks for help and the other one provides it, and at the end of the session only one of the participants will pay for the services received. The expression of anger does not endanger, it may even buttress this structure of hierarchy. Anger in itself, of course, is hostility. However, anger embedded in a general atmosphere of caring and understanding may be transmuted and experienced as a sign of interest and positive relationship. Unlike anger, erotic fantasies may endanger the hierarchic situation agreed upon by the parties. A lover, as popular psychology so well understood, "succumbs" to love. Lovers substitute their heart for their head, which is desirable and wonderful in certain circumstances, but not here. Also, confessing anger may be cathartic and lead to its dissolution; confessing love may make it stronger and more real.

Relatedness expressed by well-meant anger or by love and erotic fantasies, then, is similar in certain respects and quite different in others. "Ever since Joseph Breuer, after witnessing Anna O. in the throes of an hysterical pregnancy, fled from her house 'in a cold sweat', and abruptly terminated his previously devoted treatment of her – leaving for a second honeymoon with his wife the next day - psychoanalysts have had reason to be concerned with the striving for and the fear of intimacy in both patient and analyst ... the talking cure can arouse in one or both participants deep longings for intimacy along with the most powerful libidinal and aggressive impulses" (Kirman, 1982, p. 99). This is the truth of the matter and while, of course, I fully agree with the demand for sincerity, that the therapist should not try to suppress but rather face honestly his feelings, I have some second thoughts concerning the ways of dealing with it in psychotherapy. Since the arousal of such feelings may be expected, even if not regularly and inevitably, but from time to time, the therapist should not panic, but should also be aware that he can only help his patient if his own head and heart are hierarchically involved in the work, and the head is the *arche*, the leader.

Searles, who advised parents that if they sensed that erotic overtones were mingling with their parental love, they ought not to defend themselves against what they perceive as a threat by turning aloof and disinterested, thereby possibly endangering their children's welfare, did not demand that those parents also discuss their predicament with their children. This, I think, applies to psychotherapists too.

Having delineated, as promised, some guidelines to psychotherapy as a real meeting, I would now like to turn to an aspect of this approach which may demonstrate more than we could have shown earlier, the natural tie between the concept of trauma as the pathogenic factor and real meeting as the way to remedy it.

Luborsky and associates (1988) were engaged for years in a project pursuing some important aspects of psychoanalytic psychotherapy, one of them being the identification of "the most potent curative factors and the best fitting operational measures of each of them" (p. 146). They took stock, as they phrased it, of what had been written about curative factors based on clinical observation and on clinical-quantitative research. Eight factors emerged which they then organized into a graded series according to their probable power for potentiating positive outcomes. These were: patient's experience of a helping relationship; therapist's ability to understand and to respond; patient's gains in self-understanding; patient's decrease in pervasiveness of relationship conflicts; patient's capacity to internalize treatment benefits; patient's learning of greater tolerance for his or her thoughts and feelings; patient's motivation to change; therapist's ability to offer a technique that is clear, reasonable, and likely to be effective.

As it turned out, the least important of these curative factors was the last one, the theory adhered to, and the most important was the first one: "... relationship factors may be the most crucial for the outcome of psychoanalytic therapy ... What led to our viewing this curative factor as the most central one was the following line of reasoning: patients usually achieve benefits from psychotherapy even though we cannot predict these benefits with a *high degree of accuracy* from the pretreatment information, from the designated type of the treatment, or from samples of the sessions. Since a variety of differently designated psychotherapies showed similar percentages of benefits [60-80% improved moderately or better], common nonspecific factors in the treatments must be responsible for these benefits. One of these common elements must be the presence of a helping alliance" (pp. 148 and 150, emphasis in original).

Therapeutic alliances, Luborsky et al. explicated, are believed to develop through a therapist's empathy and supportiveness or through a fortuitous matching of patient's expectations and therapist's attributes. Similarity in age and similarity in level of religious activity, they found, may help in establishing a facilitating atmosphere between patient and therapist. "... a positive helping alliance will be increased by the existence of some basic demographic similarities [i.e., age, religion], by the opportunity of the therapist to express preference in patient assignments, and by the therapist's efforts toward facilitating the helping alliance" (p. 292).

Of these three factors promoting therapeutic alliance, two are the result of the therapist's deeds: If the therapist expresses his satisfaction with the patient being in his treatment and does not wait passively for its emergence but rather initiates and fosters an atmosphere of relatedness, the alliance between the patient and therapist may become established. It may appear that the Luborsky study supports the established psychoanalytic view which, by emphasizing interpretations and the "handling" of transference, relegates the patient to a passive-receptive role only. This kind of patient-therapist interaction may fit the medical model where the patient is only expected not to disturb the healing process controlled by medications or the surgeon's knife, but not the expectation aroused by the concept of real meeting. On second look, however, it may become apparent that Luborsky et al. found that interpretations are less important than what the theory teaches, but a positive helping alliance is important. By putting in the center the term "alliance", they also emphasized an interaction between patient-therapist and a mutual sharing of responsibilities, although admittedly, they did not explicate the patient's contributions.

Rather interestingly, a short statement of Freud (1933), anticipating the results of Luborsky et al., seems to have defined, precisely and succinctly, the contribution of the patient to this alliance. In his *New Introductory Lectures*, Freud stated: "I do not think our cures can compete with those of Lourdes. There are so many more people who believe in the miracles of the

Blessed Virgin than in the existence of the Unconscious" (p. 152). Just as his third theory of psychopathology might have helped Kohut, this momentous sentence might have helped Spence (1982), for Freud here agreed that the power and value of interpretations depends on whether or not the patient "believes" in the existence of the repressed Unconscious. Moreover, he compared this belief with that in the Blessed Virgin. In what follows here, I shall try to spell out some consequences of this comparison left in torso, as it were, by Freud.

Since Freud compared psychoanalysis with Lourdes, one should point out that Lourdes won its fame through the miraculous recovery of some patients suffering from medically documented organic diseases. Further, the percentage of cures at Lourdes, Weatherhead stated, is very low. "... though there were ten thousand pilgrims in Lourdes while I was there, no one even claimed to have been cured. It is said that six hundred thousand pilgrims go to Lourdes every year. In 1948 more than two million pilgrims visited the shrine. Fifteen thousand were patients, but only one is expected to be an official 'cure' ..." (p. 153). Lourdes then could not justify the philosophy of faith-healing. "Religious faith is clearly not enough", as Weatherhead put it (p. 157). This faith though seems to be enough to prevent some calamities which might arise at such populous gatherings. The pilgrims have to bath in the stream of water unearthed by little Bernadette. "Since there are people who have come a long way, people who are far from clean, people who are too ill to be continent, and people with discharging ulcers, skin diseases, running sores and inflamed eyes, it must take a great deal of faith to be plunged beneath water which bears only too obvious signs of its filthiness, hoping to be cured ... But, to my surprise, both the doctors in charge of the English pilgrims took daily baths themselves. They were, of course, Roman Catholics" (pp. 152-153).

While this sentence, written by an Anglican chaplain, has some easily perceivable overtones, I shall relate to it at its face value: Roman Catholics, empowered by their faith in the Blessed Virgin and her appearance to the little village-girl, are not disgusted and not infected by what one would think they might be. Thus, while Lourdes is not a test case for psychoanalysis, and in this respect Freud was unduly pessimistic, nevertheless, it may serve as a metaphor for the contention that faith in a symbol of power and wisdom, natural or preternatural, is no less helpful than interpretations are. Whom shall we credit by effecting such miracles, the symbol believed in, or perhaps the humble believer? A quick glance at the laboratory miracle called biofeedback, that is voluntary control over bodily functions which for centuries were regarded as autonomous, beyond voluntary control, may help us in finding an answer.

Biofeedback, in the felicitous formulation of Budzinsky (1971), has captured the imagination of both laymen and researchers. Even the term "bio-feedback" has acquired a charismatic quality. One of the relatively simple tasks here is to learn to control the rate of one's own brain waves. Green (1971) developed for this purpose an auditory feedback system that detects the presence of various brainwaves and multiplies their frequencies by two hundred, up to the audible range. By this procedure, beta waves are made to produce a "piccolo" type of music. Alpha sounds like a flute, theta like an oboe, and delta like a bassoon; an interesting and not unpleasant quartet, as Green put it.

Now, how shall we teach the subject to control what he thought he would never be able to? "In working with research subjects, we obviously do not say that the physiological functions they are going to control are involuntary - because if they really believed that, the training would not work. In actuality, *it is the 'belief' ... that is the controlling factor in learning to manipulate a so-called involuntary process"* (p. 157, emphasis added). "Obviously", says Green, and we may write out in full what he condensed in one word and state that biofeedback, that is, self-control of biological processes, including autonomic ones, is initiated by suggestion. In order to perform some notable feat, first you have to believe that you are able to do so. If a researcher or a parent or a therapist assures one and one believes them, one may achieve surprising levels of control of one's behavior. Who, then, is the wondermaker here? Both of them, because the wonders of biofeedback (and placebo as well) are miracles produced by the humble believer. The believer, however, needs the moral and intellectual support of the therapist, be it by means of interpretations or compassion or satisfaction expressed over the opportunity to have met and treated the patient. Taking biofeedback as our model rather than Lourdes, we may conclude that in a real meeting, both therapist and patient contribute something unique: The first provides strength and wisdom, and the other draws an impetus from his belief in this symbol of strength and wisdom, gains control over what seemed to be beyond the possibility of control. This is then the meaning of the helping alliance: to help the other to use his own inner resources, on the one side, and on the other, to feel liberated to fully become one's potential self.

If the pathogenic factors are narcissistic mortifications and/or traumata, which human life was never deficient in producing, then real meeting and its growth-inducing impact are the proper way of treatment. If, however, an unconscious conflict over some repressed sexual fantasies is the pathogenic factor, then to heal means to make these fantasies conscious by means of interpretations. Trauma and real meeting belong together as naturally as do the Oedipus construct and inter-pretations. It is not without significance that from Breuer through the early and later Freud to Ferenczi, the pioneers of psychoanalysis believed in the theory of trauma, and if not in theory but in praxis, supported the conception of real meeting.

PSYCHOLOGY AND LITERATURE

A daydreamer or an impostor?

A flower, even if it is only a daisy, must have a root, "and a work of art, however gay, precious, or severe, is in the last instance fed, however indirectly, invisibly, through delicate capillary tubes, from the ancient substrate of experience" (Koestler, 1964, p. 364). Unlike Koestler, Jung (1929) was sure that the personal life of a poet cannot be held essential to his art. "He may go the way of a philistine, a good citizen, a neurotic, a fool, or a criminal. His personal career may be inevitable and interesting, but it does not explain a poet" (p. 172). Jung admitted, however, the possibility of drawing inferences about the artist from his work and *vice versa*, but these inferences are never conclusive: "At best they are probable surmises or lucky guesses. A knowledge of Goethe's particular relation to his mother throws some light upon Faust's reclamation: 'The mothers – mothers – how very strange it sounds!' But it does not enable us to see how the attachment to his mother could produce the Faust drama itself, however unmistakably we sense in the man Goethe a deep connection between the two" (p. 152).

Yet, Jung weakened his own argument by reminding us that Wagner occasionally liked to wear womanish clothes. Here one does see a connection between "the heroic masculine world of Niebelungs and a certain pathological effeminacy in the man Wagner" (p. 152). Such a connection, indeed, is inevitable, Freud thought. In correspondence with Yvette Guilbert, a French *diseuse*, which appeared in her autobiography, *La chanson de ma vie*, but of which I learned from a paper of Gombrich (1966), Freud very clearly expressed this view. Yvette Guilbert wrote to Freud and asked for his opinion on the actor's psychology. It is obvious, Gombrich remarks, why this problem concerned her so much. "She had gained her success with *chansons* of most dubious morality, representing on the stage of prostitutes and criminals. She had been hurt and worried by the vulgar identification of the actress with the characters she portrayed, and she had naturally stressed the distance that separates the two" (p. 142). Freud, however, could not agree. In a letter dated 8 March, 1931, he wrote her:

I would think that what you assumed to be the psychological mechanism of your art has been very frequently asserted, perhaps universally so. Yet this idea of the surrender of one's own person and its replacement by an imagined one has never satisfied me very much. It says so little, it naturally does not tell how it is done and, most of all, it does not tell us why something which allegedly all artists desire succeeds so much better in one case than in another .... Not that the actor's own person is eliminated but rather that elements of it – for instance, undeveloped dispositions and suppressed wishes – are used for the representation of intended characters and thus are allowed expression which gives the character concerned its truth to life ... (p. 142).

Yvette Guilbert was dissatisfied for this letter affirmed what she wished to disprove, namely, that she portrayed prostitutes because to live as a prostitute was one of her repressed wishes. In his reply, Freud, somewhat condescendingly, "enjoys the interesting experience" to defend his thesis against the actress. "Now you will say that Madame Yvette has more than a single role, she embodies with equal mastery all possible characters; saints and sinners, coquettes, the virtuous, criminals and *ingenues*. That is true and it proves an unusually rich and adaptable psychic life. But I would not despair of tracing back her whole repertory to the experiences and conflicts of her early years" (p. 143).

Freud did not prove what he thought possible to prove, "unsolicited analyses cause annoyance," he excused himself, and we may regret his decision. As it stands, his statement seems sweeping and all-embracing, and it raises doubts as to its validity. Moreover, he seems to have contradicted himself. In the first letter, the mastery, the success, was suggested as a proof that it was as if the actress "acted out" her own unconscious conflicts. In contrast, in the second letter Freud agrees that the actress may have excelled in representing the many variants of female existence because of "an unusually rich and adaptable psychic life". This adaptability was the very argument of Yvette Guilbert, and Freud seems to have agreed with her. While in the next sentence, he returned to his original position: "But I would not despair of tracing back her whole repertory to the experiences and conflicts of her early years", one has the impression that in his second letter Freud was less confident than he seemed to have been in his first one. By any measure, "I would not despair", sounds rather cautious, whereas the first letter deemed totally useless the assumption that an actor may "replace" his own personality by an imagined one.

Such hesitations notwithstanding, one may say that it was the opinion of Freud and Koestler that a work of art, "in the last instance", is determined by, and derivable from "the ancient substrata" of the artist's experiences. Jung seems to have left the door open for opposing approaches, and Keats, if he could have participated in this exchange of views, would have supported Yvette Guilbert.

In a letter to Richard Woodhouse (October 27, 1819) Keats stated the following remarkable opinion:

As to the poetical character itself (I mean that sort of which, if I am anything, I am a member;) it is not itself – it has no self – it is everything and nothing. – It has no Character .... A Poet is the most unpoetical of anything in existence; because he has no identity – he is continually in for – and filling some other Body ... The Sun, the Moon, the Sea and Men and Women who are creatures of impulse are poetical and have about them an unchangeable attribute – the poet has none; no identity – he is certainly the most unpoetical of all God's creatures ....

Keats attended Hazlitt's famous *Lectures on the English Poets*, and a few sentences, Bate (1963) thinks, at the start of the third lecture, "On Shakespeare and Milton", may have especially struck him. Shakespeare, said Hazlitt, "was the least of an egotist that it was possible to be. He was nothing in himself;

but he was all that others were, or they could become .... He had only to think of anything in order to become that thing, with all the circumstances belonging to it." In agreement with Hazlitt and Keats, I shall here try to show, by means of an analysis of Shakespeare's *Hamlet* and Henry James' *The Turn of the Screw*, that the theory of replacement of the artist's personality by a pretended one is viable and demands serious consideration.

Hamlet, Dover Wilson (1930) argued, is the greatest of popular dramas, and has held the stage for three centuries just because of that. Not a few critics, nevertheless, found it less than perfect. Thus, for example, Lewes (1855) praised *Hamlet* by relating to the opposite view as follows: "... in spite of a prejudice current in certain circles, that if now produced for the first time it would fail, [it] is the most popular play in our language" (p. 33). Johnson (1765) too, while contending that *Hamlet* is the best of Shakespeare's dramas had to admit that "The poet is accused of having shown little regard to poetical justice, and may be charged with equal neglect of poetical probability" (p. 24). Still, the harshest of all was Voltaire (1748): "... it is a vulgar and barbarous drama, which would not be tolerated by the vilest populace of France, or Italy .... It seems as though nature had mingled in the brain of Shakespeare the greatest conceivable strength and grandeur with whatever witless vulgarity can devise that is lowest and most detestable" (p. 23).

Critics, who do highly esteem *Hamlet*, emphasize that in contrast to his other dramas here "Shakespeare created a mystery, and therefore it is for ever suggestive; for ever suggestive, and never wholly explicable" (Dowden, 1875, p. 36). Similarly, it was the opinion of Mack (1952) that "the first attribute that impresses us, I think, is mysteriousness .... We feel its presence in the numberless explanations that have been brought forward for Hamlet's delay, his madness, his ghost, his treatment of Polonius, or Ophelia, or his mother; and in the controversies that still go on about whether the play is 'undoubtedly a failure'

(Elliot's phrase) or one of the greatest artistic triumphs ..."
(p. 88).

This mysteriousness, indeed, was created by Shakespeare. As is well-documented, Shakespeare did not conceive the story of the prince of Denmark, but rather reshaped it and endowed it with his thoughts and words. Jones (1947, 1949) suggested that involuntarily, of course, Shakespeare also "embellished" it with his own neurotic conflicts. "It is", Jones (1947) wrote, "as if Shakespeare, on reading the story, had realized that had *he* been placed in a similar situation he would not have found the path of action so obvious as was supposed .... His own Oedipus complex was too strong for him to be able to repudiate it as readily as Amleth and Laertes had done, and he could only relate a hero who was unable to escape from its toils" (p. 195). In his second attempt to decipher the mystery of Hamlet, Jones (1949) formulated it even stronger: "His own 'evil' prevents him from completely denouncing his uncle's, ... *His moral fate is bound up with his uncle's for good or ill.* In reality his uncle incorporates the deepest and most buried part of his own personality, so that he cannot kill him without killing himself" (p. 59, emphasis in original).

In his study on Hamlet's madness, Lidz (1975) agrees that "the theory that Hamlet identifies with Claudius is sound enough and offers a reason for Hamlet's paralysis of will, but it is not the way the play reads" (p. 9). Besides, he observes, there are alternate ways in which Hamlet could have reacted to learning that his uncle had seduced his mother and killed his father. "As Otto Rank pointed out, Hamlet could have used his obligation to avenge his father as an excuse to get rid of that man in his mother's bed, thereby acting out his oedipal wish to eliminate a father figure" (p. 9). Thus even if one would agree that Shakespeare shaped Hamlet along the lines of his own unconscius Oedipus complex, his delay of the revenge until the last moments of Hamlet's life is not explained but rather made more enigmatic. But, how do we know that Shakespeare had such an unsolved and unconscious conflict? Jones took it for granted, and did not even attempt to prove it. Since it seemed to him that his equation between Claudius and Hamlet makes acceptable the delay of revenge, he seems to have felt that the equation between Hamlet and Shakespeare was also established.

This, however, is precisely the crux of the matter, and one would expect some indications for supporting these equations. Lidz, as we have seen, was of the opinion that "it is not the way the play reads". Indeed, James Joyce read and understood the text of *Hamlet* differently. In his *Ulysses*, Stephen Dedalus turned his attention to Hamlet's mother: "Is it possible that the player Shakespeare ... speaking his own words to his own son's name (had Hamnet Shakespeare lived he would have been Prince Hamlet's twin) is it possible, I want to know, or probable that he did not foresee the logical conclusion of these premises: You are the dispossessed son, I am the murdered father; your mother is the guilty queen, Ann Shakespeare, born Hathaway?"

Shakespeare's only son, Hamnet, died at the age of eleven. Shakespeare was then thirty years old, thus when he wrote *Hamlet*, the Danish prince was of the age of Hamnet had he lived. James Joyce thinks that Hamlet was more preoccupied with his mother's adultery than with his father's murder by Claudius, and his hatred grew to matricidal impulses:

O heart, lose not thy nature; let not ever
the soul of Nero enter this firm bosom;
Let me be cruel, not unnatural;
I will speak daggers to her, but use none;
(III. 376 - 379).

The mentioning of Nero was very appropriate, Lidz thinks, for Nero, too, had a stepfather, who was also his great uncle, and whose name was Claudius. Nero though was more cared for by his mother than Hamlet could have dreamed of. Agrippina, thus the rumor went, poisoned her husband-uncle to free the way for her son to the throne; Gertrude, by her marriage, barred the way of Hamlet. Also, in accord with another rumor, Agrippina, but not Gertrude, sought to commit incest with her son. The outcome of these associations between Claudius-Claudius and Agrippina- Gertrude is that the truly negative person is the mother and, thus, Hamlet is not an Oedipus but an Orestes.

Both Jones and Joyce assumed a continuity between the life and play of Shakespeare, the only difference between their respective suggestions being that for Joyce, Shakespeare must have been aware and for Jones, Shakespeare must not have been conscious of this continuity. We have now to choose between these possibilities: Orestes-Oedipus conscious-unconscious, but can we? Both Orestes and Oedipus are possible interpretations, and neither is proven. Moreover, they are by definition non-provable for, as Dowden (1875) so well put it, in *Hamlet* "Shakespeare created a mystery, and therefore it is for ever suggestive: for ever suggestive, and never wholly explicable". Shakespeare wrote 37 plays; were they, all of them, an outlet for his conscious and/or unconscious conflicts? In contrast to his other plays, which evolve their stories step by step in a logically acceptable form, *Hamlet* is surrounded by mist and fog, and we feel intrigued and invited to spread certainty where ambiguity prevailed. This may explain the distinguished position of *Hamlet*, and the efforts invested in explaining what demands to be explained. Still, the question posed above awaits an answer: if all the work of a writer is unconsciously determined, then are Shakespeare's conflicts displayed in *Hamlet* also reflected in his other works?

Conflicts, and not conflict, for Hamlet's madness, feigned or real, is no less a mystery than the delay of the revenge ordered by his father's ghost. It is not without significance that Lidz (1975), an expert on the theory of schizophrenia, chose his words carefully: "'Either/or' is a simplification desired by man but shunned by nature. Hamlet can - and I believe does - balance on the border. He can be somewhat psychotic or very much in control of himself, depending on the circumstance, as Hamlet intimates when he tells Rosencrantz and Guildenstern, 'I am but mad north-west; when the wind is southerly, I know a hawk from a handsaw'" (II. 360-361). Hamlet's madness is but half false, Lidz quotes Coleridge: "O that subtle trick to pretend the acting *only* when we are near *being* what we act" (p. 8).

Lidz also found that the words "mad" and "madness" appear in the play more than forty times, "ecstasy" (meaning madness) four times, "lunacy" and "distemper" three times each, "distracted" twice, and "antic-disposition", "wit-diseased", and "confusion" once each. One should add to this count of words some fifty indirect expressions concerned with loss of reason, loss of self-control, doubt of the senses, suicide, melancholy, and insanity. Clearly, "the frequency of 'mad', 'madness', and other words and expressions related to that concept underlines the need to pay specific attention to the theme of madness in *Hamlet*" (p. 28). Many interpretations, however, seemingly agreed to concentrate their attention on the procrastination of Hamlet, but the evidence brought forward by Lidz is convincing, and one cannot disregard it. If one believes that the unconscious psychic conflicts of a writer are his ghost-writer, then in the case of *Hamlet*, one should relate both to the topics of delay of revenge and madness. Was Shakespeare on the verge of losing his mind, did he intuitively understand something about himself others were not yet aware of? The alternative, and suggestive possibility is to accept Hazlitt's appreciation of Shakespeare, and agree that "he was nothing in himself; but he was all that others were, or that they could become".

Before elaborating, however, on the implications of this suggestion, let us consider *The Turn of the Screw* by Henry James, and some of its interpretations. *The Turn of the Screw* appeared originally as a serial in Colliers' Weekly in 1898, and in the same year, together with *Covering End*, in book form. It is a ghost-story, prompted by another such story, alluded to but not told by the author:

The story has held us, round the fire – [thus The Turn of the Screw begins] – sufficiently breathless, but except the obvious remark that it was gruesome, as on Christmas Eve in an old house, a strange tale should essentially be, I remember no comment uttered until somebody happened to say that it was the only case he had met in which such a visitation had fallen on a child.

Douglas, who soon will have to tell the story of a young governess and two orphans under her tutelage, agreed "in regard to Griffin's ghost, or whatever it was – that in appearing first to the little boy, at so tender an age, adds a particular touch. But it is not the first occurrence of its charming kind that I know to have involved a child. If the child gives the effect of another turn of the screw, what do you say to *two* children." Thus it happened that Douglas recalled the story received from the heroine many years ago. She was the youngest of several daughters of a poor country parson on her way to London to answer in person a want ad in a newspaper. The prospective patron proved a gentleman, a bachelor in the prime of life, such a figure as had never risen, save in dream or in an old novel, before a fluttered, anxious girl out of a Hampshire vicarage ... He was handsome and bold and pleasant, off-hand and gay and kind. ... she conceived him as rich, but as fearfully extra-vagant – saw him all in a glow of high fashion, of good looks, of expensive habits, of charming ways with women ...

Charmed, as she was, she agreed to take on the responsibili-ties of a governess of two children, orphaned relatives of the radiant gentleman, and went to the place of her employment, a country house in a distant place. One afternoon, the children "were tucked away" and she went out for a stroll. One of the thoughts that used to be with her in these wanderings was that perhaps someone might appear there at the turn of a path, stand there and smile and approve. She didn't ask for more than that. She only asked "that he should *know;* and the only way to be sure he knew would be to see it, and the kind light of it, in his handsome face".

What arrested her on the spot – and with a shock much greater than any vision had allowed for – was the sense that her imagination had, in a flash, turned real. He did stand there! ....

"It produced in me, this figure, in the clear twilight, I remember, two distinct gasps of emotion, which were, sharply, the shock of first and that of my second surprise. My second was a violent perception of the mistake of my first: the man who met my eyes was not the person I had precipitately supposed .... The gold was still in the sky, the clearness in the air, and the man who looked at me over the battlements was as definite as a picture in a frame."

Who was this man? Was there a "secret" in Bly – a mystery of Udolpho or an insane, an unmentionable relative kept in unsuspected confinement? Soon she made up her mind: it was an apparition, the ghost of the dead valet, who, she knew immediately and with certitude, came for someone else, not for her, but in fact for Miles, the boy under her charge. Rather close to this visitation, the governess saw a second ghost, that of the former governess; the ghost of Miss Jessel appeared with the intent, recognized by the heroine, to seduce Flora, the little girl, to follow her into death and "moral corruption". Although frightened to death, the governess did not flinch, and unhesitatingly entered into a strugle against the ghosts in order to save the children. Alas, Peter Quint had the upper hand. Little Miles dies in the arms of the governess; she lost him to the dead valet.

"If the strength of literature", Shoshana Felman (1982) observed, "could be defined by the intensity of its impact on the reader, by the vital energy and power of its effect, *The Turn of the Screw* would doubtless qualify as one of the strongest – i.e., most *effective* – texts of all time, judging by the quantity and intensity of the echoes it produced, of the critical literature to which it has given rise" (p. 96).

The echoes though were diversified. For the reviewer of the *Independent* (Jan. 5, 1898) it was "the most hopelessly evil story that [he has] ever read in any literature, ancient and modern" (p. 75). In contrast, Phelps (1916) found in it "a great work of art, profoundly ethical, and making to all those who are interested in he moral welfare of girls and boys an appeal terrific in its intensity. With none of the conventional machinery of melodrama, with no background of horrifying or threatening scenery, with no hysterical language, this story made my blood chill, my spine curl, and every individual hair to stand on end" (p. 245).

Henry James himself seemed to have been surprised by the strength of reactions. In a letter to Waldstein (Oct. 21, 1898) he wrote: "And as regards a presentation of things so fantastic as in that wanton little Tale, I can only rather blush to see real substance read into them .... My bogey-tale dealt with things so hideous that I felt that to save it at all needed some infusion of beauty or prettiness, and the beauty of the pathetic was the only attainable - was indeed inevitable." Then, in a letter to Myers (Dec. 19, 1898) he excused himself by saying: "... I scarce know what to say to you on the subject on which you wrote, especially as I am afraid I don't quite *understand* the principal question you put to me about "The Turn of the Screw" ... The T[urn] of the S[crew] is a very mechanical matter, I honestly thing - an inferior, a merely *pictorial* subject and rather a shameless pot-boiler." Finally in his preface to *The Aspern Papers* one reads: "'The Turn of the Screw' ... this perfectly independent and irresponsible little fiction ...".

It is the opinion of Cargill (1956) that James was here consciously trying to lead his readers astray for, in fact, *The Turn of the Screw* was inspired by the sad figure of Alice, Henry's sister. "The tenderest of men, Henry James could hardly have used the illness of his sister as the basis of a story while she lived or later, without elaborately disguising it - particularly since that illness though not concealed, was only guardedly revealed as mental" (p. 13). Indeed, among many other things, she wrote in her *Journal*, which, Cargill thinks, Henry "must have read" after her death in 1892: "As I used to sit immovable, reading in the library, with waves of violent inclination suddenly invading my muscles, taking some one of their varied forms, such as throwing myself out the window or knocking off the head of the benignant Pater, as he sat, with his silver locks, writing at his table; it used to seem to me that the only difference between me and the insane was that I had all the horrors and suffering of insanity, but the duties of doctor, nurse, and strait jacket imposed on me".

She was treated by many alienists, but to no avail. Due to Alice's illness, Henry James may have been knowledgeable enough to depict a state of mind on the verge of insanity, but, Cargill suggests, he was also "supported" by the joint work of Breuer and Freud, *Studien uber Hysterie*, in 1895. It is possible, Cargill speculates, that his friend Myers, who had written the first notice of the book in English, brought it to Henry James' attention. Such a connection could explain some remarkable similarities between *The Turn of the Screw* and the case-history of Lucy R., described by Freud. Lucy R. was an English governess in Vienna, in charge of the education of her wealthy employer's children. She was infatuated with her master, her love and hope for marriage being aroused by one single intimate interview with him, as was the case with the governess in James' story. Out of these sources, Cargill suggests, Henry James concocted "one of the greatest horror stories of all time" (p. 13).

Fagin (1941) too found a source of influence shaping *The Turn of the Screw*, but of a quite different kind. "In simple terms, *The Turn of the Screw* is an allegory which dramatizes the conflict between Good and Evil. The apparitions are the personifications of evil; ... the governess, the parson's daughter, is a sort of Guardian Angel, hovering protectively over the two innocent children placed in her charge" (p. 199). All this is reminiscent of Hawthorne, of *Young Goodman Brown* and *Rappacine's Daughter*, and it is well-known that James admired Hawthorne, and was impressed by his preoccupation with sin. It is possible, Fagin admits, "that we have read into this novelette more than its author intended to convey. Perhaps it is really nothing but a 'shameless pot-boiler' and our readings of it are merely fanciful?" Nonetheless, he thinks, "This is not the same thing as surmising 'subconscious processes' in the light of Freud" (p. 202).

While Fagin could not have related here to Katan's (1962, 1966) essays, which appeared many years later, I should prefer to discuss these essays rather than the others available to Fagin, because Katan is a psychoanalyst, known and knowledgeable, and his work was published by a psychoanalytic periodical. Integrating the two essays into one comprehensive analysis, one may say that Katan had no doubts in regard to the question this chapter deals with. To his understanding, *The Turn of the Screw* and literary works, in general, are autobiographical. "If", he (1962) stated, "James has 'turned' autobiography into a ghost story, I have tried to 'return' his production to its origin" (p. 493). Or, four years later: *"Story and autobiography supplement each other"* (1966, p. 625, emphasis in original). As the first step of this thesis, Katan (1966) reminds us of the "romance of life" fantasized by young Henry. In his *A Small Boy and Others,* James recalled as follows the "many deepening and final darknesses" of his childhood:

Our father's family was to offer such a chronicle of early deaths, arrested careers, broken promises, orphaned children. It sounds cold-blooded, but part of the charm of our grandmother's house for us - or I should perhaps but speak for myself - was in its being so much and so sociably a nurseried and playroomed orphanage. The children of her lost daughters and daughters-in-law overflowed there, mainly as girls; on whom the surviving sons-in law and sons occasionally and most trustingly looked in. *Parentally bereft cousins were somehow more thrilling than parentally provided ones; and most thrilling when, in the odd fashion of that time, they were sent to school in New York as a preliminary to their being sent to school in Europe.* They spent scraps of holidays with us in Fourteenth Street, *and I think my first childish conception of the enviable lot, formed amid these associations, was to be so little fathered or mothered, so little sunk in the short range, that the romance of life seemed to lie in some constant improvisation, by vague overhovering authorities, of new situations and horisons.* We were intensely domesticated, yet for the very reason perhaps that we felt our young bonds easy; ... my first assured conception of the richness was that we should be sent separately off among cold or even cruel aliens in order to be there thrillingly homesick (pp. 14-15, emphasis added).

What young Henry conceived as an enviable lot, namely, to be bereft of parents, to be little fathered or mothered, and taken over by vague overhovering authorities, was precisely the fate allotted to Miles and Flora in *The Turn of the Screw*. Their parents were dead, their uncle did not want to be bothered, and the responsibility for them was transferred to an inexperienced young girl, their governess. *The Turn of the Screw*, then, "is based upon Henry James's daydream. In this daydream lies the corroboration of the autobiographical nature of the story" (1966, p. 604).

The second step in Katan's analysis dealt with the question of horror. Why was Henry James so eager "to scare the whole world", as he once said to Phelps? "He wants to instill anxiety in everybody because he has so much anxiety himself. He wants to get rid of his anxiety by discharging it onto others" (1962, p. 476). The reason for James' nightmarish anxiety was his observation of his parents engaged in making love. The autobiographical data though "contains no evidence that Henry James ever observed sexual intercourse, nor is there any hint of his having performed a forbidden sexual act with another child". This however is not really an obstacle for "It would be rather naive on our part if our method of corroboration were to rely solely upon obtaining direct confirmation of our constructions" (1962, p. 584). Instead of the autobiography, we may turn to the story, and there we find allusions to sexual relations between Peter Quint and Miss Jessel, further we learn that the governess suspects that Miles and Flora knew of the connection between the two.

"So if we may take the words of the governess as being James's own, they have this meaning: if, as a child, you have witnessed intercourse between the parents or their substitutes, and if you cannot get rid of these impressions but under their influence you get 'in cahoots' with another child you are lost

.... Thus we may say that James suffered from the traumatic effects of primal-scene observations" (1962, p. 479). To say it again, Katan (1962) thinks "that infantile nightmares served as an example for James's ghost story. These terrifying dreams were based upon traumatic events of his childhood. The way in which James tried to discharge his anxiety onto his reader is too obvious for us not to accept the idea that James, in the story, is giving a distorted fantasy of important events in his life which gave rise to anxiety" (p. 489).

I have to admit having difficulty in understanding what Katan meant by James' discharging his nightmares onto his readers, but at the same time I would like also to emphasize that for our discussion here the main issue is what Katan (1966) felicitously defined as follows: *"The story fills in that part which is left open in James autobiographical account. Story and biography supplement each other"* (p. 625, emphasis in original). Are the literary works indeed a kind of sometimes intended and sometimes unintended autobiography, and by extension, is an actor, whatever his roles, only able to be his own, conscious and unconscious self? If we relate to this question by means of the evidence proffered by Katan, the answer seems to be yes and no. Henry James' "romance of life" and the circumstances which led the governess to meet Miles and Flora, indeed are symmetrical. One may also add here that, although not as a child or as an orphan, Henry James did leave his place of birth, lived in England, and eventually became an English citizen. His fantasy became lived reality; he sent himself off among aliens, and one seems justified in assuming that it was also one of the motives which influenced the conception of *The Turn of the Screw*.

In contrast, the primal scene Henry James assumedly has seen is a matter of interpretation derived from what the governess thinks Miles and Flora have seen but pretend not to: "There is a turn of the screw now", Katan (1962) explains, "for a new hallucination appears. We have already mentioned this; namely, the governess. in Flora's presence, sees an apparition of Miss Jessel, and the little girl pretends not to see it. Such hallucinations convince the governess that the children are lost, for they obviously deny that they see such apparitions. Thus the governess discovers that the children have full knowledge of the sexual relationship between the former governess and the valet .... Accordingly all three – the governess and the two children - have fantasies about the primal scene, or about scenes derived therefrom" (p. 483). This interpretation of the governess' insistence that the children should acknowledge the existence of ghosts is the basis of Katan's thesis, which he concluded in the following remarkable sentence: "In the story, primal-scene material is abundant" (p. 489).

Katan (1966) was all but unaware of the difficulty he was confronted with, and I could not have succeeded better than he in defining it: "We have searched in vain for an immediate confirmation of our constructions of early childhood events, But even if we were able to detect such an event behind a screen memory, it would be a method of verifying one construction by making another. Even a less severe critic with whom I am supposed to deal would never let this pass by!" (p. 595). I have only to add here that there are no advantages in interpreting the interpretation of an imaginary character, namely, that Flora's not seeing the ghosts, which the governess interprets as if the child is only pretending not to, be interpreted as evidence that Flora *had* seen Peter Quint and Miss Jessel in sexual intercourse, over the interpretation of a screen memory.

I am, though, well aware that many, perhaps the majority, of the experts will prefer Katan's (and Freud's) approach over the one indicated here. For example, Edel (1984) saw in parallels, like that between Henry James' romance of life and the scheme of *The Turn of the Screw*, "the silliest kind of biography" (p. 140). Yet, such belittling remarks notwithstanding, he was also of the opinion that "The act of imaginative writing is an act of expression and only incidentally an act of communication" (p. 133), and rather logically concluded that "The quest for the 'impersonal' in art is a delusion created by artists who, quite naturally, prefer the disguises bestowed on them constantly by their imagination" (p. 141).

Everybody interested in this question may welcome Edel's sweeping formulation, which in a sense echoes a similar statement by Freud, because it defines succinctly and with force the essence of the issue. A writer, he suggests, expresses himself; his art-work is a kind of internal monologue, a dream in full awareness. If that were true, writers would live in the solipsists' paradise, insensitive to the joy and suffering of mankind, moral or material. In truth however, life means interaction: expressing ourselves and being impressed by our environment are as naturally and necessarily interwoven as are inhaling and exhaling. Due to their "rich and adaptable psychic life", writers of great fiction are able to create an imaginary world, which while it does not exclude their own image, faithfully reflects the many faces of human existence.

While not stating it expressly, Greenacre (1958) seems to have supported such a view. Artists and impostors, she suggested, are kindred souls: both are eager to substitute foreign selves for their own. Thomas Mann, Greenacre wrote, was "engrossed" in this theme. It appears in *Disillusionment, The Dilettante, The Infant Prodigy, Tonio Kröger, Mario and the Magician, Royal Highness, The Holy Sinners, Doctor Faustus,* and *Felix Krull.* In *Tonio Kroger,* Thomas Mann reflects on the loneliness of a writer: "It begins by your feeling yourself set apart, in a curious sort of opposition to the nice, regular people; there is a gulf of ironic sensibility, of knowledge, skepticism, disagreement between you and the others; it grows deeper and deeper. You are alone; and from then on any reproachment is simply hopeless!" Having quoted this confession of Mann, Greenacre commented: "We might add, unless as an impostor, you find a new character for yourself" (p. 540). A new character, which represents a facet of reality, and not the hidden side of the artist's own personality.

As to the question, then, of whether the writer is a daydreamer who projects his/her repressed wishes onto imaginary figures and lets them do and feel what he was prevented from doing, or rather is a kind of impostor who temporarily appropriates some foreign lives and experiences, Greenacre, a well-known psychoanalytic author, favored the latter approach.

At the same time that Greenacre published her observations, Eiduson (1958) reported a study which compared the Rorschach Test and T.A.T. of artists (writers, actors, directors), to business-men (managers, accountants, and salesmen). Eiduson (1958) found in regard to the "emotional variables" that the artists, but not businessmen, are sensitive to moods and feelings of others, as well as of their own, are challenged by frustration and anxiety-producing situations rather than being overwhelmed by them, tend to imitate and depend on others in thinking and action, and can easily establish a multiplicity of identities. Artists, then, are sensitive, introspective, and prone to acquire, temporarily, identities other than their own. It is this ability which nurtures the artist but fails the impostor.

The writer's intentions and the truth of the narrative

Writers are able to acquire multiple identities but, of course, have their own personalities too. It also does not even need to be proved that their experiences are among the factors determining the character of the imaginary world they conceive. Yet, I have some difficulty with the attempt to restrict these experiences, first, to the early childhood, then to further limit these "ancient substrata", as Koestler put it, to the unconscious Oedipus conflict. In one of his last formulations on the genesis of psychoneuroses, Freud (1939) stated that "We give the name of *traumas* to those impressions experienced early and later forgotten, to which we attach such great importance in the aetiology of the neuroses". These traumas "relate to impressions of a sexual and aggressive nature, and no doubt also to early injuries to the ego (narcissistic mortifications)" (pp. 72 and 74). According to Freud, then, pathogenic experiences are not confined to sexual traumas, whether real or fantasized. A loveless childhood, replete with narcissistic mortifications, is no less a possible source of later neurotic development than traumas of sexual nature. It is well-known though that earlier Freud (1905) defined the unconscious Oedipal conflict as the nucleus of psychoneuroses and the acceptance of this thesis as the shibboleth which distinguishes between those who accept psychoanalysis and who oppose it (p. 226, n). In his later years, however, he admitted that the Oedipus construct and unconscious fantasies in general, are one of many possible causes of psychoneuroses, and by the same token, of literary creativity.

A further difficulty relates to the supposedly self-evident condition that the experience, which should find an expression in an art-work, must have been repressed. The writer, that is, should be unaware of the fact that his narrative is but a reflection of his own unresolved conflict(s). While people usually regard this assumption as the quintessence of psychoanalytic literary psychology, in fact, the later Freud was well aware of the impact of consciously remembered traumata upon the work of artists. For example, in his second letter to Yvette Guilbert, Freud also reminded her of Charlie Chaplin, who at that time was visiting in Vienna. "He is undoubtedly a great artist though admittedly he always acts one and the same character, the weakly, poor, helpless and awkward youth for whom however things turn out well in the end. Do you believe that he had forgotten his own ego playing this role? On the contrary he always acts himself as he was in his sad youth. He cannot get away from these experiences and still derives compensation today for the hardships and humiliations of those times. His is, as it were, a particularly transparent case" (p. 149). His case, if I may appropriate the word used by Freud, makes it transparent that Chaplin did not forget his sad childhood, he was conscious of it, and yet those gloomy conscious reminiscences were the source and inspiration for his art-work.

One may even ponder whether Chaplin's was an isolated, individual case, or, to the contrary, whether consciously recalled traumatic experiences are a typical motivating force guiding the enabled one to artistic professions. Indeed, surveying the childhood of 57 distinguished writers, mainly poets like Keats, Wordsworth, Coleridge, Swift, Edward Gibbon, Thackeray, Robert Bridges, "men who form an important part of our cultural tradition", Brown (1968) found that 55 percent of them had lost a father or mother before the age of 15, "a higher orphanhood rate than either the depressive or female delinquent cases" (p. 473). One seems justified in assuming that these artists experienced and remembered the trauma of orphanhood as consciously as any experience can be. Chaplin turned his melancholic youth into an incessant ridiculing of the evil forces he met with. Others, one may assume, reflect the world as they experienced it. Indeed, Koestler (1964) found that the most popular archetypal pattern of literature, the greatest fiction included, is *Puppet on Strings*, or *Volition against Fate*, a sin the ancient Greeks called *hubris* and personified in Prometheus. Tragedies are not only the most popular, they are, in Aristotle's view, also the "highest form of learning and the noblest one of literature" because men are not gods and human existence, by definition, is tragic.

While psychoanalytic hermeneutics would agree with this characterization of the motive force of literary creativity, that is, Volition against Fate, it would prefer to see Volition as a repressed and unconscious wish, Fate as an introjected, unconscious obstacle, and the conflict between them too as unconscious. "Freud's main contribution", Noy (1979) stated, "to the study of art was in showing that the analysis of *any* work of art always reveals that it contains a latent meaning which is reducible to the basic motives and conflicts common to all human beings: the oedipal conflict, homosexual problems etc. ... According to this approach, every art is merely a sublimated expression of the same limited number of basic human themes, and the difference between the thousands and thousands of works of art is to be found only in the way these themes are handled by the artist" (p. 231, emphasis in original). These, indeed, are Freud's well-known views, yet, as we have seen above, Freud also spoke of narcissistic mortifications as neurotogenic experiences, and consciously recalled traumata as a motivating force of art works. Literary creations, then, even in Freud's understanding, may be what they proclaim to be: pathetic-tragic stories of the bitter-sweet existence, and not difficult-to-prove disguises of an infantile Oedipus.

With the kind help of Cinderella, I shall here argue that a phenomenological approach to literary texts is, in general, preferable to the hermeneutics which would detect the unconscious motives of the writer, hinted at disguisedly in his/her art works.

The tale of Cinderella, Dundes (1982) stated, is the most beloved one in the Western world. But it is well-known in other parts of the world too. Already in the ninth century Cinderella was known in China (Jameson, 1932) and Sing (1974) reports on twenty-one variants of the tale in China and Indo-China. The extended references made to it in a sermon delivered in

Strasbourg in 1501 (Dundes, p. 4) is the first indication of the tale's popularity in Europe. Four hundred years later, Marian Roalfe Cox (1893) was able to collect 345 Cinderella stories, and a few years later Anna Birgitta Rooth (1951) published about twice the total of versions assembl~d by her predecessor. Cox suggested dividing the Cinderella tales into three categories: (1) the main variant in which the heroine suffers degradation and is ill-treated due to the viciousness of her stepmother and/or her stepsisters until eventually she is restored to her status and happily married to her prince sweetheart; (2) the heroine flees from her home and suffers till the happy end, in the manner of Cinderella, because her widower father wants to marry her; (3) a father dissatisfied with his daughter's love for him, expels the heroine and thus she becomes a Cinderella.

To these three categories one should add a fourth one, which relates to the miraculous story of a cinder-boy, instead of a cinder-girl. For example, Ralston (1879) mentions the Russian tale of "Neznaiko", in which young Ivan was persecuted by his stepmother who even tried to kill him, although unsuccessfully because a mysterious colt secretly advised him. Eventually Ivan and the colt fled together. Here the colt left, but before parting promised to return if Ivan would badly need help, but also advised him never to make any other reply to any question than "I don't know" (ne znay). This is why people became used to calling him "Neznaiko". He was accepted in the king's garden as a scarecrow. Now it happened that an Arab prince asked for the hand of the king's daughter, and when his suit was rejected, raised his army and invaded the king's realm. By the magic help of the colt, Ivan rescued the king from defeat. Immediately Ivan returned to his job of scaring the crows. The rejected prince tried again, and Ivan and his colt did wonders again. On this occasion he was slightly wounded in the arm, and by this sign he was recognized by the king's daughter as the disguised hero. The story ends with their marriage. It is quite evident, Ralston commented, that the story of the hero who is persecuted by a stepmother and aided by a supernatural horse, and whose true identity is temporarily concealed under a covering of skin and hide, corresponds with the story of the heroine who is ill-treated by a stepmother and assisted by a supernatural cow. "The tales of Goldenlocks and of Cinderella - Catskin are evidently twin forms of the same narrative, brother and sister developments of the same ... germ" (p. 48).

Any suggestion in regard to this "germ" will have to take into consideration the many reasons given for the suffering of Cinderella: a manipulative stepmother who succeeds in securing the father's consent to her scheme - an incestuous father - a King Lear-type father. Let us note that the villain in categories two and three is the father; only in the first category is the mother the evil-doer. Then one has to account for the existence of the tales of Neznaiko and Ivan Popyaloff, that is Ivan of *Pepel*, the cinder-boy, and the many other of its variants mentioned in Cosquin's (1918) study on male Cinderellas.

The quotation from Ralston cited above suggested an answer to this challenge, and it was for the sake of presentation that I withheld it temporarily. The tales of Goldenlocks and of Cinderella-Catskin are evidently twin forms of the same narrative, brother and sister developments of the same historical or mythological germ, stated Ralston. Just as it seems really true, in Ralston's opinion, that at least many of the stories of fair maidens released from the captivity in which they were kept by demoniacal beings can be traced back to mythological traditions about Spring being released from the bonds of Winter, the sun being rescued from the darkness of the night, the Dawn being brought back from the far West, the Waters being set free from the power of the Clouds, so it appears not unreasonable to suppose that the large group of tales of the Cinderella class may have origins in similar mythological traditions. "In all the numerous narrations about brave princes and beautiful princesses who, apparently without sufficient reason, conceal under a foul disguise their fair nature, emerge at times from their seclusion and obscurity, but capriciously return to their degraded positions, until they are finally revealed in their splendor by accident and destiny - in all these stories about a Rashie-Coat, a Katie Woodencloak, a Goldenlock, or any other of Cinderella's brothers and sisters, there appears to be a mythical element capable of being not unreasonably attributed to the feelings with which, at an early myth-making period, pre-scientific man regarded the effect of the forces, the splendour of the phenomena, of nature" (p. 57).

Ralston faithfully followed here the dictum of Max Muller (1859), according to which every tale must be traced back to a legend or myth "from whence it arose, and in which it had a natural meaning" (p. 237). Yet, he was ready to admit that "the 'unlawful marriage' opening of Rashie-Coat's story offers a difficulty" (p.52), but he would not regard it as impossible that the story of Rashie-Coat's proposed marriage refers to ancient ideas about the lawfulness of unions now disallowed.

There is no doubt, he argued, that the memory of obsolete customs may be long preserved in folk-lore. Eventually, Ralston turned pessimistic: "What seems to be really demanded from every interpreter of old tradition, every explorer of the dark field of popular fiction, is a wariness that will not allow itself to be hoodwinked by any prejudice in favour of this or that particular theory ... the more he becomes acquainted with popular tales, the less he will be inclined to seek for any single method of solving all their manifold problems" (p. 55).

Ralston's allowing for the possibility that the Rashie-Coat variant of Cinderella cycle may have preserved an ancient and long forgotten custom was supported by his compatriot, Hartland (1895). Critically examining the opinion forwarded by some of his contemporaries that the European folktales are of Indian origin, Hartland, like Ralston before him, was aware of the obstacle created by stories of the Catskin type. "They usually open with an attempt by a widowed father to marry his daughter, the heroine. All these stories are European, with one exception which comes from Kurdistan. The incident needlessly repulsive to the feelings of every European nation, could hardly have been imagined at a period when the marriage of father and daughter was a thing quite unheard of. More likely it was transferred from real life, at a stage in civilization when the sentiment of the community was against such a marriage, though it may not have been, or only recently have become contrary to the tribal customs" (p. 68/9). Indeed, outside of Europe even today – that is, one hundred years ago – such marriages are not unknown, and he quotes the information from Simpson's (1886) *Travels in the Wilds of Ecuador*, that among the Piojes of Ecuador a widow takes her son, a widower his daughter, to replace the deceased consort.

Whether because the Catskin-type seemed to be different in origin, or because Ralston was not the only one to realize that they are unable to find a principle which would be comprehensive enough to fit the whole Cinderella cycle, researchers and especially interpreters seem to have been content to analyze the stepmother type only. Thus, Saintyves (1923) suggested that the tale of Cinderella is a remnant of pre-Christian spring festivals, where Cinderella, the new season, was followed by the young sun, and married after proof had been obtained that she was the spouse designated by destiny. Likewise, von Franz (1927), a Jungian psychologist, completely disregarding the Catskin and the male versions, states that in the tale of Cinderella "The father does not play a great role; he is neither good nor bad and appears only at the beginning and at the end, where the problem does not seem to be very concentrated. The whole drama takes place in the feminine realm" (pp. 207-8). In her understanding, the death of the mother means, symbolically, the beginning of the process of individuation; the daughter feels that she wants to be herself, which entails going through difficulties, and this is why the stepmother appears. "Frequently just after the first intuitive realization of the self, the powers of desolation and darkness break in ... Some persecuting power starts at once to blot out the inner thing" (p. 213).

In a somewhat similar manner, Usher (1951) suggested that "the story of Cinderella, known to English children in the ...

version of Perrault's seventeenth-century *Contes de Fées* [that is to say, the step-mother-type], is a very sensitive allegory for the Soul's discovery of its Image ... Cinderella is a seed of the intuitive consciousness which, like a Creator in myth, has returned to its heaven" 9p. 195). The two step-sisters, Usher stated, represent the split and fragmented "abstractions" of the logical faculty. They are not even half-sisters, "for they are wholly bad – the second wife has imported them like bloodless concepts, ready-made, into the house of the mind" (p. 195). How this interpretation accounts for the "unlawful marriage" opening or the Ivan Popyaloff type of the Cinderella cycle, did not seem to have bothered Usher.

In contrast, Bettelheim (1976) was ready to accept the challenge of both the tales of the King Lear-type and of the incestuous father. Moreover, Bettelheim stresses precisely the variant, which seemed perplexing to the authors quoted above, the "unlawful marriage" opening. The two groups of Cinderella stories, while differing on the surface in regard to what causes her misfortune, namely a stepmother or an "unnatural father", as Marian Cox (1893) once put it, "are not at all contrary on a deeper level. They simply render separately some main aspects of the same phenomenon: the girl's oedipal desires and anxieties" (p. 248). We may say, Bettelheim suggests, that the inordinate love of a father for his daughter and hers for him come first, and her reduction to the Cinderella role by mother and sisters is the consequence. "This situation parallels the oedipal development of a girl" (p. 248). The other stories in which Cinderella is expelled by her father because she does not love him enough may be viewed "as a projection of a little girl's wish that her father should want her to love him beyond reason, as she wants to love him" (p. 246).

Although supported by a broad consensus and as well-known as this explanation of Cinderella's appeal to countless readers is, one must be aware, Bettelheim alerts us, that it would be impossible upon hearing the story of Cinderella to recognize that her suffering is due to oedipal involvement on her part, "and that by insisting on her unrivalled innocence the story is covering up her oedipal guilt. The well-known Cinderella stories consistently obscure what is oedipal, and offer nó hints to cast doubt on Cinderella's innocence" (p. 249).

This, indeed, is a problem, *the* problem, which interpretations of whatever kind should have related to more seriously than they seem to have. Granted the possibility that the main source of literary creations is the individual and/or collective unconscious, and that both of these sources for different reasons, however, prefer the indirect over the direct expression, still or rather precisely because of this circumstance, one has to deal with the question of validation. How can one prove that one's interpretation of a symbol like Cinderella's suffering correctly displays what was meant but disguised, in accord with the rules regulating communications from the unconscious? Also, how should we know whose interpretation to prefer?

I am reminded here of a simile of Freud (1900) regarding the difference between the dream-content, which is the equivalent of a tale's text, and the dream-thoughts, which is the true meaning of this content and which preceded the construction of the dream-content. Suppose, he wrote, I have a picture-puzzle, a rebus, in front of me. It depicts a house with a boat on its roof, a single letter of the alphabet, the figure of a running man whose head has been conjured away, and so on. Obviously, "we can only form a proper judgment of the rebus if we ... try to replace each separate element by a syllable or word that can be represented by that element in some way or other .... A dream is a picture-puzzle of this sort ..." (p. 278). In solving the rebus, Steele and Jacobsen (1977) commented on this statement of Freud, "We can check our solution against the original phrase, but, and this is where Freud's analogy leads us astray, there is no original text independent of interpretation to which we can compare our dream solution ... there is a confusion between an actual meaningful explanation, the dream interpretation, and a hypothetical original event, the latent dream" (p. 394).

Can we then be sure that our interpretation indeed succeeded in re-establishing the "original" text? It is quite evident, I think, that by applying these methods of interpretation to fairy tales conceived by unknown author(s) under unknown circumstances, the doubts should become even more pressing. Ricoeur (1970), a Freudian philosopher, agreed that "psychoanalysis has never quite succeeded in stating how its assertions are justified, how its interpretations are authenticated, how its theory is justified" (p. 274). This, however, he suggested, is not really important for "in analysis the real history is merely a clue to the figurative history through which the patient arrives at self-understanding" (p. 369). Such an understanding though seems to close the door to the interpreters of Cinderella for, while in the course of a psychotherapy one may find some justification for offering a "figurative" instead of a "real" history, ("psychoanalysis", Freud [1909] admitted, "is not an impartial scientific investigation, but a therapeutic measure. Its essence is not to prove anything, but merely to alter something"[p. 104]), what should exonerate such attempts with regard to fairy tales? Should we not pay more attention, and if I may say so, respect to the text rather than, as many of us prefer, discard it as a useless shell of a presumed but evasive truth?

Incidentally, I have borrowed this metaphor from Erikson (1954): "Unofficially", he wrote, "we often interpret dreams entirely or in parts on the basis of their manifest appearance. Officially, we hurry at every confrontation with a dream to crack its manifest appearance as if it were a useless shell and to hasten to discard this shell in favor of what seems to be more worthwhile core" (p. 140). Interpretation of dreams, then, do pay respect to the text of a dream, and it is an intriguing question why this approach and its important ramifications should be restricted to, one would almost say, hidden by, the confines of the therapeutic hours, as if disavowed "officially"?

Significantly, Bettelheim did make a step in the direction indicated by Erikson, for he agreed that the meaning of some tales is just what they tell. The many stories in which innocent Cinderella is claimed by her father as his marital partner, Bettelheim interprets as conforming to and expressing universal childish fantasies in which a girl wishes her father would marry her and then, out of guilt because of these fantasies, denies anything to arouse this parental desire. "But deep down a child who knows that she does want her father to prefer her to her mother feels she deserves to be punished for it - thus her flight or banishment, and degradation to a Cinderella existence. The other stories in which Cinderella is expelled by her father because she does not love him enough may be viewed as a projection of a little girl's wish that her father should want her to love him beyond reason, as she wants to love him. Or the father's expulsion of Cinderella because she does not love him enough could equally well be regarded as giving body to paternal oedipal feelings for a daughter ..." (p. 246).

Bettelheim seems not to have distinguished here between incestuous and oedipal desires, a distinction crucial to our topic. Oedipal desires relate to the incestuous wishes of sons and daughters toward their parents, and not to "seduction" of daughters by incestuous fathers. At any rate, if the King Lear-type of tale can be equally understood as the projections of a girl's wish as well as the wish of a father which, in fact, is what the tale communicates, then why not apply this same principle to the "unlawful marriage" opening too, and agree that the incestuous desire of the father may be a wish of Cinderella projected on to her father, but that it is equally possible that the tale says what its text imputes? In fact, the text and its amendations by means of interpretations are not of equal rights, for while there is always a possibility to grant interesting and even paradoxical meanings to literary narratives, one should never forget that the text of the narrative is known and real, but the interpretations are, at best, possibilities.

In this particular case, the possibility that Bettelheim's interpretation of the tale of Cinderella as the expression of a girl's oedipal involvement may be accepted, is seriously threatened by the fact that, in common with all the other interpreters quoted above, he too forgot the male variant of the Cinderella cycle. Had he not disregarded "Neznaiko" and similar tales, he would have hesitated, I assume, to interpret the Cinderella cycle as created due to a girl's oedipal involvement.

Neither the solar mythology, nor the Oedipal complex, nor the archetypes of selfhood, none of these constructs succeeded in suggesting a frame fitting the whole of the Cinderelia cycle. Yet, before one raises his hands, one might have a second look at what was rescued from oblivion by none other than Bettelheim, the text itself. The text, as Jameson (1932) already saw, does allow a comprehensive suggestion. The Chinese Cinderella he was the first to report on, was an orphan, whose father and mother died, and who lived with her father's second wife, her stepmother. Whatever the symbolism of the various parts of the story may be found to be, whatever meanings may be attached to slippers and fishes, helpful animals and dead parents, "the daydream which we call fairy tale is organized by the central situation presented near the beginning: The emotions growing out of the fact that here is a small girl who was fondly loved by a father that died and is now being mistreated by her stepmother" (p. 93). The bleak world of orphanhood, of both girls and boys, is the common theme connecting the many variants of the Cinderella cycle.

At times when, as compared with ours, life expectancy was short, orphans were a rather common phenomenon and their fate was far from being enviable. Indeed, the Bible recurrently reminds us "not to cause pain to orphans and widows", and one may assume that it was their thorny lives which prompted these warnings. Life is beautiful but also frightening and even cruel, and to quote a sage sentence of Esman (1982), one should be wary not to seek "to explain say, the power of Macbeth's 'Tomorrow and tomorrow and tomorrow' soliloquy by extracting from its text a primal scene fantasy, as though its manifest concern with such profound existential issues as death and transience were insufficient to account for its appeal" (p, 17). Neither should we think that difficult-to-prove motives explain the popularity of the Cinderella cycle better than the text, which tells us of desperate orphans who have only their dead parents to turn to for help and consolation, a fate which in earlier times every villager was acquainted with, and not a few parents were afraid their own children, too, might experience.

Goethe 1826 by Ludwig Sebbers

I would like to conclude these reflections by reproducing here three paintings of Goethe executed by different painters between the years 1826-1829.

Goethe sat for these artists, and his face was anything but a veiled message to be decoded. Yet, one of them saw before him a member of the Olympian pantheon, calm and seeing beyond the human horizon, another saw an embittered and weary human fellow, and the third artist depicted an old man, whom, if we were to meet him by chance, would probably not impress us enough to remember him. One may empathize with Mobius

Goethe 1828 by J. K. Stieler

(1898), who, it seems in exasperation, observed: "I have seen many but not all the paintings made of Goethe, and the more I see the less I know how actually Goethe looked like, since all are different" (p. 239). Nevertheless, and in contradistinction to his own statement, Mobius praised Stieler's painting, the "Olympian" one, as the best depiction of Goethe. I would like

Goethe 1829
by Pierre Jean David d'Angers

to urge interpreters of literary creations to keep in mind these pictures of Goethe, together with Mobius' preference for one of them, made deliberately, as it seems.

I don't know what Goethe's reactions were to these representations of him, but we do know of Freud's reaction to a drawing of Abraham by an Expressionist artist. In a letter to Abraham, Freud (26 December, 1922), consoled him as follows:

Dear Friend, I received the drawing which allegedly represents your head. It is ghastly. I know what an excellent person you are. I am all the more deeply shocked that such a slight flaw in your character as is your tolerance or sympathy for modern "art" should have been punished so cruelly. I hear from Lampl that the artist maintained that he saw you in this way. People such as he should be the last to be allowed access to analytic circles for they are the all-too-unwelcome illustrations of Adler's theory that it is precisely people with severe inborn defects of vision who become painters and draughtsmen. Let me forget this portrait in wishing you the very best for 1923.

It is not impossible that, metaphorically speaking, we all have inborn defects of vision, and this should encourage us to be modest and accept the "visions" of others as reflections of reality as possible as are our own "visions". But above all, this should remind us that observable facts, like the text of a literary narrative, may reflect not only the intentions of the writer but also the truth of this narrative.

REFERENCES

Arkin, A.M. (1979). *Sleep-talking*. N.Y. City University Press.

Ashwell, S. (1894). *A practical treatise on the diseases peculiar to women*. London: Samuel Highly.

Banquet, A. (1989). Inter and intrahemispheric relationships of the EEG activity during sleep in man. *EEG and Clinical Neurophysiology, 55*, 51-59.

Barratt, B. (1976). Freud's psychology as interpretation. *Psychoanalysis and Contemporary Science, 5*,

Barron, R. (1952). Personality style and perceptual choice. *Journal of Personality, 20*, 358-401.

Basch, M.F. (1983). The significance of self-psychology for a theory of psychotherapy. In *Reflections on self-psychology*, Lichtenberg, J.D. and Kaplan, S. (Eds.), Hillsdale, N.J.: L. Erlbaum.

Bate, W.F. (1963). *John Keats*. Harvard University Press.

Beecher, H.K. (1961). Surgery as placebo. *Journal of the American Medical Association, 176*, 1102-1107.

Bender, L. and Blau, L. (1937), The reaction of children to sexual relations with adults. *American Journal of Orthopsychiatry, 7*, 500-518.

Bender, L. and Grugett, A. (1952). A follow-up report on children who had atypical sexual experiences. *American Journal of Orthopsychiatry, 22*, 825-857.

Berger, R.F. (1963). Experimental modification of dream content by meaningful verbal stimuli. *British Journal of Psychiatry, 109*, 722-740.

Bernheim, H. (1884). *De la suggestion dans l'état hypnotique et dans l'état de veille* (On suggestion in the hypnotic and waking states). Paris.

Bernheim, H. (1886). *Suggestive therapeutics*. N. Y.: Putnam, 1895.

Bettelheim, B. (1960). *The informed heart*. London: Thames and Hudson.

Bettelheim, B. (1976). *The uses of enchantment.* N.Y.: Alfred Knopf.

Bischof, N. (1975). Comparative ethology of incest avoidance. In *Biosocial anthropology*, Fox, R. (ed.). London: Malaby Press.

Blight, J.G (1981). Must psychoanalysis retreat to hermeneutics? *Psychoanalysis and Contemporary Thought* 4, 147-205.

Borges, J.L. (1962). *Labyrinths.* Selected stories and other writings. N.Y.: A New Directions Book.

Bowlby, J. (1977). The making and breaking of affectional bonds. II. Some principles of psychotherapy. *British Journal of Psychiatry, 130,* 421-431.

Braid, J. (1843). *Neurohypnology: Or the rationale of nervous sleep, considered in relation with animal magnetism.* London: John Churchill.

Bramwell, J.M. (1903). *Hypnotism, its history, practice, and theory.* London: P. Richards.

Breuer, J. and Freud, S. (1895). Studies on hysteria. *Standard Edition,* vol. 2 London: Hogarth Press.

Brill, A.A. In *The basic writings of Sigmund Freud.* Translated by A.A. Brill. N.Y.: Modern Library, 1938.

Brown, R. & NcNeil, D. (1966). The "tip-of-the-tongue" phenomenon. *Journal of Verbal Learning and Verbal Behavior, 5,* 325-337.

Brown, F. (1968). Bereavement and lack of a parent in childhood, In *Foundations of child psychiatry*, F. Miller (ed.). London: Pergamon, pp. 435-455.

Bruner, J.S., Goodnow, J.Y., & Austin, G.A. (1956). *A study of thinking.* N.Y.: Wiley.

Budzinsky, T.H. (1971). Some applications of biofeedback produced in twilight states. In *Biofeedback and self-control*, Shapiro, D., Barber, T.X., DiCara, V., Kamiya, J., Miller, N.W., and Stoyva, J. (eds.). Chicago: Aldine, 1973, pp. 145-151.

Bugental, J. (1965). *The search for authenticity.* N.Y.: Holt, Rinehart, & Winston.

Calef, quoted from Langs, R. (1976) *Therapeutic interactions.* N.Y.: Basic Books.

Cargill, O. (1956). Henry James as Freudian pioneer, *Chicago Review, 10,* 13-29.

Chase, M.H. (ed.) (1972). *The sleeping brain.* Los Angeles: Brain Information Service.

Codignola (1974). *Essay on the logical structure of psychoanalytic interpretation.*

Cohen, D.B. & Wolfe, G. (1973). Dream recall and repression: Evidence for an alternative hypothesis. *Journal of Consulting and Clinical Psychology, 41,* 349-355.

Cohen, D.B. & MacNeilage, P.F. (1974). Test of the salience hypothesis of dream recall. *Journal of Consulting and Clinical Psychology, 42,* 699-703.

Corner, T. (1984). Maturation of sleep mechanisms in the central nervous system. In *Sleep Mechanisms,* Borbely, A. and Valatx, J.L. (eds.). N.Y. Springer, pp. 50-66.

Cory, T.R., Orniston, D.W., Simmel, E., & Dainoff, M. (1975). Predicting the frequency of dream recall. *Journal of Abnormal Psychology, 84,* 261-266.

Cosquin, E. (1918). Le "Cendrillon" masculin, *Reuve des Traditions Populaires 35,* 193-202.

Cox, M.R. (1893). *Cinderella.* London: David Nutt.

Descartes. *Philosophical works* of. London, Cambridge University Press, 1912.

Domhoff, B. & Kamiya, J. (1964). Problems in dream content study with objective indicators. A comparison of home and laboratory dream reports. *Archives of General Psychiatry, 11,* 519-524.

Dorus, E., Dorus, W., & Rechtschaffen, A. (1971). The incidence of novelty in dreams. *Archives of General Psychiatry, 25,* 364-368.

Dover Wilson, F. (1930). *What happens in Hamlet,* In *Hamlet: A casebook,* Jump, J. (ed.). London: Macmillan, pp. 44-45.

Dowden, E. (1875). *Shakespeare: A critical study of his mind and art,* in *Hamlet: A casebook,* Jump, F. (ed.). London: Macmillan, pp. 35-36.

Dundes, A. (ed.) (1982). *Cinderella: A casebook*. N.Y. Wildman Press.

Dupee, F.W. (1956). *Henry James, Autobiography*, ed., with an Introduction by F.W. Dupee. N.Y.: Criterion Books.

DuPrel (1885). *Die Philosophie der Mystik* (The philosophy of mysticism). Leipzig.

Eagle, M. (1984). *Recent developments in psychoanalysis: A critical evaluation*, N.Y.: McGraw-Hill.

Eagle, M.N. and Wolitzky, D.L. (1986). Book review: *The process of psychoanalytic therapy: Models and strategies* by Emanuel Peterfreund. *Psychoanalysis and Contemporary Thought, 9*, 79-102.

Edel, E. (1973). Toward a theory of literary psychology, in *Interpersonal explorations in psychoanalysis*, Witenberg, E.G. (ed.), N.Y.: Basic.

Edel, E. (1984). *Writing lives*. N. Y.: Norton.

Edelson, M. (1973). Language and dreams. *The Psychoanalytic Study of the Child, 27*, 203-282.

Eiduson, B.T. (1958). Artist and nonartist: A comparative study. *Journal of Personality, 26*, 13-28.

Eiduson, B.T. (1962). *Scientists: Their psychological world*. N.Y. Basic Books.

Ellenberger, H. (1970). *The discovery of the Unconscious*. N.Y.: Basic Books.

Ellis, H. (1899). The stuff that dreams are made of. *Popular Science Monthly, 54*, 721-735.

Erikson, E.H. (1954). The dream specimen of psychoanalysis. *Journal of American Psychoanalytic Association, 2*, 5-56.

Esman, A.A. (1982) Psychoanalysis and literary criticism – A limited partnership. *Psychoanalysis and Contemporary Thought, 5*, 17-25.

Evans, F.J., Gustafson, R.A., O'Connell, D.N., Drue, M.T., & Shor, R.E. (1970). Verbally induced responses during sleep. *Journal of Nervous and Mental Diseases, 150*, 171-187.

Exner, G. (1894). *Entwurf zu einer physiologischen Erklärung der psychischen Erscheinungen* (A draft to a physiological explanation of pychological phenomena.) Vienna, Deuticke.

Fagin, N.B. (1941). Another reading of The Turn of the Screw. *Modern Language Notes, 56*, 196-202.

Faravelli, C., Webb, T., Ambonetti, A., Fonnesu, F., and Sessarego, A. (1985). Prevalence of traumatic early life events in 31 agoraphobic patients with panic attacks. *American Journal of Psychiatry, 142*, 1493-1495.

Felman, S. (1982). Turning the screw of interpretation. *Yale French Studies, 55/6*. 94-207. .

Ferenczi, F. (1930). The principle of relaxation and neocatharsis. *International Journal of Psychoanalysis, 11*, 428-43.

Ferenczi, F. (1932). Confusion of tongues between adults and the child; in Masson, F.M. (1984), *The assault on truth.* N.Y.: Farrar, Straus, and Giroux.

Fine, R. (1982). *The healing of the mind. The technique of the psychoanalytic therapy.* N.Y.: The Free Press.

Finkelhor, D. (1979). What's wrong with sex between adults and children? *American Journal of Orthopsychiatry, 49*, 642-697.

Forel, A. (1907). *Hypnotism: or suggestion and psychotherapy.* N.Y.: Rebman.

Foulkes, D. (1962). Dream reports from different stages of sleep. *Journal of Abnormal and Social Psychology, 65*, 14-25.

Foulkes, D. (1978). *A grammar of dreams.* N.Y.: Basic Books.

Foulkes, D. & Vogel, G.W. (1965). Mental activity at sleep onset. *Journal of Abnormal and Social Psychology, 70*, 231-243.

Foulkes, D. & Fleisher, S. (1975). Mental activity in relaxed wakefulness. *Journal of Abnormal Psychology, 84*, 66-75.

Freud, S. (1895) in Breuer, J. and Freud, S. (1895)

Freud, S. (1896). The aetiology of hysteria. *Standard Edition,* London, Hogarth Press, Vol. 3, pp. 191-221.

Freud, S. (1900). The Interpretation of Dreams. *Standard Edition,* London, Hogarth Press, 1953, Vols. 4 and 5.

Freud, S. (1901). On dreams. *Standard Edition,* London, Hogarth Press, 1953, Vol. 5, pp. 633-686.

Freud, S. (1901). The Psychopathology of Everyday Life. *Standard Edition,* London, Hogarth Press, Vol. 6.

Freud, S. (1905/a). Fragment of an analysis of hysteria. *Standard Edition,* London: Hogarth Press, vol. 17, pp. 7-122.

Freud, S. (1905/b), Three essays on sexuality. *Standard Edition,* London: Hogarth Press, vol. 7, pp. 125-243.

Freud, S. (1905/c), My views on the part played by sexuality in the aetiology of neuroses. *Standard Edition,* London: Hogarth Press, vol. 7, pp. 271-279.

Freud, S. (1909). Analysis of a phobia in a five-year old boy. *Standard Edition,* London: Hogarth Press, vol. 10, pp. 3-149.

Freud, S. (1910). Five lectures of psychoanalysis. *Standard Edition,* London: Hogarth Press, vol. 11, pp. 9-55.

Freud, S. (1912/a). The dynamics of transference. *Standard Edition,* London: Hogarth Press, vol. 12, pp. 97-108.

Freud, S (1912/b). Recommendations to physicians practicing psychoanalysis. *Standard Edition,* London: Hogarth Press, vol. 12, pp. 109-120.

Freud, S. (1912/c). A note on the unconscious in psychoanalysis. *Standard Edition,* London, Hogarth Press, Vol. 12, pp. 260-266.

Freud, S. (1913). On beginning the treatment. *Standard Edition,* London: Hogarth Press vol. 12. pp. 121-144.

Freud, S. (1914). On the history of the psychoanalytic movement. *Standard Edition,* London, Hogarth Press, Vol. 14, pp. 7-66.

Freud, S. (1915). Observations on transference love. *Standard Edition,* London: Hogarth Press, Vol. 12, pp. 159-171.

Freud, S. (1915). The unconscious. *Standard Edition,* London, Hogarth Press, Vol. 14, pp. 166-215.

Freud, S. (1916/17). Introductory Lectures on Psychoanalysis. *Standard Edition,* London, Hogarth Press, Vols. 15-16.

Freud, S. (1918). From the history of an infantile neurosis. *Standard Edition,* London, Hogarth Press, Vol. 17, pp. 7-122.

Freud, S. (1919). A child is being beaten. *Standard Edition.* London: Hogarth Press, vol 17, pp. 177-204.

Freud, S. (1920). Beyond the pleasure principle. *Standard Edition,* London: Hogarth Press, vol. 18, pp. 4-65.

Freud, S. (1921). Group psychology and the psychology of the ego. *Standard Edition,* London: Hogarth Press, vol. 18, pp. 67-143.

Freud, S. (1923). Joseph Popper-Lynkeus and the theory of dreams. *Standard Edition,* London, Hogarth Press, Vol. 18, pp. 261-263.

Freud, S. (1924). A short account of psycho-analysis. London, *Standard Edition,* London, Hogarth Press, vol. 19, pp. 191-209.

Freud, S. (1925). An autobiographical study. *Standard Edition,* London: Hogarth Press, vol. 19, pp. 7-74.

Freud, S. (1933). New introductory lectures on psychoanalysis. *Standard Edition,* London: Hogarth Press, vol. 22.

Freud, S. (1937/a). Analysis terminable and interminable. *Standard Edition,* London: Hogarth Press, vol. 23, pp. 216-253.

Freud, S. (1937/b). On constructions in psychoanalysis. *Standard Edition,* London: Hogarth Press, vol. 23, pp. 255-269.

Freud, S. (1939). Moses and monotheism. *Standard Edition.* London, Hogarth Press, v. 23, pp. 77-137.

Freud, S. (1940). An outline of psychoanalysis. *Standard Edition,* London, Hogarth Press, 1964, Vol. 23, pp. 144-207.

Fromm, E. (1960). Psychoanalysis and Zen Buddhism. In *Zen Buddhism and psychoanalysis.* Suzuki, D.D., Fromm, E. and de Martino (eds.). N.Y.: Harper and Row.

Galton, F. (1879). Psychometric experiments. *Brain, 2,* 148-162.

Gardiner, M. (ed.) (1971). *The Wolfman and Sigmund Freud.* N.Y.: Basic Books.

Gardner, R.W. & Long, R.J. (1962). Control, defense, and centration effect: A study of scanning behavior. *British Journal of Psychology, 53,* 129-140.

Gauthier, A. (1845). *Traité pratique du magnétisme et du somnam-*

bulisme (A practical treatise of magnetism and somnambulism). Paris: Baillière. Quoted after Ellenberger, H. (1970). *The Discovery of the Unconscious.* N.Y.: Basic Books.

Gelinas, D. Z (1983). The persisting negative effects of incest, *Psychiatry, 46,* 312-332.

Gill, M.M. (1979). The analysis of transference. *Journal of American Pychoanalytic Association, 4,* 263-268.

Gill, M.M. (1982). Analysis of transference. Vol. 1. *Psychological Issues, 53.* N.Y.: International Universities Press.

Giora, Z. (1981). Dream styles and dreaming. *Journal of Psychoanalysis and Contemporary Thought, 4,* 291-379.

Giora, Z. (1989). *The Unconscious and the theory of Psychoneuroses.* N.Y.: New York University Press.

Glover, E. (1931). The therapeutic effect of inexact interpretation. *International Journal of Psychoanalysis,*12, 405-414.

Glover, E. (1955). *The technique of psycho-analysis.* N.Y.: International Universities Press.

Gombrich, E.H. (1966). Freud's aesthetics, *Encounter, 26,* 30-39. Also in *Literature and psychoanalysis,* Kurzweil, E. and Philips, W. (eds.). N.Y. Columbia University Press, 1983.

Goodenough, D.R. (1986). History of the field dependence construct. In *Field dependence in psychological theory, research and application,* Bertini, M., Pizzamoglio, L., and Wagner, S. (eds.). N.Y.: Erlbaum, pp. 5-13.

Goodwin, F., Simms, M., and Bergman, R. (1979). Hysterical seizures: A sequel to incest. *American Journal of Orthopsychiatry, 49,* 698-703.

Goody, F. (1956). A comparative approach to incest and adultery. *British Journal of Sociology, 7,* 286-305.

Green, E. (1971). Biofeedback for mind-body regulation: Healing and creativity. In *Biofeedback and self-control,* Shapiro, D., Barber, T.X., DiCara, V., Kamiya, J., Miller, N.E., and Stoyva, J. (Eds.). Chicago: Aldine, 1973, pp. 152-166.

Greenacre, Ph. (1958). The relation of the impostor to the artist. *The Psychoanalytic Study of the Child, 13,* 521-540.

Grinstein, A. (1983). *Freud's rules of dream interpretation.* N.Y. International University Press.

Gross, M. (1979). Incestuous rape: A cause for hysterical seizures in four adolescent girls. *American Journal of Orthopsychiatry, 49,* 704-708.

Grunbaum, A. (1983). Explication and implications of the placebo concept, in *Placebo,* White, L., Tursky, B., and Schwartz, G.E. N.Y.: Guilford Press, 1983.

Guntrip, H. (1974). *Schizoid phenomena, object relations, and the self.* London: Hogarth Press.

Halász, P., Pál, J., & Rajna, P. (1985). K-Complex formation of the EEG in sleep. A survey and new examinations. *Acta Physiologica Hungarica, 65,* 3-35.

Harper, R.C., Kenigsberg, K., Sia, G., Horn, D., Stern, D.N., & Bongiovi, V. (1980). Ziphophagus conjoined twins. *American Journal of Obstetrics and Gynecology, 137,* 617-629.

Hartland, E.S. (1893). Notes on Cinderella. The International Folklore Congress, in *Cinderella: A casebook,* Dundes (ed.). N.Y.: Wildman Press, pp. 57-71.

Hartmann, H. (1958). *Ego psychology and the problem of adaptation.* N.Y.: International Universities Press.

Herbart, J.F. (1816). *Lehrbuch der Psychologie* (A textbook of psychology). Königsberg und Leipzig, Unzer.

Herbart, J.F. (1824). *Psychologie als Wissenschaft.* (Psychology as science.) Hamburg and Leipzig: L. Voss, 1886.

Herman, J,H., Ellman, S.J., & Roffwarg, H.P. (1978). The problem of NREM recall–re-examined. In *The Mind in Sleep: Psychology and Psychophysiology.* A.M. Arkin, J.S. Antrobus, & S.J. Ellman (eds.). Hillsdale, N.J.: Erlbaum.

Herman, J.R., Perry, Chr., and Van der Kolk, B. (1989). Childhood trauma in borderline personality disorder. *American Journal of Psychiatry, 146,* 490-495.

Hilgard, J. (1972). Evidence for a developmental-interactive theory of hypnotic susceptibility. In *Hypnosis: Research developments and perspectives.* Fromm, E. and Shor, R.E. (eds.). London: Paul Elek, pp. 387-397.

Hiscock, M. & Cohen, D.B. (1973). Visual imagery and dream recall. *Journal of Research in Personality, 7*, 179-188.

Hobson, J.A. (1988). *The dreaming brain.* New York: Basic Books.

Holloway, F.A. & Wansley, R. (1973). Multiphasic retention deficits at periodic intervals after passive avoidance learning. *Science, 180*, 208-210.

Hopkins, K. (1980). Brother-sister marriage in Roman Egypt. *Comparative Studies in Society and History, 22*, 303-354.

Horne, J.A. (1985). Tissue restitution and sleep. In *Endogenous sleep substances and sleep regulation*, Jouvet, S. and Borbely, A. (eds.). Tokyo, Japan Scientific Societies Press, pp. 25-39.

Hufeland, F. (1811). *Ueber Sympathie* (On Sympathy). Weimar: Verlag des Landes – Industrie – Comptoir. Quoted after Ellenberger, H. (1970), *The discovery of the Unconscious.* N.Y.: Basic Books.

James, H. (1879). *Hawthorne*, London.

Jameson, R.D. (1932). *Three lectures in Chinese folklore.* Peking, North China Language School.

Janet, P. (1897). L'influence somnambulique et le besoin de direction. (The somnambulic influence and the need to be directed.) *Revue Philosophique, 43*, 113-143.

Joelson Segal, S. (1972). Assimilation of a stimulus in the construction of an image: the Perky effect revisited. In *The functions and nature of imagery*. P.W. Sheehan (ed.). N.Y. Academic Press, pp. 203-230.

Johnson, N. F. (1970). Chunking and organization in the process of recall. In *The psychology of learning and motivation*, G.H. Bower (ed.). N.Y. Academic Press, Vol. 4, pp. 171-247.

Johnson, N. F. (1972). Organization and the concept of a memory code. In *Coding processes in human memory*, Melton, A.W. and Martin, E. (eds.). Washington D.C.: Winston and Sons, pp. 125-159.

Johnson, S. (1965). His edition of Shakespeare's plays, in *Hamlet: A casebook*, Jump, F. (ed.). London: Macmillan, pp. 23-24.

Jones, E. (1947), *Hamlet, Prince of Denmark, by William Shakespeare, with a psycho-analytical study by E. Jones*, In *Interpreting Hamlet*, R.E. Leavenworth (ed.). San Francisco, 1960, pp. 173-196.

Jones, E. (1949). *Hamlet and Oedipus*. London: Gollancz, In *Hamlet: A casebook*, Jump, F. (ed.). London: Macmillan, pp. 51-63.

Jones, E. (1953). *The life and work of S. Freud*. N.Y. Basic Books, Vol. 1.

Joseph, E.D. (ed.) '1967). The place of the dream in clinical psychoanalysis. *Monograph II of the Kris Study Group of the New York Psychoanalytical Institute*. N.Y. International Universities Press.

Jump, J. (ed.). *Hamlet: A casebook*. London: Macmillan, 1968.

Jung, C.G. (1928). The relations between the Ego and the Unconscious. In *The basic writings of C.G. Jung*. N.Y. Modern Library., pp. 105-182.

Jung, C.G. (1929). *Modern man in search of a soul*. N.Y. Harcourt, Brace and World 1933.

Jung, C.G. (1933). Dream-analysis in its practical application. In *Modern man in search of a soul*. N.Y. Harcourt, Brace and World, 1933, pp. 1-27.

Jung, C.G. (1938). Psychology and religion. In *The basic writings of C.G. Jung*. N.Y. Modern Library, 1959. pp. 469-528.

Jung, C.G. (1945). On the nature of dreams. In *The basic writings of C.G. Jung*. N.Y. Modern Library, 1959. pp. 363-379.

Kagan, J. & Kogan, N. (1970). Individuality and cognitive performances. In *Carmichael's Manual of Child Psychology*. Vol. 1, 3rd ed. P. Mussen (ed.). N.Y.: Wiley, pp. 1273-1365.

Kalnins, J.V. & Bruner, J. (1974). Infant sucking used to change the clarity of a visual display. In *The competent infant*, Stone, J., Smith, H.J., and Murphy, L.B. (eds.). London: Tavistock, pp. 713-718.

Kaplan, M. and Kloss, R. (1973). *The unspoken motive.* N.Y.: Free Press.

Katan, M. (1962). A causerie on Henry James's "The Turn of the Screw". *Psychoanalytic Study of the Child, 17,* 475-493.

Katan, M. (1966). The Origin of the Turn of the Screw. *Psychoanalytic Study of the Child, 21,* 583-635.

Katz, D. (1951). Zur Geschichtlichen Entwicklung der Psychologie, in *Handbuch der Psychologie* (A Handbook of psychology). D.Katz und Rosa Katz (eds.), Basel, Schwabe.

Kirchhoff, Th. (1924). *Deutsche Irrenaerzte* (German psychiatrists). 2 Vol. Berlin.

Kirman, J.H. (1982). Modern psychoanalysis and intimacy. In *Intimacy,* Fisher, M. and Stricker, G. (eds.). N.Y.: Plenum, pp. 99-114.

Klein, M. (1981). On Mahler's autistic and symbolic phases: An exposition and evaluation. *Psychoanalysis and contemporary Thought, 4,* 69-105.

Koestler, A. (1964). *The act of creation.* London: Pan Books.

Kohut, H. (1959). *The search for the self.* Vol. 1. N.Y.: International Universities Press.

Kramer, R., Winget, C., & Whitman, R.M. (1971). A city dreams: A survey approach to normative dream content. *American Journal of Psychiatry, 127,* 1350-1356.

Kubie, L.S. (1954). The fundamental nature of the distinction between normality and neurosis. *Psychoanalytic Quarterly,23,* 167-185.

Kwawer, J.S. (1982). Object relations theory and intimacy. In *Intimacy,* Fisher, M. and Stricker, G. (eds.). N.Y.: Plenum, pp. 53-64.

Laberge, S. and Gackenbach, T. (1986). Lucid dreaming. In *Handbook of States of consciousness.* In Wolman, B.B. and Ullman, M. (eds.). New York: Von Nostrand, pp. 159-198.

Lacan, J. (1977). *Ecrits.* A selection. N.Y. Norton.

Langs, R. (1976). *Therapeutic interactions.* 2 Vols. N.Y.: Basic Books.

Lapkin, B., and Lury, F. (1985). Transference and counter-transference in the light of developmental considerations. *American Journal of Psychoanalysis, 43, pp.* 345-359.

Lashley, K.S. (1950). In search of the engram. *Proceedings of the Society for experimental biology* (Great Britain). Cambridge University Press.

Lavi, N. (1988). The relationship between styles of dreaming, personality characteristics, and aesthetic preferences (in Hebrew). Unpublished M.A. thesis, Tel-Aviv University.

Leavenworth, R.E. (1960). *Interpreting Hamlet.* San Francisco: Chandler Publishing Co.

Lewes, G.H. (1855). *Life and works of Goethe,* in *Hamlet: A casebook,* Jump, F. (ed.). London: Macmillan, pp. 3-34.

Lidz, T. (1975). *Hamlet's enemy.* Madness and myth in *Hamlet.* N.Y.: Vision.

Liébault, A.A. (1866). Du sommeil et des états analogues, considérés surtout au point de vue de l'action du la morale sur la physique (On sleep and analogous states, considered from the point of view of the action of the mind on the body).

Lindner, G.A. (1858). *Lehrbuch der empirischen Psychologie nach genetischer Methode* (Textbook of empirical psychology by genetic method) quoted from Jones, E. *The life and work of Sigmund Freud,* v. 1, N.Y.: Basic Books (1953).

Lipps, T. (1883). *Grundtatsachen des Seelenlebens* (The basic facts of mental life), Munich.

Lipps, T. (1897). Der Begriff des Unbewussten in der Psychologie. (The concept of unconscious in psychology.) *Records of the Third International Congress of Psychology.* Munich.

Little, M. (1979). Counter-transference and the patient's response to it. *International Journal of Psychoanalysis, 32,* 32-40.

Loftus, E. (1979). *Eyewitness testimony.* Harvard University Press.

Loomis, A., Harvey, E.N., Hobart, G. (1936). Electrical potentials of the human brain. Journal of experimental Psychology, 19, 249-279.

Lubbock, Q. (ed.). *The letters of Henry James.* 1 vol. N.Y. Charles Scribner's Sons, 1920.

Luborsky, L., Critx-Christoph, P., Mintz, J., Auerbach, A. (1988). *Who will benefit from psychotherapy?* N.Y.: Basic Books.

Macalpine, I. (1950). The development of transference. *Psychoanalytic Quarterly, 19,* 501-539.

Mack, M. (1952). The world of Hamlet. *Yale Review, 41,* 502-523, In *Hamlet: A casebook,* Jump, F. (ed.). London: Macmillan, pp. 86-107.

Malcolm, J. (1982). *Psychoanalysis: The impossible profession.* N.Y.: Vintage.

Mamon, A. (1988). The relationship between styles of dreaming and personality characteristics (in Hebrew). Unpublished M.A. thesis, Tel-Aviv University.

Mann, Th. (1933). *The story of Jacob in Joseph and his brothers.* Tr. Lowe-Porter. London: Secker and Warburg.

Masson, J. (1984). *The assault on truth.* Farrar, Straus and Giroux.

Masson, J.M. (1988). *Against therapy.* London: Fontana, 1990.

Maudsley, H. (1967). *Psychology and pathology of the mind.* London.

McCarley, R. and Hobson, J.A. (1977). The neurobiological origins of psychoanalytic dream theory. *American Journal of Psychiatry, 134,* 1211-1211.

McCarley, R.W. & Hoffman, E. (1981). REM sleep dreams and the activation-synthesis hypothesis. *American Journal of Psychiatry, 138,* 904-912.

Meddis, R. (1979). The evolution and function of sleep. In *Brain, Behavior and Evolution,* Oakley, D.A. and Plotkin, H.C. (eds.). London: Methuen. pp. 99-125.

Meissner, S.J. (1981). Metapsychology - who needs it. *Journal of American Psychoanalytic Association, 29,* 921-938.

Mesmer, F.A. (1779). Mémoire sur la découverte du magnétisme animal. Paris, Didot. (Essay on the discovery of animal magnetism). Quoted after Ellenberger, H. (1970). *The discovery of the unconscious*. N.Y.: Basic Books.

Messick, G. (1986). Herman Witkin and the meaning of style. In *Field dependence in psychological theory, research and application*, Bertini, M., Pizzamiglio, R., & Wapner, S. (eds.). N.J. Erlbaum, pp. 115-117.

Miller, G.A. (1956). The magical number of seven, plus or minus two: limits of our capacity for processing information. *Psychological Review*, *63*, 81-97.

Mills, Ch.K. (1883). *A system of practical medicine by American authors*. William Pepper (ed.). Philadelphia: Lea Brothers and Co.

Möbius, P.J. (1898). *Über das Pathologische bei Goethe* (On the pathological in Goethe). München, Matthes u. Seitz, 1989.

Muller, M. (1859). *Chips from a German Workshop*. Oxford.

Nai-Tung Ting (1974). *The Cinderella cycle in China and Indo-China*. Helsinki: Academia Scientiarum Fennica.

Newirth, J.N. (1982). Intimacy in interpersonal psychoanalysis. In *Intimacy*, Fisher, M. and Stricker, G. (eds.). N.Y.: Plenum Press, pp. 76-9.

Nietzsche, Fr. (1878). *Human, all–too–human*. N.Y.: Russell and Russell.

Noy, P. (1979). Form creation in art: An ego-psychological approach to creativity, *The Psychoanalytic Quarterly*, *48*, 229-256.

Orne, M.T. (1972). The simulating subject in hypnosis research. In *Hypnosis. Research developments and perspectives*, Fromm, E. and Shor, R.E. (eds.), London: Paul Elek, pp. 399-423.

Ornstein, P.H. (1979). Remarks on the central position empathy in psychoanalysis. *Bulletin of the Association for Psychoanalytic Medicine*, *18*, 95-108.

Ornstein, P.H. (1981). The impact of self psychology on the conduct and process of psychoanalytic psychotherapy. The Lydia Rapoport Lectures.

Ornstein, P.H. (1983). Discussion in *Reflections on self-psychology*, Lichtenberg, J.D., and Kaplan, S. (eds.). Hillsdale, N.J.: L. Erlbaum.

Ornstein, P.H. and Ornstein, A. (1980). Formulating interpretations in clinical psychoanalysis. *International Journal of Psychoanalysis, 61*, 203-211.

Osler, W. (1892). Quoted from Thornton, E.M. (1976). *Hypnotism, hysteria and epilepsy.* London: Heineman.

Overton, D.A. (1964). State-dependent or „dissociated" learning produced with pentobarbital. *Journal of comparative and physiological Psychology, 57*, 3-12.

Perky, C.W. (1910). An experimental study of imagination. *American Journal of Psychology, 21*, 422-452.

Peterfreund, E. (1983). *The process of psychoanalytic therapy.* Hillsdale, N.J.: Analytic Press.

Phelps, W.E. (1916) quoted from Kenton, E. (1924). Henry James to the ruminant reader: The Turn of the Screw, *The Arts, 6*, 245-255.

Piaget, J. (1951). *Play, dreams, and imitation.* N.Y.: Norton.

Politzer, H. (1965). *Franz Kafka, der Künstler.* Frankfurt a.M.

Popper–Lynkeus, J. (1899). *Phantasien eines Realisten* (Phantasien of a realist). Vienna.

Pribram, K. (1980). Mind, brain, and consciousness: The organization of competence and conduct. In *The Psychology of consciousness*, Davidson, F.M., and Davidson, R.J. (eds.). N.Y.: Plenum, pp. 47-64.

Pribram, K., Nuwer, M., & Baron, R.J. (1974). The holographic hypothesis of memory structure in brain function and perception. In *Contemporary developments in mathematical psychology.* Krantz, D., Atkinson, H., and P. Suppes (eds.). San Francisco: Freeman, Vol. 2, pp. 416-457.

Puységur (1784). Détails des cures opérées à Buzancy près de Soissons, par le magnétisme animal. Soissons. Quoted after Ellenberger, H. (1970). *The discovery of the Unconscious.* London: Penguin.

Racker, H. (1969). *Transference and countertransference.* N.Y.: International Universities Press.

Ralston, R.S. (1879). Cinderella. *The Nineteenth Century, 6,* 832-853.

Rapaport, D. (1959). The structure of psychoanalytic theory. In *Psychology: A study of science,* Koch, S. (ed.), Vol. 3. N.Y.: McGraw-Hill, pp. 55-183.

Rascovsky, A. and Rascovsky, M. W. (1949). On consummated incest. *International Journal of Psychoanalysis, 30.* 194.

Rass, M. (1983). Styles in dreaming and their relation to cognitive styles (in Hebrew). Unpublished M.A. thesis, Tel-Aviv University.

Rechtschaffen, A. (1978). The single-mindedness and isolation of dreams. *Sleep, 1,* 907-909.

Rechtschaffen, A. & Foulkes, D. (1965). Effect of visual stimuli on dream content. *Perceptual and Motor Skills, 20,* 1149-1160.

Reeves, J.W. (1966). *Thinking about thinking.* N.Y.: Braziller.

Reich, W. (1933). *Character Analysis.* N.Y.: Farrar, Strauss, and Cudahy, 1949.

Reil, J. Ch. (1803). *Rhapsodien ueber die Anwendung der psychischen Kurmethoden aud Geisteszerruttungen* (Rhapsodies on the application of the psychic methods for curing mental disorders). Halle: Curt.

Richardson, G.A. & Moore, R.A. (1963). On the manifest dream in schizophrenia. *Journal of the American Psychoanalytic Association, 11,* 281-302.

Ricoeur, P. (1974). *The conflict of interpretations: Essays in hermeneutics.* Ed. by Ihde, D., Evanston, Ill. Northwestern University Press.

Rogers, C.R. (1962). Some learnings from a study of psychotherapy with schizophrenics. *Pennsylvania Psychiatric Quarterly,* 3-15.

Rooth, A.B. (1951). *The Cinderella cycle.* Lund, C.W.K. Glearup.

Saintyves, P. (1923). *Les contes de Perrault* (The fables of Perrault), Paris.

Sander, F. (1928). Experimentelle Ergebnisse der Gestalt-Psychologie (The experimental results of the psychology of Gestalt.) In *10. Kongress Bericht der experimentellen Psychologie*. E. Becher & J. Fisher (eds.).

Sander, F. (1930). Structure, totality of experience and Gestalt. In *Psychologies of 1930*. C. Murchison (ed.). Worchester: Clark University Press.

Sartre, J.P. (1940). *The psychology of imagination*. N.Y.: Citadel Press, 1961.

Sato, S. Dreifuss, F.E. and Perky, J.K. (1975). Photic sensitivity of children with absence seizures in slow wave sleep. Electroencephalography and Clinical Neurophysiology. 39. 479-489.

Schiegl, H. (1983). *Healing magnetism. The transference of vital force through polarity therapy*. London: Century Books, 1987.

Schilder, P. (1920). On the development of thoughts. In *Organization and pathology of thought*, D. Rapaport (ed.), N.Y. Columbia University Press, pp. 497-518.

Schimek, F.G. (1987). Fact and fantasy in the seduction theory: A historical review. *Journal of the American Psychoanalytic Association, 35*, 937-965.

Schopenhauer, quoted from Ellenberger, (1970).

Schwartz, D.G., Weinstein, L.N., & Arkin, A.M. (1978). Qualitative aspects of sleep mentation. In *The mind in sleep: Psychology and Psychophysiology*. A.M. Arkin, J.S. Antrobus, and S.J. Ellman (eds.). Hillsdale, N.J.: Erlbaum. pp. 143-244.

Searles, H.F.S. (1965). *Selected papers on schizophrenia and related subjects*. N.Y.: International Universities Press.

Searles, H.F.S. (1977). The analyst's participant observation as influenced by the patient's transference. *Contemporary Psychoanalysis, 13*, 367-371.

Shapiro, D. (1965). *Neurotic styles*. N.Y.: Basic Books.

Shepher, J. (1975). Mate selection among second generation Kibbutz adolescents and adults. *Archives of Sexual Behavior, 1*, 293-327.

Sherwood, M. (1969). *The logic of explanation in Psychoanalysis.* N.Y.: Academic Press.

Shouksmith, G. (1965). A sequential guessing game for studying problem solving. *Psychological Reports, 17,* 127-130.

Silverberg, W.V. (1948). The concept of transference. *Psychoanalytic Quarterly, 17,* 303.

Simpson, A. (1886). *Travels in the Wilds of Ecuador.* London.

Snyder, F. (1970). The phenomenology of dreaming. In *The Psychodynamic implications of the physiological studies on dreams,* Madow, L., and Snow, L. (eds.). Springfield, Ill.: Thomas, pp. 124-131.

Spence, D.P. (1982). *Narrative truth, historical truth.* N.Y.: Norton.

Starker, S. (1973). Aspects of inner experience: Autokinesis, daydreaming, dream recall and cognitive style. *Perceptual and Motor Skills, 36,* 663-673.

Starker, S. (1974). Daydreaming stages and nocturnal dreaming. *Journal of Abnormal Psychology, 83,* 52-55.

Steele, R.S. and Jacobsen, P.B. (1977). From present to past: the development of Freudian theory. *International Review of Psychoanalysis, 5,* 393-411.

Stekel, W. (1913). Neurosis as it is represented in dreams. In *The meaning and psychology of dreams,* Stekel, W. (ed.). N.Y.: Avon, 1951.

Stern, D. (1985). *The interpersonal world of the infant.* N.Y.: Basic Books.

Stone, J., Smith, H.T., & Murphy, L. (eds.). *The competent infant.* N.Y.: Basic Books, 1973.

Storr, A. (1966). The concept of cure. In *Psychoanalysis Observed.* Rycroft, Ch. (ed.). London: Constable, 48, 237-251.

Sullivan, H.S. (1940). *Conceptions of modern psychiatry.* N.Y.: Norton.

Sullivan, H.S. (1953). *The interpersonal theory of psychiatry.* N.Y.: Norton.

Summit, R. and Kryso, J. (1978). Sexual abuse of children. *American Journal of Orthopsychiatry, 48,* 237-251.

Sydenham (1676). *Observationes Medicae.* London.

Tart (1969). Discussion. In *Dream psychology and the new biology of dreaming*, Kramer, M., Whitman, R.M., Baldridge, B.J. Ornstein, P.H. (eds.). Springfield, Illinois: C.C. Thomas, pp. 344-359.

Timpanaro, S. (1974). *The Freudian slip.* London: Verso, 1985.

Tolpin, M. (1970). The infantile neurosis. *Psychoanalytic Study of the Child*, 25, 273-305.

Tower (1956), quoted from Searles, H.F.S. (1965).

Ullman, M. and Krippner, S. (1978). Experimental dream studies. In *The Signet Handbook of Parapsychology.* N.Y.: New American Library, pp. 409-422

Undeutsch, H. (1942). Die Aktualgenese und ihrer charakterologischen Bedeutung. *Scientia.*

Usher, A. (1951). The slipper on the stair. *World Review, 25,* 50-52.

Varendonck, J. (1915). The psychology of daydreams. In Rapaport, D., *Organization and pathology of thought.* N.Y.: Columbia University Press, pp. 451-473.

Velasco, F., Velasco, M., Cepeda, C., and Munoz, H. (1980). Wakefulness-sleep modulation of cortical subcortical evoked potentials in man. *EEG and Clinical Neurophysiology,* 48, 64-72.

Viderman, S. (1979). The analytic space. *Psychoanalytic Quarterly, 5,* 45-62.

Völgyesi, F.A. (1954). "School for patients", hypnosis- therapy and psycho-prophylaxis. *British Journal of medical hypnotism,* 5, 8-17.

Voltaire (1748). *Semiramis,* In *Hamlet: A casebook,* Jump, F. (ed.). London: Macmillan, p. 23.

Von Franz, M.L. (1972). *Problems of the feminine in fairy tales.* N.Y.: Spring Publications.

Wallerstein, R.S.W. (1981). Foreword. In Spence, D.P. *Narrative truth and historical truth,* N.Y.: Norton (1982).

Weatherhead, E.D.W. (1951). *Psychology, religion and healing.* London: Hodder and Stoughton.

Weingartner, H. (1978). Human state dependent learning. In *Drug discrimination and state dependent learning,* Ho, B.T., Richards, D.W., and Chute, D.L. (eds.). Academic, pp. 361-382.

Werner, H. (1956). Microgenesis and aphasia. *Journal of Abnormal and Social Psychology, 52,* 347-353.

Wertham, F. (1941). *Dark Legend: A study in murder.* N.Y.: Duell, Sloan, and Pearce.

Westcott, M.R. & Ranzoni, J.H. (1963). Correlates of intuitive thinking. *Psychological Reports, 12,* 593-612.

Westermarck, E. (1926). *A short history of human marriage.* N.Y.: Macmillan.

Winfree, A.T. (1984). Exploratory data analysis. In *Mathematical models of the circadian sleep-wake cycle,* Moore-Ede, M.C. and Czeisler, C.A. (eds.). N.Y.: Raven, pp. 187-200.

Witkin, H.A. (1969). Influencing dream content. In *Dream psychology and the new biology of dreaming,* Kramer, M., Whitman, R.M., Baldridge, B.J., and Ornstein, P.H. (eds.). Springfield, Illinois: C.C. Thoman, pp. 285-345.

Wolf, S. (1950). Effects of suggestion and conditioning on the action of chemical agents in human subjects - the pharmacology of placebos. *Journal of clinical investigations, 29,* 100-109.

Zimmerman, W.B. (1970). Sleep mentation and auditory awakening thresholds. *Psychophysiology, 6,* 540-549.

INDEX

Non-recaller
    of dreams 11
NREM
    dreams 7, 92
    sleep 92, 108, 111

Objectivity 10
Oedipus
    complex 126, 133, 136, 137, 141, 143, 148, 149, 150,
        163–165, 172, 175, 196, 221
    construct 130, 132, 134, 176, 189, 210

Parapraxes 44, 45, 52, 53, 84, 87, 119–121, 124
Passion
    somnambulic 154–156, 158
Patient
    schizophrenic 98, 99, 131
Pattern of literature
    archetypal 211
Personality
    dimensions of 22
    field-dependent 29, 30
    field-independent 29, 30
    replacement of the artist's 195
Phenomenology 7, 212
Processes
    primary 44–46, 48, 51, 52, 55, 59, 60, 63
    secondary 44, 48, 51
Psychoanalysis
    cornerstones of 132
Psychology
    dynamic 64, 121
    Herbartian 58, 59
Psychotherapist
    as surgeon 162, 163, 173, 177, 179
    observant participant 180

Printed and bound by CPI Group (UK) Ltd, Croydon, CR0 4YY

09/06/2025

14685737-0001